the *Life* she once *Knew*

THE INCREDIBLE TRUE STORY OF QUEENA,
The Bloomingdale Library Attack Survivor

as told
by her mother
Vanna Nguyen

AMBASSADOR INTERNATIONAL
GREENVILLE, SOUTH CAROLINA & BELFAST, NORTHERN IRELAND
www.ambassador-international.com

The Life She Once Knew

The Incredible True Story of Queena,
The Bloomingdale Library Attack Survivor
©2020 by Join Queena LLC
All rights reserved

ISBN: 978-1-62020-727-7
eISBN: 978-1-62020-746-8
Library of Congress Control Number: 2020942832

Cover Design and Interior Typesetting by Hannah Nichols
eBook edition by Anna Riebe Raats

AMBASSADOR INTERNATIONAL
Emerald House
411 University Ridge, Suite B14
Greenville, SC 29601, USA
www.ambassador-international.com

AMBASSADOR BOOKS
The Mount
2 Woodstock Link
Belfast, BT6 8DD, Northern Ireland, UK
www.ambassadormedia.co.uk

The colophon is a trademark of Ambassador, a Christian publishing company.

the *Life* she once
Knew

The Life She Once Knew is an inspiring account of heart-wrenching, compounded trauma and miraculous triumph over evil. Vanna Nguyen leads us through her victorious journey over crises which could destroy the strongest among us. As she shares her sacrificial love for her daughter and faith in her Savior, she motivates us all to rise as champions of life and forgiveness.

—**Tina Yeager, LMHC**
Award-Winning Author, Speaker,
Flourish-Meant Podcast Host, Life Coach

The Life She Once Knew is a very compelling and uplifting book. It seems to capture the spirit of Queena and her loving family. I don't believe I have ever met a person and family whose faith is so extraordinary especially under the circumstances that were put upon them. We can all learn from Queena, and I believe you will also better appreciate your life and your family after reading her story in *The Life She Once Knew: The Incredible True Story of Queena, The Bloomingdale Library Attack Survivor.*

—**Steve Stock**
CEO, Guy Harvey Inc.

This family has endured tragedy and horrific events that most Americans would find inconceivable. The resilience and courage shown in the face of these events gives us an enormously inspiring story and will change your life for the better. What happened to Queena was unthinkable, but it happened. Her entire bright future was stolen in what seemed like moments. However, what happened after that, through the love of her sister Anna, her mom Vanna, her countless friends and more, will give you chills. If you need an example of the love, courage, and determination people can show, even in unfathomable circumstances, read this book.

—**Caryn McDermott**
IB Coordinator/Assistant Principal (retired)
Land O'Lakes High School
Land O'Lakes, Florida

Vanna Nguyen's book is an amazing parallel account of two real-life stories of courage and survival. If you wonder how much a person can endure and still come out on top, wonder no more. This story of an inspiring mother-daughter relationship of relentless love will show you.

—DAVID YATES
Producer, *Dolphin Tale* and *Dolphin Tale 2*
Former CEO: Clearwater Marine Aquarium
and Ironman Triathlon Company

This powerful account of courage in response to evil chronicles the birth and maturing of faith in the wake of this world's shocking malevolence. Vanna Nguyen's haunting account of her innocent daughter's attack, set against the backdrop of Vanna's own struggle as a young Vietnamese "boat person" fleeing for her life, is gripping from the first to the very last word. My mom-heart was touched by this mother's anguish and need to defend her beloved daughter. My cry for rigid justice was challenged by her extraordinary efforts to forgive the attacker, based on her submission to God's Word. And my sense of hope was buoyed by the way God upheld this precious family through the process of redefining and finding joy in each moment. Profound, life-changing truths in every chapter. Truly a must-read.

—DEBORA M. COTY
Inspirational speaker and award-winning author of over
40 books, including the best-selling *Too Blessed to be Stressed*
series with over 1.3 million copies sold in
multiple languages worldwide
www.DeboraCoty.com

Riveting! An emotional rollercoaster! Three women's lives changed forever over a gruesome incident at a library. Hope, faith, and love kept them together and their lights bright. A must read!

—THUTRUNG ALEXIS NGUYEN
Healthcare executive, CEO, Board Member

I was riveted by this book that masterfully weaves together the back story of Queena's family's escape from communism, and her journey of survival following the horrific attack that left her blind and in a wheelchair.

If you think the focus of *The Life She Once Knew* will be mere sadness and tragedy, you are sorely mistaken. It instead serves as an anthem for female empowerment; proof of the commitment that a community has for a survivor; and a testament to the love Jesus Christ has for us all.

I recommend this book to anyone who needs inspiration, and to those who want to learn what it means to NEVER give up.

—RENEE WARMACK, MPA
Producer | Speaker | Coach
Renee Warmack Productions, LLC

I was assigned by Hillsborough County Pubic Schools to be Queena's homebound teacher from the Visually Impaired Program. As part of her therapy team I experienced first hand the strength and faith of both of these two strong women who will never give up. I feel fortunate to have met this determined family and know that readers will be equally inspired by their journey. This is the most motivated family I have ever met in my career.

—ELIZABETH P. UNDERWOOD, BS, M.ED, COMS
Teacher of Students with Visual Impairments (retired), School District of Hillsborough County, Tampa, FL

In my prosecution career I have had the honor of speaking on behalf of many victims in court. During this time, I got to know Queena's family and soon realized that Queena had the strongest voice of all her family. Vanna's retelling of her life and her devotion to Queena is an emotional journey that continues to leave me in awe of her strength, perseverance, and devotion.

—RITA PETERS
Prosecutor

For Queena
and her angels

Contents

Anna, Vanna, and Queena - 2007

IN THE BLINK OF AN EYE

I am Vanna, fierce defender of my daughter's quality of life. After she was brutally attacked one night, Queena suffered severe traumatic brain injury, causing her to need continual care. I invite you to share the most tragic and truthful moments of my life as Queena's champion. I expose the depths of my soul as testimony to the idea that kindness and gratitude can soften even the most horrendous events.

It is my hope that the memories shared within this book will inspire people to get up and fight no matter what their current battles might be. As human beings, we may not be able to change what led to our current circumstances, but we can turn pain into purpose from this moment forward.

We can trust that we are not alone—that love will bind our wounds and conquer the fear that we might not survive another day.

> *"For I hold you by your right hand—I, the LORD your God. And I say to you, 'Don't be afraid. I am here to help you"* (Isa. 41:13).

Decades earlier, I had survived my own trauma, escaping to America to raise my family. I worked hard to make a home for my girls that was safe and secure. Before the attack, the daily routine of our family life felt normal—*rhythmic*. I focused my time and energy on my business in order to support my two girls. I went to work in the mornings and shuttled kids around throughout the week. On weekends, I treated my family to dinner at a local restaurant.

As a single mother, my desire was to set my two daughters on a healthy path in life and protect them from danger. I encouraged them to be responsible, independent girls. As they grew, I felt as though my hopes and expectations for them—which I'd focused on since their births—were coming to fruition. My daughters had become young adults. Ordinary life felt fabulous.

Then in the blink of an eye, all sense of normalcy vanished. In an instant, I became a person who couldn't function. I turned cold, numb, and lifeless. My life shifted from feeling normal to being utterly scared out of my mind. The "me" I knew disappeared *forever.*

Something horrible happened.

My teenage daughter Queena looked into the eyes of evil—just as I had decades earlier. She fought with all her might for her right to live. Ultimately, she was victorious, but she would never be the same Queena. Our entire family changed as we muddled through the aftermath of an unspeakable crime. Over the course of twenty-five horrific minutes, we lost Queena—not to death, but to a new life no one was prepared to face.

My story involves a tragedy so frightening that most parents can't bear even imagining it, let alone living it. From a parent's perspective, it's too painful to acknowledge that we can't keep our children safe. It's too unsettling to ponder an uncertain future. We avoid thinking about these potential realities because "horrible things always happen to other people." So, we push away the idea that something horrible could happen to us—to *our* child.

The events that transpired for my Queena brought back painful memories of my own trauma from when I was younger and reminded me that life is never how we plan it. Just as the life I once knew was no more, my daughter Queena was about to experience a complete change from the life she once knew.

I want to share my experiences for all who need encouragement and reassurance that families can make it through unimaginable tragedies and come out whole. I write on behalf of those who have experienced catastrophes similar to mine, for those who have been forced to wrestle with the same helpless feelings I've faced time and again . . .

If only I could turn back the clock.

If only I could have done *something* different.

If only I could've warned her to be safe—and then assured her safety.

But how? Even if we could turn back time—even if we could *will* something to be different—would disaster elude our children? Life does not provide us with this degree of certainty. Repeated pleas for the safety of our loved ones cannot possibly prevent all tragedies. Such is reality.

Within these pages, you will discover my inner strength: that of a mother who exhumes the buried memories of her past in Vietnam while coping with a newly inflicted dagger to her heart. Amid feelings of profound anger, devastation, and heaviness, I wished for nothing less than a chance to switch places with my child. But in the absence of that possibility, I share the changing relationships in my family while facing insurmountable hurdles and finding the resolution to overcome—*together.*

In the end, I conclude that no sinful act is too evil to forgive. Yet by my own admission, the ongoing need to purge feelings of bitterness toward Queena's attacker continues to be a lifelong effort, upheld by the goodness of God's mercy. To reach the point of believing that no soul is too lost or too unworthy of love and redemption is to understand the true definition of God's amazing grace. *I want to win this most difficult spiritual battle.*

I believe you will find my book to be a remarkable journey of survival. My life story is a testament to the notion that faith, community, and the unending grace of God provide us with the power to do things we never thought possible. Physical and spiritual healings—despite the hardships that threaten to undo us—can, and will, restore our souls. Love will surely prevail.

> *"Three things will last forever—faith, hope, and love—*
> *and the greatest of these is love"* (1 Cor. 13:13).

My memoir offers hope. Following the brutal assault on Queena's life, my family was forced to alter our view of the world. Yet in a multitude of ways, our picture changed for the better. Our circumstances became a catalyst for spreading encouragement to other victims of traumatic brain injuries. Today, the light of hope shines in the eyes of many people around the world who have chosen to "JoinQueena.com"—one *incredible* survivor—on her path forward.

Queena and I—along with my older daughter, Anna, and all our supporters—have come to believe that whenever hope fills the heart, life becomes worth living again. For though our lives are not what we once knew, we have a future and a hope that one day we will be made completely whole again.

> Look here, you who say "Today or tomorrow we are going to a certain town and will stay there a year. We will do business there and make a profit." How do you know what your life will be like tomorrow? Your life is like the morning fog—it's here a little while, then it's gone. What you ought to say is, "If the Lord wants us to, we will live and do this or that" (James 4:13-17).

Part One
TRAVERSING THROUGH TRAGEDY

Queena's senior picture - 2008

CHAPTER 1
APRIL 24, 2008

A FEW NIGHTS BEFORE THE turmoil to come, a frightening dream awoke my Queena. She couldn't remember the details, only a feeling that something terrible had happened. Someone had tried to harm her.

I soothed her. Reassured her. It was just a dream. No one would hurt my sweet girl. At least, that's what I told myself. I'd made sure of that.

On that sunny day in April, I pushed any troubling thoughts out of my head as I lay on the beach near our home in the Tampa area. Everything felt right in my world. My oldest daughter, Anna, was doing well in college. And Queena had just turned eighteen two days earlier. She was a beautiful young woman, who had earned all *A*'s and a scholarship to the University of Florida to study international business.

As a birthday treat, Queena wanted to spend the weekend with her friends at the TradeWinds Island Resort. So, my partner, Robert, and I checked in to get the girls' room key. I couldn't resist taking a moment to enjoy the ocean breeze, basking in the joy that my girls had made it. As a single mother, I'd wanted Anna and Queena to have privileges and opportunities that I didn't while growing up in Vietnam. Now with Queena's graduation from East Bay High School inching closer, my heart swelled with pride—and relief, too.

Queena was not only bright and kind, with family and friends who loved her, but also safe, no matter what that dream had shown her. I didn't allow her to stay out too late. She didn't hang around with the "wrong crowd." She was a responsible teenager, who didn't put herself in dangerous situations.

I'd raised my daughters in a strict household with the same strong values I'd learned in Vietnam, and my girls trusted these boundaries.

Once home from the beach, I changed into comfortable clothes. Queena said she was going to eat something, then head to her job at the Abercrombie & Fitch clothing store in the mall. She didn't say anything about returning books to the library on her way home from work.

Looking back, I wonder what I would have said if she had. Would I have told her it was okay, or would my mother's intuition have kicked in? Would I have said, "No, it might be too dangerous after hours"?

About 9:15 p.m., I expected Queena home from the mall. Robert and I had spent the earlier part of the evening searching online for cruise deals for us and the girls. We always rewarded my daughters with a cruise—our favorite affordable vacation—whenever they maintained straight *A*'s throughout the entire school year. I was so excited to plan this trip for her last summer before college.

By about 9:20 p.m., I began to wonder if she had stopped at Panera Bread, as she sometimes did. Her drive home took about fifteen minutes. I always cautioned her to walk to her car with her coworkers at night so she wouldn't be in the parking lot alone.

An hour later, at precisely 10:26 p.m., my cell phone rang. It was Rachel, one of Queena's best friends. I immediately felt anxious. Her friends *never* called me directly.

"Hi, Ms. Vanna," Rachel said, her voice trembling. "I think something happened to Queena. I was on the phone with her when I heard her scream, and the line suddenly went dead. I tried to call her back, but it keeps going to her voicemail."

I tried to remain calm and think of a best-case scenario. "Maybe her phone died, or she was talking on another line with someone else. Tell me everything that happened!"

Rachel told me that Queena had stayed at work later than usual to cover for another employee, who had called in sick. When she finally did leave, just after ten p.m., she'd called Rachel, and the two of them had talked as Queena drove. She was on her way to the Bloomingdale Regional Library. It was closed by then, but Rachel told me Queena planned to return some books through the book drop to avoid paying late fees.

The two were still chatting on the phone when Queena arrived at the library around 10:20 p.m. She told Rachel she saw a weird guy sitting on the bench in front of the library. Rachel suggested Queena stay seated in the car, roll down the window, and slide the books through the slot of the book drop without getting out of the car. But Queena told her that wouldn't work because the books were in the back seat.

"I heard sounds of the door opening," Rachel told me. "Queena said the dropbox was too full. The books were stuck, and Queena was trying to squeeze them in. Then I heard her scream, and the phone cut off."

I quickly ended the call, telling Rachel that I would go to the library myself, trying not to think the worst.

But I knew. Something bad had happened to my little girl.

I called my sister, Tina, who lived closer to the library. When her husband, Hoang, answered, I told him to rush to the library because Queena might need help.

Robert and I headed out in our car. I called Queena's phone repeatedly, but each call went straight to voicemail. Maybe she'd simply dropped her cell phone, I thought desperately. Maybe the battery had died.

I told Robert to watch for Queena's Toyota RAV4, hoping to see it traveling in the opposite direction, bringing her home—back to the safe haven I'd created for our family.

Robert and I strained to see beyond our headlights in the dark. We tried to make out Queena's face behind the windshields of cars zooming by. The seven-mile drive seemed like an eternity.

While we were still en route, Tina called. She and Hoang had just arrived. "Vanna, come quick!" she yelled into the phone. "Queena's car is here, but she's not—and the door is open. Her cell phone is on the ground. Blood is everywhere!"

"Call 911!" I screamed, now in a full panic.

Queena's friend Priscilla, along with her mother and her sister, had also arrived at the library ahead of us. Rachel had called Priscilla after talking to me, and Priscilla's family had sped to the scene. Priscilla called the police.

Moments later, I pulled up behind Queena's RAV4, still parked alongside the book drop with the engine running. The driver's door and rear passenger door were wide-open. The beeping alert, signaling an open door, sounded continuously inside the car. The left turn signal blinked, and music played through the car speakers, as if Queena was about to drive away.

But Queena wasn't there.

Where was she? Her cell phone obviously had been knocked out of her hand. It had landed just beneath the car. Blood spattered the pavement.

I kept screaming, "Call 911! Call 911!"

That's all I could do. My cry for help while feeling utterly helpless. Everyone who rushed to the library felt helpless. *Queena was gone!* Tina, along with Priscilla and her family, cried while waiting for the authorities to come.

Robert cautioned us not to touch anything while we waited for the police. We ran around the property, calling out her name. "Queena! Queena!" My brother-in-law, Hoang, wondered if Queena had been kidnapped.

Robert and I hopped into my car and drove to the back of the library. It was pitch-black, but we spotted where the parking lot's pavement ended and a grassy area merged with a bog. Robert pulled a flashlight out of the glove compartment and walked into the darkness. I left him and returned to the front of the building to be with the others.

Finally, a security guard pulled up to the library, followed by two cars with flashing red lights. The deputies from the Hillsborough County Sheriff's Office spoke with the guard first. Meanwhile, word of Queena's disappearance had spread among her friends, and more teenagers from her school arrived, including two of her best friends, Kristen and Crystal. They wept in each other's arms.

Priscilla said that earlier in the evening, Queena had asked her to wait until she got off from work, so they could go to the library together. Priscilla also worked at Abercrombie & Fitch, but she didn't want to wait. Now, she was overcome with remorse.

"It's my fault!" she screamed. "I feel so guilty."

Poor girl. It wasn't her fault! Yet at that moment, I didn't have it in me to comfort her.

The deputies turned to me for more information.

"What happened?" they asked.

One of Queena's friends overheard the question and stepped up, saying, "I am Vietnamese. I can translate."

"I don't need translation," I said. "I can speak English." The truth is, I can understand English better than I can speak it. Anxious, I might have stumbled to express myself.

Just then, my cell phone rang. I saw Robert's number on the caller ID.

"I found her!" he exclaimed, almost breathless. "She is lying in the grass behind the library at the edge of a pond. She's not moving."

I yelled to the others. Everyone ran to the back of the building. I screamed my daughter's name over and over as I ran toward the grassy area.

"Queena! Queena!"

As I hurried along, my phone rang again. This time it was my older daughter, Anna. She was frantic about an earlier message I'd left.

"We found her!" I said. "Get to the library."

That was all I could say. There was no time for details and no sense in trying to explain something I didn't yet understand myself.

For the first time that night, I felt a chill in the air, like the fear of what was happening sent ice through my veins. I ran until I reached the grassy area that sloped downward toward the woods where Queena lay. But a deputy stopped me in my tracks and would not allow me to go any farther. I tried to push him away. I wanted to run to my Queena. I wanted to touch her, to see her face, to hold her and comfort her. I wanted to make everything all right. But the deputy wouldn't budge.

"This is a crime scene, and nothing should be touched," he said.

From about ten feet away, I saw Robert kneeling on the ground.

Yes, I thought, *that must be Queena, right there, lying motionless beside him.*

It was dark, so I couldn't quite see her, but Hoang and Priscilla were with her, too. They had made it to Queena's side before the deputies could stop them.

I begged the man restraining me to release his hold. I needed to get to my daughter. Why couldn't he understand that?

"She needs me," I pleaded. "I am her mom."

Still, he held me tight, and all I could do was watch and listen as Priscilla knelt on the grass, crying. "Queena, we are all here," I could hear her saying. "We found you. Don't worry. Do you hear me, Queena? Queena?"

Robert reassured her, too. "Queena, Mom is here. The police and everyone are here. Keep breathing, Queena."

By now, Hoang was helping the officer hold me back. My heart broke into a thousand pieces. Why wouldn't they let me get close to my daughter? My eyes fought to get a clear view of her, but I couldn't make out the smooth features of her face.

More deputies arrived, many of them kneeling or standing beside my daughter. It felt like chaos—the chatter of the police radios, flashlights shining over her frail body, investigators searching for evidence. I felt strangely numb, as if this were something that I was watching in slow motion on a television screen.

I believed in God, but I had never been a religious person. Yet while staring at Queena lying motionless in the dark, my only solace came from thinking she was in God's hands. A hush fell over the crowd, as we silently—almost reverently—watched the deputies at work. I turned my head to look at everyone who had rushed to the library. All around me, our family, Queena's friends, and their parents were crying.

Tina's daughter, Amy, cried out repeatedly, hoping her older cousin, Queena, would stand up and miraculously walk away. Somehow, I found the strength to compose myself for a moment in order to comfort my niece. I assured her Queena would be okay. I spoke these words to comfort my own soul, too.

Tina cried hard, her voice barely breaking through her sobs. Then in her anguish, she yelled at me, "Why did you let Queena go to the library so late? Why didn't you return the books for her?"

Something inside of me froze. I didn't respond. I couldn't muster the will to explain that Queena hadn't mentioned her trip to the library. *I didn't know.*

At one point, Hoang knelt on the ground, gazed up toward the sky, and screamed. He begged God not to let Queena die. Then he looked around and yelled to no one in particular, "Where is the ambulance? Why is it taking so long?"

Everyone looked for someone, *something*, to blame.

I turned back to my motionless daughter on the ground in the cool night air. There was nothing I could do except watch and wait. Speechless and numb, I couldn't cry out to God, or yell, or sob—at least, not then.

Looking back on my reaction, I realize I was most likely in shock—my body's way of protecting me from a dangerous overload of psychological and emotional trauma. My frozen silence saved me from having to process all the chaos and pain around me.

At last, two fire trucks, three more police cars, and an ambulance pulled into the library parking lot. The loud sirens and red lights hushed us. The paramedics swiftly treated Queena while preparing her for transport to the hospital. It seemed like hours had passed; but in truth, it had been only minutes since Robert, the others, and I had arrived.

After paramedics positioned Queena on a stretcher, Robert rejoined me and explained how he'd found her. With the flashlight, he'd spotted her backpack, purse, and wallet on the ground. He followed their trail to Queena. Then, he told me again that he hadn't seen her move.

I grabbed his arms. "Can you tell me if she was still breathing?"

"Yes," he said. "I saw her breathing very strong."

I held so many questions inside.

How did this happen?

Who took my baby?

What did they do to her?

If Queena was breathing, why couldn't she move?

A deputy approached to say that a helicopter would arrive soon to transport Queena to Tampa General Hospital. It was the nearest Level I trauma center. Paramedics feared she had suffered a brain injury. I could barely nod to communicate that I understood what he was saying. The deputy assured us she would be all right.

Anna finally arrived at the library, just as the helicopter was about to take off with her sister. Pain and confusion showed all over her face. She was just three years older than Queena, and she and Queena had always been close. We stood together, looking at Queena's body on the stretcher—both of us shattered inside.

"I am so cold," I quietly said to Anna. She stood on the sidewalk, holding me tightly as the paramedics muscled through the crowd to get to Queena.

Just then, the Vietnamese boy who had offered to translate turned to me and asked, "Are you okay?"

"Nothing I can do now," I told him.

Looking back on that moment, I wish I had been nicer to this kindhearted teenager. He obviously just wanted to help me. Yet at the time, I was so scared. Shaken to my core. None of my responses seemed appropriate.

As the stretcher disappeared into the helicopter, I wondered if my daughter might actually die. Was it possible her life would end this way—so soon?

I turned to Priscilla's mother. "Did you hear Queena breathing?" I asked. "Yes," she assured me.

Later, Priscilla told me she had seen Queena raise her arm when she initially ran over to her in the marsh. And when she told Queena, "We found you," she saw Queena put her arm down and then slip into a deep sleep.

"I think she feels safe because we finally found her. Ms. Vanna, don't worry," she said. "She won't die."

Don't worry?

Priscilla may as well have told me to stop being Vietnamese. *Impossible.* My eyes burned with anxiety, and the walls of my throat stuck together. The only thing calming my distress a bit was knowing that Queena had heard Priscilla's voice—that she knew we had found her and were there to help her. She had fought to stay conscious long enough to be assured she was safe and could rest from the horror she had just experienced, the details of which we would never know. Yet as these thoughts swirled in my head, I could only manage to say, "I hope she's okay."

Robert, Anna, and I watched the helicopter ascend, carrying my precious daughter, who was fighting for her life. *Without me.* I had no control over whether she would win or lose the battle. The only thing to do now was to get in our cars and drive to Tampa General Hospital.

We had no idea then that our family life as we knew it had changed forever.

Queena (2) and Anna (5) - 1992

CHAPTER 2

ER—UNSPEAKABLE TRAUMA

WHEN ROBERT AND I ARRIVED at the trauma center, we learned that thirteen doctors were attending to Queena. But we were not allowed to see her.

"She is in good hands," the woman at the registration desk assured us. I didn't argue. I knew I had lost all control over this crisis.

In the waiting area, we spoke to some of Queena's friends and their parents. "They told us Queena is okay," I said. "But we don't know how much longer it will be until we can see her." I thanked them for coming to be with us but encouraged them to go home and rest. We would update them when we could. They were just as powerless as we were.

We waited along with Anna, who had arrived with her friend, Alex, who had driven her to the library. Time moved more slowly than I'd ever experienced.

Before long, a detective approached us, asking for details about Queena's actions that night. He escorted us into a private room. I looked straight into his eyes and answered each question with short, clear responses. I was like a robot, speaking in a stoic, matter-of-fact tone.

"Queena got off from work at the mall. She stopped by the library to return books. She was on the phone with a friend."

He interrupted. "Does Queena have a boyfriend?"

"Never," I answered.

My hands and feet felt so cold. My stomach was in an uproar. Yet, somehow, my voice resonated strength. I wondered if the detective could tell I wasn't as strong as I sounded.

"Did she have any disputes with friends?"

"No, Queena is loved by everyone she knows. She is a good girl. She has excellent grades, and she volunteers for many extracurricular programs."

He gave us his business card and told us to call him if we needed anything. He wanted us to contact him when Queena was able to talk. Then, he told me that my composure surprised him.

"You are holding yourself together very well for all you have been through tonight."

"Not really," I confessed. "I feel numb."

After the detective left, we returned to the waiting room, where I tried to keep my thoughts positive. I envisioned my daughter's face. My heart spoke to hers, even though the hospital walls separated us.

Queena, my dear daughter, you are a fighting girl. I know you are going to fight for your life. I know you have so many dreams and goals that you haven't started yet. I know you are a winner every time. You are going to be okay. You would never leave me, or Anna. You love us too much to leave us, right? So, you are going to fight for your life. You must fight. Okay? You cannot die. You have more to do in this world than what you have already accomplished.

Still, no tears.

Around 3:00 a.m., the doctor finally emerged with news. "Queena is stable," he said. Then he rattled off a list of injuries. Her nose was broken. Her face was bruised and swollen. Her forehead was fractured.

"She'll be okay," he said optimistically. There was no need for surgery. The nurses would clean her up and move her to another room, where she was expected to wake up in about two hours.

I felt puzzled. The doctor mentioned nothing of the possible brain injury that had worried the paramedics who had provided first aid behind the library. Was this list of injuries really all she had suffered? Could I allow myself to hope that everything might be right again? She could certainly heal from these injuries much faster than from a brain injury. So, Queena was *not* going to die, after all? She would live through this and overcome her injuries? What a relief!

The doctor turned to escort us to Queena's room in the trauma center. Robert, Anna, and I followed anxiously. I had no idea what to expect.

When we entered the room, we found Queena in a deep sleep. The skin on her face looked raw. Her beautiful, long, dark hair was abnormally messy. I rushed toward her bedside, but a nurse stopped me, just as the deputies had done behind the library.

"Queena needs to rest," the nurse quickly cautioned. "She has been through a lot and is exhausted. Sleep will help her heal."

Like every other time that night, I could do nothing except comply with the latest instruction to stay away from *my* Queena. I sat down in a chair next to her bed. In the quiet of the room, I whispered to her, hoping she could hear my voice.

"I'm here. I won't leave you. You survived, Queena. You're still with us. Keep fighting. I'm here now."

I reached over to squeeze her hand between both of mine.

The numbness that had protected me for many hours began to wear off. A sense of heaviness took its place. For the first time since Rachel had called me many hours earlier, tears welled up in my eyes.

Still, no tears fell.

Queena's eyes, face, and neck were purple and black with bruises. My child had been beaten. She had been hit and punched so hard that she had been knocked to the ground. She'd likely writhed in pain inflicted by a cruel man. No—*a beast, a monster*—something less than human.

This *can't* be my life. This *couldn't* have happened to my daughter, the upcoming graduate who, just yesterday, was looking forward to celebrating her birthday at a beach resort with her friends. Only twelve hours earlier, I had been lying on the sand, soaking up the sun, thinking everything was right in my world.

I tried not to imagine the horror my daughter had lived through. I tried to stop my mind from flashing back to the library. I didn't want to envision how those bruises got on her skin. The doctor had assured us she would be okay, so I needed to focus on a full recovery. That's what Anna and I could think about—the things *to come,* not what had already happened and couldn't be undone.

We shifted our thinking.

We began to wonder how Queena might *feel* once she woke up. The senior prom was just one week away. She had spent months planning for it. She'd bought a dress, some accessories, and matching shoes. She'd also rented a limousine to chauffeur her and a group of her girlfriends. Queena was in the prime of her young life—a time when everything is possible and opportunities are endless. Now, she would need to deal with a broken nose and bruises on her face when getting ready for the prom.

The contusions were the visible injuries. Queena likely would need professional counseling to cope with the psychological trauma. She also would have invisible injuries—the kind of emotional pain that would stay with her long after the bruises healed.

While gazing at Queena, my thoughts circled back to the mysterious attacker. I couldn't help but wonder if this beast had done anything else when he'd had her under his control. Had there been time to rape her, too?

No! Please, God—no.

Detectives eventually came to Queena's room to take pictures of various parts of her body. They asked us to identify a bag of clothing and a few other items to confirm they were hers. Anna agreed to identify the items. My oldest daughter knew me so well. On top of everything I'd been forced to see, I couldn't bear to look at Queena's belongings that had been scattered around the library grounds during the attack. I was barely holding myself together.

When Anna returned from identifying Queena's things, her eyes were red. She'd confirmed the items were Queena's, but the depth of her sadness came from a different place. Deputies had given Anna more details about the attack.

"He sexually violated her," Anna said sorrowfully.

I didn't want to know the details behind her words. I *couldn't* know. Not then.

All that I had held inside until that moment could no longer be contained. The tears finally came streaming down my face, and soon I was sobbing out my grief.

Why did this happen? Why Queena?

She had been such a shy girl, never bold enough even to flirt with a boy. Now, her sweet innocence was lost. My beautiful child had been robbed of her right to say no. Her most intimate sense of self, now sunken and buried forever in the marshy ground behind a library.

Why?

This new picture of reality looked nothing like the journey I'd envisioned for my baby girl. Oh, believe me, I was fully aware that life seldom goes as planned. Many obstacles, detours, and bad things stand in the way of everyone's dreams. I was far from naïve.

I was Queena's age when I left my family in Vietnam to flee to the United States by myself. Leaving Vietnam certainly wasn't part of my plan. I'd faced serious challenges along the way, but future opportunities always appeared with the roadblocks. These were the unexpected bumps in the road of life that I thought my daughters would experience—the typical struggles that led to something better than they could ever imagine.

But a violent beating and a *rape*? What good could ever come from this?

I knew my questions had no answers. Yet as Queena's mother, it was my job to make things all better again, as I had always done. I had applied the healing balm on all her childhood scrapes and scabs. I had soothed her disappointments and wiped away her tears. Now, I would need to treat these new injuries. But how? What type of bandage binds a wounded soul?

Maybe I could absorb the pain and horror *for* her. Yes. If I could *feel* the torment, I would be able to empathize. I might not be able to erase the pain, but somehow, I could soften the unspeakable trauma. At least, I could *try*. Her life had changed. Mine had to change, too.

I will be more courageous than I was during my escape from Vietnam. I will be stronger than I was when I became a single mother. Queena will need me to be strong. She will need hope and encouragement.

To start, I could hope that the details of her attack would not be remembered.

With this newfound conviction in mind, I finally stopped sobbing and looked over at Anna. "We will overcome this together—all three of us."

Anna and I continued to sit in Queena's room, watching and waiting. Five hours passed, and Queena was still unconscious. I grew increasingly concerned. Every couple of hours, I asked the nurse why Queena wasn't waking up, but I was told not to worry. The nurse encouraged me to get some sleep in a nearby room for visitors, but I couldn't leave Queena's side. Anna couldn't leave either. It wasn't only my pain that I felt so deeply. I felt Anna's pain, too, as we kept vigil together into the early morning hours.

Queena still showed no signs of waking, even as the afternoon wore on. The time passed *so* slowly as we waited by her side, hoping to see any sign of her coming back to life.

At 3:00 p.m., Queena finally awoke. It was now twenty-four hours since she'd told me she would eat something and head to work at Abercrombie & Fitch. I thought it would be a relief when she woke up, but I was terribly wrong. Her waking state was even more disconcerting than her prolonged sleep. Queena's body began to move in small, fitful motions. Then the movements became more pronounced. Her arms and fists started swinging as if she were in a struggle.

We immediately called the nurses. Laura, a female deputy, joined us inside Queena's room. She had been posted outside at the door due to the open criminal case.

Queena's movements grew fierce. Her eyes were closed, but she fought hard, as if she were battling a lion. All of us—Robert, Anna, Laura, the nurses, and I—tried to hold her down, but it was difficult. Her entire body lurched randomly. We called out her name in an attempt to soothe her, but nothing worked.

I stared at my daughter in disbelief. *Queena thinks she is still under attack. She is struggling to defend herself!*

I replayed the horror of the library scene. Thoughts flashed in my mind like a newsreel. The blood-spattered pavement, the sound of the open-door signal in her car, the radio playing, and her absence—her mysterious absence. I shuddered to imagine the scenes playing in her mind in that moment.

What terror she must have felt as she was dragged into the woods. Seeing her fighting now, I became convinced that she hadn't given in to the beast. She'd fought back with every ounce of her being.

Queena had always been a fighter, even as a little girl. We'd lived in Los Angeles when she'd started preschool. She had made it quite clear back then that she wanted to stay with her grandmother, who took care of her while I worked. My mother, who'd joined me from Vietnam, and I had expected Queena to be upset when I took her to school; but she'd cried so hard, she vomited. The preschool teacher had told us how Queena had refused to get down on the floor to play with the other kids. She'd clung to the teacher's lap the entire time school was in session. Despite our daily efforts to reassure her that she was safe, that determined little girl kicked and screamed every day. We finally removed her from preschool in favor of staying at home with Grandma.

The fear Queena had felt at preschool was baseless. No one wanted to hurt her. She was in a safe environment. Yet, she couldn't comprehend those truths as a small child. Now that she was a young woman, someone had hurt my Queena. Even though she was safe in a hospital room surrounded by the people who loved her, her fear was no longer baseless.

Queena's body relaxed after about fifteen minutes. Her eyes opened slowly. Then, she started to sob. These were not gentle sobs. They were angry ones—full of pain and fear and frustration.

"Why can't I see?" Queena asked.

Anna and I just stood there, stunned and confused.

Again, Queena cried out, "Why can't I see?"

The doctor had not mentioned the possibility of injury to her eyes. With this new information, my tears gushed like a waterfall.

"Stay calm, Queena," I said. "The blindness may be temporary. You are waking up after a long sleep. Later, you will see again."

Queena began screaming questions at us. "Where am I?"

Laura, the deputy, stood beside the bed and spoke calmly. "You are safe. You are in the hospital, and your family is here with you."

Anna and I both held Queena's hands and spoke encouraging words to her.

"Don't worry, Queena. It is over. You are safe. We are safe here."

"What happened to me?" she asked.

Queena spoke more softly now, as if she had run out of energy. Laura asked Queena if she remembered talking on the phone with Rachel while driving to the library.

"I remember being at the library, trying to return my books. I was talking to Rachel. That's all I remember."

Laura told Queena that she'd been "beaten up by a big guy." She assured her that the authorities were staying with her at the hospital to protect her around the clock.

"We will catch him," she said confidently.

"What did he want from me?" Queena asked, sounding like a curious child. She had no recollection of the brutality she had endured, and now wasn't the time to spell it all out.

"Maybe he wanted your money?" Laura asked, hoping to get some details that might help the criminal investigation.

"I only had five dollars in my wallet for lunch," Queena said. She began to cry again.

The doctor came in and examined Queena briefly. He said he would send an optometrist to test her vision, as well as a neurologist.

After the doctor left, I noticed that Queena's shoulders were swollen, blistered, and red with what looked like a million small bites. Queena told us she felt painful and itchy. Later, a nurse mentioned that the doctors were aware of the problem—ant bites. She'd been lying on an anthill during the attack. The bites had already been sanitized, and the nurse planned an intravenous administration of an antibiotic soon.

Throughout the remainder of the day, my girls talked quietly with one another. In those moments, I thought Queena needed a sister more than a mother. Later, Anna told me she had reassured Queena that her bruises would go away and the swelling would subside. Any scars would be covered with makeup, so she would still look beautiful for the senior prom the following weekend.

Queena asked Anna who did this to her and why. She asked if she would be okay. Anna didn't tell her about the rape, just that Queena would be fine and that she needed to stay in the hospital for a little while to heal. Based on what the doctors said, we believed this was true. Queena would be all right, and we would be prepping for the prom in a week's time.

Queena complained of thirst, so Anna put pieces of crushed ice into her mouth. The doctors didn't want her to drink anything because she might throw up.

Later, an optometrist arrived to test Queena's vision. She began by shining a light into Queena's eyes, which Queena was able see. But when the doctor put two fingers in front of her face, Queena saw only a blurry shadow. Outside the room, I asked the optometrist for more information. She thought a portion of Queena's brain might have been damaged. Her eyes and optic nerve were still good, but her occipital lobe didn't seem to be interpreting visual images or pictures. This could have been due to a lack of oxygen to the brain during the attack. If there were such an injury, Queena's vision would hopefully improve as her brain healed.

When the neurologist came, he asked Queena to move parts of her body, one at a time. She succeeded until he asked her to lift her left leg. She couldn't. The same thing happened with her left arm. She could not move the entire left side of her body. Determined to think positively, I reasoned that her body was still too weak after her long sleep.

The neurologist didn't speculate about the cause. He immediately ordered a CT scan and an MRI to examine Queena's brain. Soon, a radiologist wheeled Queena out of the room for testing. We waited eagerly for the results.

The tests brought more troubling news.

Queena had suffered a stroke in the right part of her brain, which controls the left side of her body. The neurologist told us that she could undergo physical therapy at home to retrain the left side of her body. It was one more unexpected consequence of her injuries, but it sounded doable. We could overcome this latest blow.

It became clear at this point that Queena would not make it to the prom in a week. But in my mind, she could still become the young woman she had been before this ordeal. A little therapy, and she would be back on track toward achieving her goals.

I was wrong.

Recovery would not be swift. In fact, it would be a long, long road to healing, and we hadn't yet begun.

Queena grew weaker as the hours passed. Her voice softened to a whisper that we could barely hear. Her thirst continued, so Anna frequently put ice chips in her mouth as they talked.

At one point, I promised to take Queena to the Cheesecake Factory when all of this ended. She smiled. It was one of her favorite restaurants. I reminded my girls of something funny that happened just after Queena obtained her driver's license. To celebrate her newfound independence, she'd driven Anna to the Cheesecake Factory for dinner. Queena had parked the car, got out, locked the door, and instantly realized the keys were in the ignition—the engine still running. A little embarrassed, they had called me to ask, "Could you please bring us a spare key?"

For the first time since arriving at the hospital, *we laughed.*

I will always cherish that moment—the three of us laughing in spite of it all. In the past, we had taken the simple, poignant times for granted. Not anymore. We could no longer afford to forget the bonds between us. The memories, the smiles, and the love that we feel for one another are the treasures no one can ever snatch from us. Not even the beast.

The good feelings that filled the hospital room quickly vanished when Anna gently stretched Queena's left arm, as the nurse had demonstrated earlier. She'd told Anna not to be alarmed if she saw Queena's muscles reflex or "jump" while stretching them. That was to be expected. So, we didn't become concerned as her muscles jumped slightly, time and again.

By midnight, however, while Queena slept, I saw what looked like quaking motions in her left leg. These were involuntary movements that migrated up her legs to her arms and, finally, throughout her whole body. Surely, these were no ordinary reflexes.

I called to the night doctor as he was making rounds to tell him Queena might be having seizures. He checked on her and said, "No, just routine muscle reflexes."

Queena's muscles continued jerking with increasing intensity throughout the night. Her face continued to twitch as well. I *knew* she was experiencing seizures. Again, I asked for help. This time, another physician took a closer look and immediately ordered an electroencephalogram, or EEG. By then, Queena was no longer responding when we spoke to her. She just kept twitching and growing weaker.

An EEG technician brought a large monitor, electrodes, and wires into the room. He attached the electrodes to Queena's scalp with a glue-like substance. Squiggly lines appeared in haphazard directions on the monitor, representing Queena's brain activity.

"Yes," he said. "It's possible she had a seizure, but we need to confirm this with the neurologist."

It was now Saturday morning, April 26. The neurologist wouldn't be back until Monday, so we were forced to wait again.

We later referred to the events that unfolded that weekend as Queena's "second injury."

Even today, I wonder if things would have turned out differently if the night doctor had paid more attention to *me*—his patient's mother. Would he have been able to stop the seizure and, perhaps, lessen the long-term damage to Queena's brain?

For a while, I felt anger toward him. I saw his face in my mind many times. I recalled his casual tone, assuring us that Queena's movements amounted to normal muscle reflexes. I even looked up his name in case we wanted to sue him someday. We never did.

I also questioned why a brain specialist hadn't evaluated Queena immediately upon her arrival. I thought back to the paramedics who had met us behind the library. Hadn't they been concerned about a brain injury? My daughter had been severely beaten and raped. Her nose was broken. Her skull was fractured. Why were we in a trauma center without a brain specialist?

On top of that list of injuries, she had suffered a stroke while in the trauma center! She couldn't move her left limbs. All of these symptoms were followed by a surprise seizure, while her body deteriorated in front of our eyes. Yet, we were told to wait until Monday, when the neurologist started his regular workweek?

It all seemed so *unacceptable.*

Perhaps there were logical reasons for the deterioration in Queena's condition that we didn't understand at the time. Regardless, we couldn't afford the added heartache and stress that accompanies feelings of doubt, mistrust, anger, or bitterness.

We couldn't keep looking back in time. What happened . . . *happened.*

After the second injury, I regretted not spending more time talking with Queena during her waking hours. I realized that I hadn't made the most of a brief window of time when my daughter could still speak clearly and laugh with me.

Now, I feared we might never have the chance to talk like mother and daughter again.

Queena (11) and Vanna (39) in Cancun - 2001

CHAPTER 3

"WE GOT HIM"

ON SATURDAY MORNING, WHILE WE tried to make sense of Queena's latest injury, Hillsborough County Sheriff David Gee and Chief Deputy Jose Docobo came to her hospital room. Initially, I didn't grasp the significance of the county sheriff making a personal appearance to talk with me. I was so focused on my daughter's recovery that I hadn't kept up with the news. Only later did I learn that the attack on my daughter had been the top news story for twenty-four hours, since Queena had been discovered lying in the grass behind the library.

The sheriff had commissioned an intense manhunt. Authorities had dispatched a helicopter while seventy deputies scoured the crime scene and canvassed the neighborhood, knocking on doors. A dive team had searched murky waters near the library.

Now Sheriff Gee and Chief Deputy Docobo said they had good news for us: "We got him. His name is Kendrick Morris. He is a sixteen-year-old freshman at Bloomingdale High School."

Earlier that Saturday morning, about 4:15 a.m., authorities had arrested him and placed him in a juvenile facility. The deputies were so sure of their arrest that they wouldn't need to question Queena. They had already recovered all the evidence they needed.

I didn't say much. What was there to say? His capture couldn't heal her. It couldn't bring back her sight or remedy whatever was happening in her brain. I did feel a degree of relief, knowing he couldn't hurt Queena, or anyone else, but nothing more. I hadn't thought much about his actual identity over the past two days. I hadn't really thought of him as a human being at all.

One thing did strike me, however. He was a teenager! Just a boy—even younger than Queena. A few weeks following his arrest, he would be charged as an adult and moved to the county jail. His charges included kidnapping, aggravated battery with great bodily harm, and two counts of sexual battery with force causing injury. Much later, we learned from media reports that Morris enjoyed spending time at the library and often went there after school.

At the time, I stayed focused on my daughter. I had to.

Queena's condition continued to decline. She stopped responding to us completely. We struggled to stay positive. Somehow, I was able to give thanks for the doctors who had gotten her seizures under control. Each day, they ordered CT scans and MRIs to monitor her brain activity. The hours that followed the scans dragged wearily. I walked around like a mindless zombie, wondering when my daughter would be able to go home.

I wasn't the only one functioning like a robot. Anna had watched over Queena for two nights straight without any sleep. The timing couldn't have been worse. Her third year of college was ending. Final exams were just a few days away. While I waited for the neurologist to return, Anna's friend Alex drove her back to Lakeland, near Southeastern University, so she could pick up some belongings. She returned a couple of hours later, her bookbag weighed down with textbooks.

I never saw her study as she sat by Queena's side. When I asked her about it, she assured me that every time she left the room for restroom breaks, she also grabbed a little study time. "Don't worry, Mom," she told me.

At one point, I met a woman whose brother was in the room next to Queena's. She and I took breaks and talked in an outdoor garden area, where she told me about her brother's stomach illness. I didn't want to tell her that my daughter was the rape victim whose attack had been all over the news. "My daughter has a head injury," I said.

The woman had an upbeat personality and encouraged me to stay hopeful. Then, a few days after we met, I saw her again in the garden. She ran to me, crying inconsolably. Her brother had passed away. The news broke my heart.

Soon, it would be my turn to cry.

The weekend finally passed, and the neurologist came back on duty. After examining Queena, he told us that her brain activity didn't look good. By Wednesday, nearly a week after the attack, Robert, Anna, and I sat in a private room with the head of the hospital's neurology department. We were anxious about what he would say but also eager to learn what course of action to take.

Queena's brain was overloaded with activity and swelling badly, he told us. It was as if the "electricity" in her brain had gone haywire. That's why she'd had the seizures. The swelling had begun early Saturday. Drugs intended to stop the swelling hadn't worked well, and her worsening condition could not be prevented. He apologized that this had happened to my daughter. When doctors initially examined her, they hadn't seen this coming, he said.

He used film from three scans to demonstrate how her condition had worsened. The first scan showed a dark area where a mass of brain cells had died as a result of the stroke in her right brain. But the damaged area had swollen, putting pressure on the left side, causing brain cells there to die, too. In the third scan, taken the day before our meeting, the mass of dead cells was larger. If doctors couldn't stop this soon, her whole brain could die, he said.

The blood drained from my face. What happened to the assurances that Queena would be okay? That she could go home soon? Somehow, I still expected her to rise from her hospital bed and prepare for the prom, graduation, and college. Now, we were faced with the real possibility that she might not make it out of her hospital bed alive. I couldn't think.

"But she woke up!" I spat out the words, my mind reeling. "This means she is getting better. Right?"

We learned she'd been responsive, but when her attacker had choked her, he cut off the flow of oxygen to her brain. Without oxygen, some brain cells started to die within minutes, causing a condition called anoxic brain injury. In plain English, when Queena's oxygen-carrying blood could not reach her brain, she suffered oxygen deprivation.

The doctor gave us two treatment options. The first was a medically induced coma lasting about a week to ten days to reduce the brain's activity to zero. That would reduce the pressure, decreasing the cells which were dying. That would slow the swelling and prevent further brain damage. The second option involved removing part of the skull to relieve intracranial pressure, which also could help reduce the swelling.

Robert, Anna, and I looked at each other, not knowing which path to take. Ultimately, as Queena's mother, the decision was mine. Neither choice seemed ideal, but the third possibility—my daughter's death—was unthinkable. She had so many dreams, so many reasons to live. I wished I had time to study all the pros and cons in detail. Listening to the doctor felt like hearing a foreign language. The terms—*coma, sedative, breathing machine, brain activity monitor*—were all so new to me. Why hadn't I gone to medical school instead of beauty college?

I asked the doctor what he would recommend. He explained that both options carried some degree of risk. Queena might not wake up from the coma. On the other hand, he typically avoided surgical removal of the skull in cases like this. I gave it some thought, then told him we would go with inducing the coma. Anna and Robert sighed with relief. That was the choice they had leaned toward as well.

Nurses soon provided us with more information on the procedure, and the doctor scheduled it for the next day. "We shouldn't wait," he said.

After he left the room, Anna hugged me tight. "I think Queena will be okay," she said. "Trust the doctor, Mom."

I nodded, thinking, *Do I have a choice?* What ability did I have to be the mother who made everything right again? I was forced into trusting others with my daughter's life.

Afterward, Robert and I took the elevator to the highest floor of the hospital, where I found the door leading to the roof. I flung it open and stepped out into the open air. I so desperately needed to release the tension, the anxiety, and the fear that had burdened me for nearly a week. I cried out for my daughter's life. I felt devastated, torn, and violated. I had lost all sense of safety and security for our future. *Queena's future.* I sobbed until I couldn't stand up anymore.

On that rooftop, I knew I had to let go of the feelings inside of me. Those emotions caused me to feel weak; yet I couldn't afford to wallow in such weakness. I had to release them, as much for my daughter's sake as my own. Queena needed me—the strong me, the mother who would be a rock for her. She needed a mother who would encourage her and tell her that, no matter what, she would be all right, and we would get through this.

I knew I didn't have that kind of strength. Not yet. That strength would have to come from another place. As I stood on the roof of the hospital sobbing and crying, I felt an unusual surge of power rise within me. It was just enough power to continue onward, enough to see me through the next day, enough to be who my daughter needed me to be. Tomorrow would provide Queena with another chance to overcome the beast. It would also provide me with another chance to regain my own strength.

I didn't realize it then, but the surge of power was the first of many meaningful encounters I would experience with God's love. Eventually, those encounters would mend my broken heart. I would come to terms with the fact that I could not protect my child from every danger, no matter how much I wished I could.

My own parents had learned this lesson well. They had tried to shield me when I was eighteen years old, and they, too, relinquished their ability to determine my destiny. Now, it was my turn to let go of my desire to control my daughter's fate. The only thing I could offer Queena was the same thing my parents had offered me—love and hope for a better future.

Vanna's family (left to right): brother Dung (1), mother, sister Tina (3), father,
and Vanna (9) - Saigon, 1971

CHAPTER 4

LIFE IN VIETNAM

(1962-1981)

As I struggled to process Queena's fight for life, I couldn't help but think back on my own battles. For years, I'd told myself that my past had led me to provide my girls with the security and opportunities that came with living in the United States. But now . . .

I remembered how Queena once came home from school with newfound curiosity about my native land. She was in tenth grade and took great interest in the tiny country where I'd grown up. "Mom," she said, "today in my history class, I learned about Vietnam."

I'd shared some details about my childhood with my girls, but I'd never told them the full story. Certain memories were too painful to relive.

What mother wants to tell her daughters about the horrors of the Vietnam War? Bombs exploding in the night? Her family hiding underground just to stay alive? I thought it best to move on—to focus on our new life in America. Yet history has a way of forcing itself into the present. When questions arise, they demand answers.

"What city did you live in, Mom?" Queena asked. She had no clue of the wounds her words pricked.

"Saigon," I said without elaborating.

"I don't see Saigon on the map."

"That's because the name of the city was changed. It is no longer there," I said.

Three decades after my own distressing story began, it still hurt to recall. Now I wondered if Queena would feel the same way about her assault someday. Would she recover from this ordeal, have children, and then keep the most horrific moments of her life buried in a mental casket of bitter secrets?

My own casket held the story of Communist forces from North Vietnam steadily advancing in South Vietnam, including the capital city of Saigon in 1975. I was born in 1962 in Da Nang, Vietnam's third largest city, which was better protected by the presence of the U.S. Air Force and U.S. Navy. On the coast of the Eastern Sea, Da Nang, in my memory, had the best beaches and a relaxed pace. This beautiful city by the bay provided an outlet to the South China Sea via a delta at the mouth of the Han River. Its large, natural harbor helped to make it a major port for the country. Our family lived inside of Da Nang Air Base, and that was the most precious time of my life. My dad was a security guard for the army by that time, so of course, I felt like a princess of the city.

In 1970, when I was about eight years old, my dad received an assignment at Can Tho Air Base. Our family moved to Saigon, where my dad bought a house in the hope of keeping us safe. My dad was often away from home for weeks because the distance between Can Tho and Saigon was about a two-hour drive. In the summer of 1972, my paternal grandparents came to live with us to escape the heavy fighting in Quang Tri. That year is known as the "Red Fiery Summer." The Communists once again tried to take over Quang Tri and the imperial city of Hue. My grandparents escaped with their lives, taking with them everything they could carry. They were lucky to escape unharmed as their house was reduced to rubble. Tens of thousands of people died fleeing when Communist troops fired directly into the line of people running on National Highway 1 that led south. We heard reports of one dead body for every meter on that road.

I didn't understand much about war and government back then. I knew that my father was the security chief of the Bureau of Armed Forces in the

Vietnam People's Armed Forces. He took pride in putting on his uniform each day. He wanted to help keep South Vietnam its own state. He did not want his country controlled by the Northern Vietnamese.

I knew my father liked the United States, the big country in the West that initially had helped our cause. He did not like the Viet Cong that fought with the Northern army against us. The battle went on for a long time. My entire young life was spent listening to the strategies and arguments of government conflict, of Communism versus capitalism, of the Cold War, of the Soviet Union versus the United States. I couldn't always grasp the terms or the concepts, but I knew somehow these things all mattered to our comfortable life in Saigon.

Like so many teenagers of my generation, I had witnessed the war on television. In late April, 1975, the North Vietnamese Army (NVA) reached the outskirts of Saigon. The TV news showed daily stories about the NVA winning this or that battle against the South. Everywhere we went in the city, people cried and argued about people from other cities who had lost all their money, their homes—everything. Some even lost hope or committed suicide. I did not understand. I would listen as the grownups whispered about acquaintances who told them all the cities looked like ruins. Xuan Loc, Phuoc Long, Quang Tri, Hue, and Da Nang—everywhere, buildings and homes were destroyed, rubble littering the streets.

"Why are they bombing us?" I asked my mother in my native language of Vietnamese. She tried to explain that the Communists had broken their peace truce and were attacking cities throughout South Vietnam. Still, it didn't make much sense to my childhood mind.

Then one day, our president called for all armed forces to go home to their families. They didn't understand why they were commanded to give up the city without a fight. My father left his station in Can Tho and traveled eighty miles to return home to Saigon. We feared we would lose the war. Many people who could afford to do so—like my family—left the country by airplane or boat. I heard Dad talking on the phone to my uncle about a plan to fly straight to Guam, which the United States controlled. By that time, my aunt and her children had already flown to Guam, and my uncle planned to fly our family out as well. He was a squadron leader at the Tan Son Nhut Air Base in Saigon and had reserved an airplane for the trip.

My dad turned to Mom and my grandmother and said, "We need to leave." He told Mom to pack, so we could go to the airport the next day. We loaded our bags and boxes. My two sisters, my brother, my parents, my grandmother, and I rode to the air base. When we arrived, it was closed to civilians. The last few flights to leave were military planes evacuating U.S. personnel and high-ranking military officer's families. Access to the runway was closed to all civilians, and heavily armed military police guarded the gate. Only those with special passes were permitted entry. Angry and desperate people gathered outside the fence, screaming and pushing to make their way inside. Soldiers aimed their long rifles at the crowds in an attempt to stop them from going farther. Because of my dad's and my uncle's military status, the guards allowed our car to enter.

We stayed overnight at my aunt and uncle's empty house near the airport grounds. There, we waited for the plane my uncle had reserved to take us to Guam the next day.

As we prepared to leave, however, my grandmother realized another of her sons had decided not to come. He had reluctantly agreed to fly out with us, but he never showed up at the airport. He was a famous singer in Vietnam and couldn't bear to leave the country that had shown him so much love. We waited for him, and my father called every number he could think of to find him. Finally, Grandma said stubbornly that if he did not go, she would not leave without him.

Through the tension, I sensed that my father didn't really want to leave, either. Despite the destruction all around us, he still hoped desperately that South Vietnam would emerge from defeat and win the war. He stopped dialing numbers to find my uncle. We all knew by then that he would stay, too. Finally, he spoke it aloud.

"We should stay in our own country," my father declared.

Our family roots in Vietnam ran deep. I am a descendant of the Nguyen family kings who ruled under the domination of French conquerors. My paternal great-great-great-grandfather, Nguyen Van Tuong, was the Mandarin prime minister under the Nguyen dynasty in Vietnam from 1824 to 1886.[1] My father was proud of our native land. His love for his country and family heritage was so strong that he felt homesick the entire time he attended college in France.

Despite our history, my mother still wanted to get out, afraid of what would happen to us if we stayed. Because my grandmother and my father insisted on staying, however, the decision was made. Dad drove all of us back home, where we found our housekeeper cleaning the vacant rooms. She looked at us with surprise, thinking that, by then, we were on the plane.

My father walked right by her and didn't say a word. He headed straight to the phone and dialed the numbers of his old friends—men who had fought alongside him to keep South Vietnam free. These were men who, like Dad, said they would never give up, never give in to the Communists. Yet, one call after another, he heard only the voices of housekeepers, telling him their bosses had already left Vietnam to start their lives in a new country. I never saw my father cry before that day; but after the last call, he hung up the phone, and he wept. For twenty years, they all had fought together. Now, his friends had given up. Should he have given up, too?

A few days later, on April 30, 1975, the explosions finally ended. South Vietnam officially surrendered. The North seized Saigon, and the presidency changed hands. Despite the warning signs, it all happened so quickly that we weren't expecting it. At least, not on that day. I ran out to the main street, where a line of armored cars crept along in the direction of the president's mansion. I eyed the men, but to my surprise, they didn't look like men at all. The North Vietnamese troops were teenagers with slim bodies and wide eyes—youthful like mine. They wore camouflage that looked like jungle uniforms and steel helmets ringed with branches. I think they were surprised to enter the capital without any resistance or a shot fired.

When they reached the mansion, they plowed through walls of security, and Gen. Duong Van Minh surrendered. Eventually, the troops captured all South Vietnamese soldiers, including my father.

They came to our home, arrested him, and took him to a prison in North Vietnam, leaving my mother to raise four children on her own.

My father was sent to the concentration camps, along with tens of thousands of other officers. In order to entice them to surrender, the Communist authorities initially told them they would need clothing and food for only thirty days. My father ended up staying in various camps for more than five years. He suffered very poor living conditions, forced labor, starvation, hard punishment, and daily Communist indoctrination. The Communists moved prisoners around to different locations so they wouldn't get too familiar with the surrounding areas and people, which might make it easier for them to escape. My father was singled out as a "dangerous" individual and was kept in camps in isolated regions of Northern Vietnamese provinces to make it even more difficult to escape.

About a year after Saigon was captured, the Communist government began to implement a merciless policy against Southerners, and they especially targeted intellectuals, wealthy individuals, and those who had ties to the United States or former South Vietnamese government. They established "new economic zones" located in remote highland areas, where living conditions were harsh. People there received no food and were reduced to eating the leaves off the trees and bushes. Some suffered from starvation. In many cases, people died from eating manioc leaves (also called cassava leaves) that they had cooked.

The government assigned my mom to one of these zones as forced labor. She stayed with a group of men and women in a big house with no walls, only a roof. My mom said it was very cold and scary in the nighttime because they were in the middle of nowhere. The government trained my mom to produce crops with no equipment. I remembered when she came back home, her hands and feet were so swollen and broken out. I had to soak her hands and feet in salt water to help reduce the swelling and horrible rash and pain. But I didn't know how to help reduce her anxiety.

Before the intense days of the war and our move to Saigon, my family had lived in Da Nang among the middle-class elite. My younger siblings and I rose from warm beds each morning and dressed in nice clothes. We ate ham and bread for breakfast, then sat comfortably in the backseat of our parents' car as a hired driver took us to school. Housekeepers cooked our meals and tidied our rooms.

All of that changed after the North won the war. With my father in prison and no longer able to support us, our income plummeted. The Communists said the South Vietnamese people had earned too much money, that our wealth was unfair to others. They ordered everyone to hand over the old South Vietnamese currency and everything of value that we had. We were taught that everyone in society was equal. That meant, for example, there were no more school janitors. We took our turns cleaning school toilets, and we had to bring our own cleaning supplies. On Labor Day, we all awoke at five a.m. to clean the streets. Our family went from wealthy to destitute.

Mother visited my father in prison, but not often. She had to travel by train to the countryside, where she boarded an old bus that took her to a small village. From there, she hiked up a mountain to reach the prison. She packed dry and salted food for the journey—all for a visit that lasted just a few hours. For the rest of our time in Saigon, the Communist government allowed her to see Dad only once a year. My siblings and I didn't see him for five years.

The reality of living under the Communist regime affected us in other ways as well. Children were classified in accordance with their family's allegiance, so children of Communist party members received special treatment and automatic passing grades in spite of their academic performance. Children of non-intellectuals—such as laborers, taxi drivers, and peasants—were in the middle category that neither received preferential treatment nor discrimination. Children of South Vietnamese officers, like me, were penalized. My grades were negatively weighed by the fact that my father was in a concentration camp.

I went from wearing fancy clothes to wearing the same outfit every day. One day in school, a boy was playing with fireworks when one of them got on my pants and made a big hole. We had no money for a new pair. My mom closed the hole with needle and thread, leaving obvious patchwork. I tried to hide it in front of my classmates, but I know some of them saw it. I also used the same recycled school supplies. I held onto them from one year to the next.

We could no longer afford bread and ham for breakfast. Instead, we started off the day with cassava or sweet potatoes, the cheapest food in the country. Rather than high-quality white rice, we ate cheap barley—the worst I'd ever tasted—and a dish called *bobo*. Food was rationed, and there were always long lines at the government distribution center. Many days, we didn't have anything to eat for breakfast or lunch.

The Communists kept detailed files of every family—your parents' occupations in the previous era, the number of people in your household, information about your siblings. They collected data through many organizations—schools, local police stations, workplaces—to look for inconsistencies. They used the information to decide how much food you could purchase, determine the outcome of your school application, choose which job was available to you. The Communists would knock on doors of houses in the middle of the night to check for anyone living there who was not listed in the files. Soon, neighbors began disappearing, never to be heard from again.

Somehow, our next-door neighbors were allowed to have a piano, which the two sisters there played often. The drastic change in what had been ordinary comforts of living caused me to dream that someday, I would have enough money to buy new clothes and school supplies for my own children. I dreamed that my children would learn to play the piano, play sports for fun, and would go away to college.

By 2008, half of that dream had come true—Anna was an exceptional college student. Queena, I thought, would soon follow.

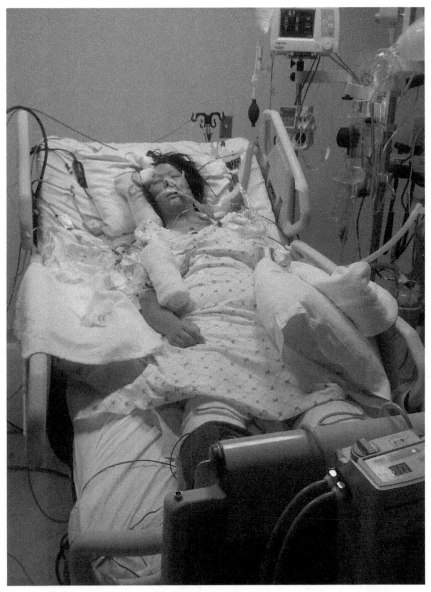

Queena in an induced coma - 2008

CHAPTER 5

ICU—DEAR GOD, WHY US?

THE MEDIA DUG INTO QUEENA'S story and wouldn't let go. Reporters learned her identity and tracked down close family members. Queena's name had not been released to the public because she was a rape victim. Still, journalists from just about every local newspaper, TV, and news radio station wanted to interview me and Anna. Reporters came to the hospital to find us, but the staff stopped them at the registration desk. They left business cards along with notes, pleading to speak with us.

They promised not to use Queena's name in print, nor would they speak it on air. They just wanted to relay our side of the tragedy, details of Queena's medical condition, and how we felt about Kendrick Morris. They wanted to put my grief into words, to capture my thoughts about my daughter being attacked just days before graduation, months before the next stage of her life at the University of Florida.

I collected their notes and business cards but did not respond. Despite the emotional release I'd experienced on the rooftop of the hospital, some degree of fear lingered inside of me. Yes, I was letting go of my weakness to be stronger for my daughter, but how could I open up to strangers? How could I expose my grief to a world where so much evil lurked? I shuddered thinking of the depth of the malevolence that had harmed Queena.

I wanted to remain focused on the next phase in Queena's recovery. On Thursday, a week after the attack, hospital staff transferred her to the intensive care unit. Located in a new wing of the hospital, Queena's private room in the ICU was spacious and tidy. Everyone needed a password to enter. Although authorities already had a suspect in custody, deputies remained posted outside her door in twelve-hour shifts. Once she was there, doctors prepared for the medically-induced coma by placing a small bolt in her skull to measure intracranial pressure.

Robert and I settled in a waiting room in the new wing. A couple of hours passed before the nurse came out to tell us they had successfully induced the coma. We could go in and see Queena. The nurse warned us not to be alarmed when we saw the bolt in her head. We held our breaths and walked inside.

Queena lay there motionless, soundless. In addition to the bolt, there were tubes that had been inserted into her throat. I noted her swollen features and couldn't help thinking that she didn't look like herself. Even so, she looked better than I had imagined.

"Not bad," I said, trying to calm myself and find peace after the shock faded. "She doesn't look that scary."

The nurse encouraged us to go home and rest, since Queena wouldn't come out of the coma for a week or more. Go home? I wouldn't have it. I couldn't leave her there alone.

"I want to stay here with her. Give me a recliner, anything. I don't mind."

The nurse told us hospital policy forbade anyone from staying overnight in the ICU because the patients needed silence to rest. On the verge of tears, I assured her I would be very quiet and begged her to let me stay. After some back-and-forth, she relented. Soon, I sat on a soft leather chair next to the window in Queena's room, overlooking Tampa Bay. No one else could stay, however. Robert and Anna would have to go.

Anna went back to Lakeland, since she had already missed several days of school and needed to continue studying for final exams. Robert and I went home to shower and returned later that day. Although Robert couldn't stay in Queena's room with me, he was close by, sleeping in our van parked in the hospital's garage.

At that point in my life, I believed in God, but faith wasn't a major part of how I lived. I couldn't remember the last time I'd thought about God before Queena was attacked, and I didn't attend a church. Yet when her life was on the line, I found myself wandering out to the garden area on the hospital grounds, believing that no one but God had the power to save her. The hospital staff and doctors were smart, but they weren't perfect. If they were, they would have been prepared for possible seizures. No, they were imperfect humans, but I had heard that our Creator was all-knowing and all-powerful. Would God listen to someone like me? Would my prayers be heard? Could God's healing power save my little girl?

For hours, I watched Queena lie in stillness, attached to the various machines keeping her alive. I could hear her spirit talk to me at times in her usual voice: *Mom, I am very sleepy. I just need to sleep.*

Sometimes, I took a break and found comfort in the hospital chapel. On one of my trips to the chapel, I spontaneously knelt in prayer. I'd felt God's presence on the rooftop of the hospital, but now, I needed God to do more than hear my cry for strength. This time, I needed answers to questions that crowded my mind—questions that only a Higher Power could answer. When I opened my mouth, words shot forth from someplace deep in my heart.

"Dear God, how could You have allowed this to happen? How could You have let my child be robbed of her future? *Why Queena? Why us?*"

I started praying desperately for a miracle. I begged the Lord for strength, for courage, and for mercy, but mostly for God to allow my daughter to live. I had believed that when we needed God to show up, God showed up. But for years, I'd prided myself in being a strong, independent woman. I had endured and fought through so much hardship during my childhood that I thought I could handle anything on my own. It was evident now, more than ever, that I couldn't do it alone.

I prayed for a long time on my knees that day, until I sensed something begin to change—not in my daughter's condition but within me. The questions I posed about why God would allow such evil to harm Queena and our family went unanswered. There was no miracle. She still rested in a coma. But I received something precious nonetheless. *Faith.* In the midst of my uncertainty and pain, God offered peace and an assurance that everything would be all right.

I had come into the chapel burdened and weighed down in spirit, but now, on my knees, my spirit felt light. With the weight of worry lifted, I began to believe in the power of God—the God who had placed my beautiful Queena inside my womb eighteen years earlier. That same God would make my family right again somehow, someday. I didn't need to try to do it all by myself. I couldn't anyway. What I needed was a greater understanding of God's help in my time of trouble. I began to recognize that the more I relied on God's Divine Spirit as my source of strength, the more I would see exponential growth in my faith. In turn, as my faith in God grew, all the answers I needed would be given to me.

During Queena's stay in the ICU, media requests for interviews were frequent. I accepted only two visitation requests, but not from journalists. The first was from Queena's friend Cristina; her mom, Dalia; and her sister Stephanie. Cristina was Queena's first friend when we moved from Maryland to Florida in 2005. They had ridden the same bus to high school. It had been Queena's first time riding on this particular bus. She had been a little afraid because the students had seemed so different from her classmates at the private Baptist school she'd attended in Glen Burnie, Maryland.

But later that day, Queena had said, "I looked around on the bus and found a nice girl sitting in the corner." The girl had allowed Queena to sit next to her, and their friendship began.

The day after Queena's attack, Cristina called me from school.

"Ms. Vanna," she said through sobs, "what happened to Queena? Why does everybody know but not me?"

Friday morning after the attack, when Cristina arrived at school, she had heard students talking about the Bloomingdale Library incident. "Who are you talking about?" she had asked them. When they'd said Queena's name, Cristina had been crushed. Now with Queena in a coma, Cristina wanted to see her. We couldn't let visitors into the ICU room, so Cristina and her family stood in the hall, staring teary-eyed at Queena through a glass window.

Cristina told me that during an assembly at school, students had lit candles in Queena's honor. "Everyone prayed and cried for her," she said.

Our second hospital visit came from the prosecutors, Chief Assistant State Attorney Michael Sinacore and Assistant State Attorney Rita Peters. Police had collected a lot of evidence in the case, but the state needed more information to prepare for a criminal trial.

Rita Peters greeted me with a warm smile. She let me know that Cheryl, the mother of Queena's friend Kristen, was a friend of hers. She had actually seen Kristen and Queena together many times and remembered my daughter.

"The State Attorney's Office wants to help you," she said. "They want to get to know you, so they can be your voice in court."

Later, I asked Cheryl's husband about Rita.

"Is she really as nice as she seems?"

"Gentle" was the word he used. "But in a courtroom, she's a tiger. She is the person you need in your corner," he said.

I didn't know what the future held, but I felt safe having Rita on my side after hearing his endorsement.

Robert usually joined me in the mornings. We sat together drinking coffee outside the ICU wing throughout the days Queena was in a coma. For lunch and dinner, we'd grab a bite to eat, or a coworker from my nail salon would drop food off for us. But every day, while away from Robert, I visited the chapel alone to talk with God.

Once in a while, I ventured behind the chapel to the garden area—the same place where I'd met the woman whose brother had died. I sometimes encountered others like me, going through the hardest situations, racked with fear and grief for their family members in the ICU. We told each other stories of the tragedies that had brought us there.

Through them, I acknowledged that Queena and I were not alone or unique. Every day, many others suffered through disappointment and uncertainty. They needed prayer, too. I learned how to pray for them and for their loved ones. Often, we prayed together. Sometimes the same faces that smiled with relief because of a positive doctor's report or signs of improvement turned into faces of sorrow after their loved ones suddenly took a turn for the worse.

We learned from each other. We leaned on each other. We supported each other out of a common understanding. Through them, God answered my questions—one embrace and one prayer at a time. I couldn't handle this alone, so others were sent to walk through tragedy with me. Individually, we were weak, but together, we found the strength we needed to show our precious children, our sisters and brothers, our husbands and wives.

Queena's condition failed to improve. By her fifth day in a coma, doctors said the swelling in her brain still had not gone down. She lay in her room, hooked up to machines with wires and tubes everywhere, able to breathe only with the help of a ventilator. I wondered about the challenges she would face when she woke up. What skills would she have to relearn? Would she be like a baby wobbling through her first steps?

I researched brain injury rehabilitation centers and treatment programs around the country and read up on anoxic brain injury. I learned that the brain consumes around one-fifth of the body's oxygen supply. I didn't know exactly how long the attacker had strangled Queena, but it takes only a few minutes of oxygen deprivation before cells start to die. The research proved painful and enlightening at the same time. The more information I gained, the better I could face the details of what happened to Queena.

As the days went by, I feared losing track of time. What happened, and when did it happen? I needed to remember. So, I sat down one day and used cell phone records and comments from Queena's friends to chart a timeline of events.

Thursday, April 24, 2008
10:04 p.m. Queena called Rachel.
10:20 p.m. Queena arrived at the library.
10:26 p.m. Rachel called me.
10:32 p.m. I left our house and drove to the library.
10:45 p.m. Priscilla, her mother, and sister arrived at library.
10:46 p.m. My sister Tina, her husband, and her daughter arrived at the library.
10:48 p.m. I arrived at the library.

Queena had been attacked during a span of about twenty-five minutes. These details did nothing for my daughter at that point, but for some reason, I had to get a handle on the timeline. My spirit was stronger now, enabling me to confront the truth of her attack. I took in the information about that day, just as I'd absorbed the details of Queena's injuries. The facts before me read hard and cold as I logged the chronology of events. But as Queena's mother, it was my responsibility to bear the truth of those facts.

Soon, I received a thoughtful goody bag from an organization called Mothers Against Brain Injury. I smiled for the first time in four days. The bag contained reading material and encouraging stories about people in similar situations. It also included a blanket, pillow, soap, and Tylenol for those nights when people like me sleep on chairs to be near their loved ones. At that time, the gestures of kindness comforted me, reminding me that others related to my struggles.

The good feeling didn't last long, though. I had begun to record all of Queena's brain activity and medical data. Each day, I noticed that her brain remained very active. The doctor wanted the activity lessened to zero, or close to it, to control the swelling.

Then, more problems came. I received a phone call about Queena's Medicaid benefits. When we first moved to Florida, Queena was eligible for Medicaid because I wasn't earning much money at the time. But she had turned eighteen two days before the attack; and having reached the age of adulthood, she no longer qualified for Medicaid. Insurance coverage had been the last thing on my mind. I told the caller that Queena was in a coma, and I couldn't afford these medical expenses without coverage. The caller responded simply that I had sixty days to transition to another insurer.

I didn't know what to do. My only hope seemed to be Queena's complete recovery in two months' time. The next day, a social worker affiliated with the hospital came and suggested that I apply for Supplemental Security Income, or SSI, for disabled people with little or no income. For some reason, the suggestion offended me. I never thought about Queena being permanently disabled. In my mind, the only question was, "How long will it take for her to recover?"

I answered the woman with an edge to my voice, "Queena is *not* disabled. This is just a roadblock in her life right now. She will walk again. She will go to college and walk at her graduation, just as we planned."

A gentle smile came over her face. "Of course, you need to stay positive," she said. "I hope you're right." She told me to let her know if I needed any help.

That night, after thinking about her words, I found myself searching for an SSI application. Was I being realistically hopeful about Queena's swift recovery, or was I in denial? I couldn't decide.

I filled out the application and submitted it to the government. I'd learned long before then that sometimes relief doesn't come the way we expect. Perhaps, the social worker's advice was God's way of sending additional help my way.

Vanna (10), brother Dung (2), and parents at Vinh Nghiem Pagoda - Saigon, 1972

CHAPTER 6

ESCAPE ON THE OPEN SEAS

(1981)

The situation in Vietnam grew worse. We didn't have enough to eat; so through the years, we sold off most of the things we had to buy food.

Then, in 1980, five years after the Vietnam War ended, my father suddenly showed up at our front door. He'd been released from the North Vietnamese prison. I had just finished high school and planned to go to college for a degree in business. Dad pulled me close one night and whispered in my ear.

"We can't survive here," he said. "It was my fault that we didn't leave five years ago."

He had been naïve to trust that the North would have a heart for fighters captured in South Vietnam. Now, he realized our family would never have a future—no education, no freedom—in our homeland.

"You need to leave," he told me.

The charge shook me. Yes, I wanted a future. I wanted an education and to be successful. I knew I would have no future under the Communist regime. I had seen photos of people living in America and Europe and dreamed of being able to live in such places. We knew families with relatives fortunate to leave Vietnam before the Communists had taken over the country. Every few months, those who remained behind would receive packages with clothes, medicine, and candies. I thought if I left Vietnam and found a job somewhere, I would be able to help my family back home. I thought I could help my younger brother and sisters, so we could all be happy. Before, I had always thought, even after the war, success would come in Vietnam. I, too, had been naïve. Now, my father was steering me toward another way—a route that I had never planned to travel.

He had already made a deal with a local fisherman to get me out of the country, along with other refugees who faced potential persecution from the new government. He planned for me to travel by motorboat for free with a group of others who were also escaping. My father would flee as well, but on a separate, smaller boat. At some point, Dad would pay the fisherman and jump onto my boat, so we could be together. He didn't want to leave my mother and siblings behind, but he couldn't allow me to travel to a foreign country alone. We would go to the United States together, and later, he would send for the rest of the family to join us there.

"You will be okay," he said. "I will be next to you the whole time. Don't be scared. Think about Mom and your younger brother and sisters. They need to be freed."

"Yes, Dad," I said. "I have to be brave. I have to survive. I will fight for my future."

I saw pride in his eyes when he said, "Never give up?"

I straightened my back and answered, "Never give up."

I had no idea exactly where we would go or how long it would take to get there—and I didn't know about the dangers at sea.

Shortly after the Chinese New Year, February 11, 1981, the day came for us to fight for our freedom. At eighteen years old, I carried the weight of my family's future. My father and I left what had been our sweet home of Saigon. Mom held me tight. She cried and told my father to keep me safe. She had heard stories of the danger involved with an escape like ours—people drowning in the South China Sea. She said she would pray until she heard from us.

Dad told her not to worry. He would watch over me every minute. Somehow, I wasn't scared, at least not in that moment. An amazing sense of strength came over me. Perhaps it was genetic, from the kings and rulers in my family line. Or maybe I just didn't realize the true dangers that awaited.

After leaving my mother and siblings, Dad and I arrived at Can Tho, the small city west of Saigon where Dad had been stationed in the Air Force. I felt both excited and nervous. I was hopeful for a new horizon but also sad about leaving the rest of my family behind. I wondered if I would ever see them again.

It was early in the morning. I stayed at the home of my great-uncle for most of the day. We did activities together, and I tried to enjoy my last hours in the only country I had ever called home.

Dad took me to an outdoor market, where we ate fish soup, but I accidentally swallowed a fishbone, causing excruciating pain. As the bone stuck to my throat, I felt badly for my father. I saw pain in his eyes because he didn't know how to help me. He never knew how to help when it came to situations like that. His job had always been to provide financially while my mother stayed home to care for our aches and pains. The bone eventually worked itself loose, and the pain subsided.

Then, in the early evening, Dad took me to the Ninh Kieu port, where a small boat, about thirty feet long and no wider than six feet, had docked. It had a roofed cabin in the middle to which we were directed. About twenty-six of us had gathered, including my two younger cousins, Tuan and Tuyen, who were seventeen and fifteen at the time.

Before getting into the boat, Dad pulled a metal chain from his pocket. On the end hung a summoning tablet, or a dog tag, that had his service number from when he'd worked with the U.S. Central Intelligence Agency during the Vietnam War. The chain also held a tag with my aunt's address in Anaheim, California. She had escaped on the plane to Guam in 1975.

Dad put the chain around my neck, just in case we were separated.

"That won't happen," he assured me. "Don't worry."

The boat was to head to Pulau Bidong, a refugee camp in Malaysia. The Americans would have a big boat waiting for refugees entering international waters. All I had to do was show those in charge my necklace with Dad's service number, and they would help me get to the United States. More specifically, they would help me get to California and my aunt. I held tightly onto my father's hand that afternoon, just before the sun went down, and tried to sound brave.

"Okay, Dad. I'll see you soon," I said in Vietnamese. "Be careful."

He grabbed me and hugged me. "I love you."

I stepped onto the boat and immediately felt seasick. I had never been on a boat before, and I vomited right away. Eventually, my stomach and my nerves settled. As the boat sailed along, I sat inside the covered area beside my cousins. Everyone on the boat was quiet, with not even a whisper to disturb the silence. We huddled in the cramped cabin in two rows, one on each side of the boat, facing each other.

By late evening, I looked outside and saw my father in the smaller boat sailing alongside ours, just as planned. I lay down to relax. The sky above me shone like a black blanket. No light from the moon or stars made it a good night for our escape. All the lights on the boat were off, and it seemed as if everyone held their breath and prayed silently.

I don't know how much time passed before loud sounds of gunfire awakened me. Boom! Boom! We turned and saw a coast guard boat slicing through the waves, quickly moving toward us. The captain screamed, "All women and children get down to the bottom! Hide!"

We moved as fast as we could. The captain of our boat revved the engine to full speed to make a run for the sea. The shots came from Vietnamese authorities in another boat. The crackle of bullets sounded like firecrackers. I tried pulling one of my cousins along with me to a lower part of the boat, even as he was throwing up.

Bullets volleyed back and forth for a long time, and I feared our journey would end before it began. Then, out of nowhere, came a huge rainstorm, which was very unusual for February. Our boat bobbed up and down through the waters of the Mekong River that empties into the South China Sea. The storm scared me, but it also helped our escape. The rain and constant whipping of our boat made it a tough target for shooters. They didn't give up easily, however. Shots rang out sparingly for a few more hours as we sailed on. As the rough winds nudged us farther from the Vietnam border, the shots eventually ceased.

By morning, a man came to the lower deck where my cousin, Tuyen, and I had crouched down beneath a cover. "We made it into international waters approximately two hundred nautical miles from the shoreline," he said. "We survived."

But it was unknown if everyone had survived. I looked around, trying to spot the smaller boat with my father inside.

"Where's my dad?"

The man looked at me intensely, then shook his head.

"I am sorry," he said.

The smaller boat had gotten away from us amid the shots and the storm. He had no idea what had happened to it or the people onboard.

"We lost him," the man said.

At that point, I did not know if my father was still alive—if he'd been swallowed by the sea or shot down by the country he once fought to save. My only certainty was I would need to be brave and complete the journey alone.

Detail of Queena's prom dress, purchased only weeks before her attack

CHAPTER 7
SO MANY LOSSES

SENIORS AT EAST BAY HIGH School donned taffeta dresses and tuxedoes. They wore corsages and cummerbunds. Smiling parents took pictures. It was May 3, 2008—prom night. The theme for the event was "Red Carpet Romance." Students rode in limousines and borrowed cars to a scene filled with decorations and loud music at Raymond James Stadium.

Queena's ticket, No. 0068, went unused. She'd paid sixty dollars for it three weeks earlier. The chic lavender gown with crimson beading and silver embroidery stayed on its hanger, tucked safely away in her closet, along with the matching shoes and dainty white handbag. Everything she had chosen to wear to the prom was exactly where she'd put it—except her birthday pearls.

Queena loved pearls. For some reason, once she grew old enough to care about accessories and such, she'd clasp a set of pearls around her neck every day, no matter the outfit. Those were fake, of course. But two days before the attack, I'd given her a genuine set of pearls for her eighteenth birthday. The pearls cost about $150, but they were worth the price for my baby, who had grown into a lovely young woman. Queena adored them. Her mouth spread into a wide grin when she opened the box at the birthday party I'd planned at home.

I'd invited her friends over as a surprise, complete with a dinner of Queena's favorite Vietnamese food. They'd snuck into the house that afternoon while Queena lay in bed, exhausted from the senior class trip to Walt Disney World the day earlier. I woke Queena up at three o'clock that afternoon. As she walked down the stairs, however, I noticed she was fully dressed, makeup done, and hair neatly brushed and styled. Clearly, she'd already known about the party and wanted to make sure she looked good for the inevitable pictures.

"Mom, you're not good at surprises," she'd said with a big smile.

Her friends had erupted into laughter. I'd thought I was doing such a good job; but they knew otherwise, and the joke was on me. I'd felt such joy as I watched them eat, talk, and laugh together outside on the lanai.

Many of the gifts Queena received for her birthday were things she needed for college. Anna had bought a decorative utility bin and filled it with goods for Queena's dorm room, including a pink mini vacuum cleaner and cute flip-flops for the shower. Queena's friend Cristina had given her a sweet birthday card, declaring her love and forever friendship. Other friends had given cards and gifts as well.

I'd given her a new pink laptop from Apple and the pearls. But the pearls were now gone. The investigators had shown us many of Queena's belongings they'd recovered that had been scattered on the ground around the library that night. Yet they never found the pearls.

I'd assumed she would wear her new pearls to the prom. I had never been to a high school prom. No such thing in Vietnam. I had heard other adults talk about their prom nights, though, and I embraced the tradition for my daughter. Queena would have been the first in our family to attend an American prom. Anna had attended a private Baptist school that prohibited a prom night. Instead, her school had hosted a nice dinner, where she'd dressed in a modest gown and listened to a special message from a faculty member. Not the same as being able to dance the night away with her friends.

Just three days before the attack, Queena asked me to take her to CC's Bridal Boutique in St. Petersburg because she knew none of her girlfriends would shop there. That way, her dress would be unlike anyone else's at the prom. I remember Queena trying on so many dresses that day, asking me which was the best fit, before finding the lavender one she liked.

I'd thought this night would add so many good memories to Queena's life. She preferred to go with her girlfriends, not that she had no other option. A Vietnamese boy in her class had sheepishly asked her to be his date, but by that time, she already had made other plans.

"Thank you for asking," she'd told him, "but our limo is all packed."

I'd planned to be the typical prom mother and take lots of pictures. Queena would be beautiful. I envisioned her in the back of that limo with her friends, all of them giggling in their elegant clothes. I imagined her on the dance floor, dancing to her favorite songs.

But now her legs were not moving. Her eyes were not opening. She lay motionless, oblivious on a hospital bed, as the music of everyday life played on without her. I stared out of the window in her hospital room, needing a fresh dose of that peace I'd felt on my knees in the chapel. As if God didn't know exactly what I felt, I protested that it wasn't just Queena who lost so much. *You took my life, too.*

In that moment, a welcome surprise entered the room: Queena's friend Priscilla. Her hair and makeup were done for the prom, but she wore regular clothes, no gown.

"What happened?" I asked. "I thought you would be at the prom."

"I couldn't go," she said. "I'm staying here with Queena."

She smiled, as if missing her senior prom was no big deal. I stared at Priscilla for a moment in disbelief. Part of me felt badly for her. She would not have a second chance to attend her high school prom. At the same time, I rejoiced that Queena had a friend who truly loved her. Instead of dancing and giggling and taking pictures with her classmates, she sat with Queena throughout the night, watching over my daughter like an angel. God had shone a light on my dark mood and revealed an example of sacred love.

Two days after the prom, the doctor told us the swelling in Queena's brain had not receded. We agreed to keep her in a coma for a few more days, hoping for a change. But another week passed, and the swelling still hadn't reduced as much as the doctor felt necessary.

"Give it another few days," he said.

My frustration overflowed. I had spent days mostly in silent prayer, keeping my own vigil over Queena. I tried not to let Anna see my discouragement. She put on a brave face, too, wanting to be as strong for me as I tried to be for her.

Then on Sunday, May 11, with Queena still in bed, Anna came into the room and whispered into my ear: "Happy Mother's Day, Mom."

I'd forgotten all about the holiday. In the hospital, we didn't look at calendars; we just counted days. Anna's thoughtfulness touched me, but I couldn't help crying a little inside. Usually, I would hear both her and Queena wishing me a happy Mother's Day.

The year before, Queena had called my mother in California several times, asking for advice on what gift to get for me. She had just started working for Abercrombie & Fitch and had earned her first check for $150. With a big grin on her face, she'd handed me a gift box that morning. Inside, I found a crystal heart—larger than any crystal I had ever seen. Queena knew how much I believed in feng shui. Crystal was supposed to bring health, safety, and luck. When I opened the gift, she proudly announced that it was a *real* crystal. She beamed brighter than the crystal I held in my hands. I cherished her thoughtful gift and proudly hung it from my rearview mirror. The next day, I went to the store in the mall where she purchased the crystal heart. Judging by the brand name on the box, it seemed rather expensive, especially for a teenager on her first job. I browsed until I found another one. When I turned over the price tag, the cost stunned me. It was one hundred dollars! My sweet, thoughtful child had spent almost her entire first paycheck on something for me. I felt humbled and proud to know that I had raised such a caring girl.

This year, the best gift she could give me would be much simpler. I wanted her to open her eyes again, to smile, to speak, to laugh, or even to cry.

Anna's gift was heartfelt and timely. She gave me a beautiful purple-framed picture taken of the three of us on our cruise the prior summer. The frame had the letters *M-O-M* on it. Phrases from Bible verses in Philemon 1:7 and Philippians 1:7 lined the side the frame: "Your love has given me great joy" and "for you have a special place in my heart."

I had cherished being a mom since Anna's birth. I had wanted nothing more than to be the most loving, caring, attentive mother who ever lived. I was determined that both girls would lack nothing they needed. And just as their love had given me such great joy, I realized that God has a special place for me, Queena, and Anna in His heart and that He hadn't abandoned us. He would take care of us.

During the coma, spirituality filtered into our lives in ways I never expected. I grew well-acquainted with the hospital chaplain. Every day when I stopped by the chapel, he said special prayers for Queena's healing and for my strength. Also, a woman from India came to our room almost daily. She stood beside Queena's bed and made certain flowing motions with her hands around my daughter's body, coming close but never actually touching her. Then, she placed a gemstone by the window. I later came to understand that this was the practice of reiki, or "healing touch." Whatever it was, I was open to anything that might help heal my baby. I allowed her to carry on in the hopes that something, anything would lead to genuine healing.

On one occasion, while walking down the hallway, I came across a group of people. I did not know them, so I just greeted them and kept walking. Later, one of the women approached me and asked if they could pray for me and my loved one. I did not hesitate. The power of prayer had been foreign to me in the past, but now I saw these spiritual offerings as opportunities to help Queena. By this time, I felt that my daughter needed prayers, no matter the religion of those who offered them. Everyone in the group stood, formed a circle, and held hands. Their prayers wrapped me like a cozy blanket. They opened their mouths and let out cries for Queena's healing, for strength, and for wisdom. They prayed in the name of Jesus and said, "There is power in His name."

With each prayer encounter—from the people in the garden, to the chaplain, to the group in the hallway—I learned something new about God. Judging from how others prayed, I realized that the most important thing was not that my words were perfect, but that they were sincere and from my heart.

I wished I could talk with Queena about all of this, because I knew she could teach me so much more when it came to faith. She had long been in tune with her own spirituality, even as a child. When she was eleven years old, we lived in Maryland. I remember her riding in the car with me on my way home from work. Snow covered the ground, so I drove slowly, fearing for our safety. I reached over and said to assure her, and to comfort myself, "Queena, you are a *good* daughter. I want you to be my daughter again when we are in Heaven. We can be a family again up there."

I didn't expect her reaction. "Mom, how can you be sure you will be in Heaven?" she asked. "You cannot go to Heaven just by being a *good* person." Her expression turned serious. "You need to believe Jesus is God's Son and accept Him as your Savior."

My daughter's words shocked me. I'd thought niceness and good behavior were all that was needed for acceptance into Heaven, in line with the Buddhist tradition that I grew up believing. Now, years later, the praying strangers at the hospital helped me understand my daughter's devout commitment to the Christian faith as she perceived it and its importance to her. I sat in Queena's room and prayed in the manner Queena would have desired. I made sure to end my prayers with "in Jesus' name," as the group in the hallway had done. I spent my days and my nights praying for Queena's healing, petitioning the Lord for strength and wisdom.

One morning, I came upon a group of teenagers in the hallway. I recognized at least one girl from Queena's school and asked why they were there.

She said another student had been injured in a car accident on his way to football practice. His friends had gathered at the hospital, just like Queena's friends had done for her.

Many teenagers roamed all around. *He must be popular*, I thought. Probably a nice young man who was well-liked by everyone. I asked the girl to show me his parents, and she pointed to a woman nearby. I walked over to her and briefly introduced myself. Then I hugged her tight and whispered into her ear. "He will be okay," I said. "He is in God's hands."

My heart felt heavy as I identified with this mother's pain, a grief so deep and so painful that no parent should ever have to experience. The next morning, students milled about with red eyes, and the football player's mother cried hard against her husband's chest. From my experience with Queena, I knew that sometimes words were useless. I left them alone and went away to pray for them by myself.

Later, hospital staff moved the boy into the room next to Queena's. Like the others who had gathered for him, I peered at him through the viewing window, just like the one in Queena's room. I feared he might not recover. My heart broke for his parents and for all of his young friends. I kept the curtains to the window in Queena's room closed. She still couldn't have visitors, so I didn't want students from her high school to see her.

The next day, the boy's parents agreed with doctors to take him off life support, and I witnessed what true bravery looked like as the mother watched her son slip away forever. I cried for her. It took unimaginable strength to let him go. I refused to leave Queena's side and clung to her more tightly that day. I never told the boy's mother that in her grief, she inspired me. She made me even more grateful to have Queena alive, despite her grave condition. His mother gave me courage to weather the storms sure to come. She showed me that I had so much to be grateful for, even in the midst of so much loss.

On May 12, the day after Mother's Day, Queena's doctor finally discontinued the drugs that kept her in a coma. He kept her breathing and feeding tubes operating. I sat nervously by her bedside, waiting and hoping her eyes would slowly open. I imagined her sitting up and spreading her arms to give me a big hug.

It didn't happen that way at all. Not even close.

Queena regained consciousness slowly and eventually opened her eyes. As she awoke, she had these terrible coughing fits, so severe they triggered the alarms from the brain monitor. The breathing tube that kept her alive wreaked havoc on her throat. The doctor didn't want the heavy coughing to increase her brain activity again, so he ordered a sedative to calm her. She stayed heavily medicated for days. Rather than the joyous reunion I had hoped for, Queena fell back into a deep sleep.

By May 23, Queena's coughing lessened, and doctors took her off the heavy sedatives. In the days afterward, the doctor entered her room every morning at six to administer alertness tests.

"Queena, wake up!" he would say in a booming voice.

She would not respond.

"Queena, wiggle your toes for me!"

Again, no response.

After a few days, doctors concluded that Queena's brain simply could not function. Their efforts to calm her brain activity and bring her back to me had failed. Her injuries had caused too many brain cells to die.

The news was almost unbearable. I had waited so long, my faith insisting on the opposite result. I didn't know what to think or feel now.

Hospital staff replaced temporary tubes that had kept Queena alive during the scheduled coma with more permanent tubes to be used indefinitely. They took the temporary oxygen tube from her mouth and replaced it with a tracheostomy (trach) tube for the long term. They took the feeding tube out of her nose and inserted a gastronomy tube, or G-tube, through her stomach. It seemed that they all gave up on her.

Through the changes, Queena stayed just as silent and still as she had during her coma, with the occasional flutter of her eyelids. My child. My baby. Unresponsive at eighteen.

Vanna and her mother visiting City Hall - Saigon, 1969

CHAPTER 8
MIRACLES AT SEA

(1981)

The night my father vanished at sea, no one on my boat knew what happened. No one talked about him or tried to find out if he'd lived through the night. They simply gave up on him, just as I thought the hospital staff was giving up on Queena years later. Is it really that easy to give up on another human being?

I cried because of my father's absence. I secretly hoped that the government didn't capture him—or worse, kill him with the gunfire that had crackled through the night. Maybe he somehow made it safely back to shore. I felt the thin metal of the necklace he had given me. As my fingertips touched the cold silver, I remembered his parting words to me and the service number imprinted there. My parents could no longer protect or guide me. I held tightly to the necklace. It was the only thing I had to take with me into the future.

We were now in open waters, the silence broken. Everyone talked about what they would do when they settled in a new country, the anxiety and stress evaporating. I felt hope but mostly relief to be free, outside the yoke of the Communists.

Then at one end of the boat, a woman screamed, "Water, water everywhere!" Only then did I realize my pants were soaked. Bullets from the shots fired overnight had hit our boat. The water rose slowly and had reached about five inches at that point. We found a dipper onboard and scooped out the water, dumping it back into the sea. I had packed a few changes of clothes, but the water soaked my bag as well. I worried about being chilly later. Then I imagined the worst.

Would the boat sink and leave me to drown? I didn't know how to swim, and I imagined my body giving way to the cold, relentless waves.

Our troubles didn't end with the water at our ankles, however. I heard the captain shout, "Oh, no! The engine is no longer working," he said. The floodwaters had filtered into the fuel tank. With no power to steer forward, the boat could only float. If we kept heading west, we would end up either in Malaysia or Thailand—or Singapore if we strayed too far south. We navigated by looking at the sun during the day and the stars at night. We kept a fire going in the smokestack and blew pipes, hoping friendly boaters would see us and rescue us. The remainder of that day, we simply floated on the sea. Yet I wondered where the big American boat my dad talked about was.

Two more days passed while our tiny boat sputtered along on the great openness with water as far as the eye could see. Scanning the horizon, we saw in the distance what looked like a group of lights. By their spacing, the lights appeared to be part of a very large ship. Someone grabbed a flare gun and fired a shot that interrupted the parade of stars above. After a few minutes, we noticed the group of lights were moving toward us. Our hearts jumped, thinking that it might be a naval vessel or a freighter coming to save us. I moved to the front of the cabin so I could peek outside.

As the lights drew closer, we realized it was a ship of Thai pirates. The bandits easily caught up to us and paired their large ship alongside our tiny boat. With guns, knives, hammers and axes, the pirates quickly swarmed over our boat. They ransacked our possessions, searching for gold and silver, taking watches and rings. They pried up the wooden planks along the wall and floor of the boat, hoping to find hidden treasure.

When the raiders failed to be satisfied by the booty they'd gathered, they became upset and turned their attention toward the women. They dragged all the women to climb onto their ship's deck. I was shaking, hiding in a dark corner of the boat. One pirate saw me, grabbed my wrist, and pulled me to the front of our boat. I cried out loud like a baby, struggling, and was able to slip away, scurrying back into the cabin. Fortunately, the pirate decided to leave me alone.

In the darkness, the sound of terrified screams filled the cold night air. At last, after these animals finished with the women, they threw all our food, water bottles, and gasoline containers into the ocean. They then climbed back onto their ship and tried to scuttle ours, pitching our little boat from side to side as they rammed us repeatedly so we could not report the crime should we reach land.

After about half an hour, the pirate ship abandoned us and left. We were stranded in the middle of the ocean with no food, water, or gasoline aboard a boat full of cracks.

Everyone took turns using small buckets to bail the water from the floor of the boat. At daybreak, the men on the boat put up a sail. When the wind died, our boat began to drift aimlessly. Over the course of many days of drifting, we grew weary and hungry, beaten down by the burning heat of the tropical sun. Our fate seemed sealed by the vastness of the water that stretched to the horizon in all directions. By a small miracle, we found a canister of water left on the boat, and each had a few sips a day to stay alive.

I suppressed thoughts of my father's disappearance by focusing on those around me, listening to their stories and telling them mine. We all believed in different religions. My family followed Buddhism. I grew up riding my bike to temple. On the boat, one person prayed to Jesus, someone else to Mother Mary, another to Muhammad. Not secure in the specifics of my faith at the time, I just looked up to the sky at one point and talked to the Creator.

"You are going to make the final decision," I said. "We leave our lives in Your hands."

Later, as we floated through the darkness, hoping for rescue again, I closed my eyes and wondered what tomorrow would bring. I had no idea. None of us did. We sat and talked to ease our tensions and strengthen our faith, no matter which god we believed in.

By midnight, some managed to fall asleep, despite the uncertainty of what lay ahead. I couldn't, though. My eyes stayed open, and I thought about Dad and the future he left around my neck, about my mother and siblings back home, and whether I would ever see them again. The longer I sat thinking about my family, the more the quiet of the night seemed to smother me. I saw nothing but darkness. I could hear nothing but the muffled sounds of those who had drifted into their own world of dreams.

Suddenly, loud booms sounded from the other side of the boat. BOOM! I couldn't figure out what might be causing the noises, but I knew it wasn't the sound of waves. BOOM! I had listened to crashing waves for two days. I also knew that it wasn't the sound of gunfire. This sound was different, and I was curious. BOOM! I crawled closer to the location of the noise. Carefully, oh, so carefully, I peered over the boat's edge and saw total blackness. The water looked like ink that stretched for miles and miles.

Then, I saw an image grow clearer. A shiny object burst through the palette of ink before me. BOOM! I couldn't believe it—a whale, about half the size of our boat, pushed our vessel forward. Too shocked to be afraid, I just stared with my mouth wide open. As if taking turns, the same sound came from the other side of the boat. BOOM! I scurried to the opposite side to take a look. Yes, another whale doing the same thing. Our boat was being nudged along in the water by two whales! Unbelievable!

I hurried to wake up the others. "Wake up! Whales are pushing our boat!"

They didn't believe me at first. Who would? They had to experience the vision for themselves. Rubbing sleep from their eyes, they jumped up and ran to either side of the boat. They stood wide-eyed just as I had moments before. Awe overtook our fear. Oddly, we didn't perceive the whales as a danger. We thought of them as the answer to our prayers. God's way of ushering us to safety.

When morning came, the captain checked his chart and calculated that our floating boat had not veered off-course but indeed stayed on track to reach Pulau Bidong in a day or two. Two frolicking whales had been our engine—our saving grace.

But the whales were gone now, and we wouldn't make it much longer without more help. We still needed another vessel to come along and rescue us. A few more hours passed, and the morning light surrounded us.

Then, at some point, a man looking through binoculars screamed, "I see a black point!"

We all ran to him, asking if we could look through his lenses and see for ourselves. One by one, we did, straining to see a tiny point of hope in the distance. Another man saw it, too.

"It's getting bigger," he said. "It's another boat."

"I think they saw us," the captain said, adding that the vessel looked to be heading our way. We hoped those onboard were the "good ones," people who were willing to help refugees, rather than ignore us or, worse, turn us in to the Vietnamese government.

The savior whales had long vanished, and our powerless boat remained stationary, bobbing back and forth. The black dot seemed so far away, inching toward us across miles of sea. Hours passed, and late morning greeted us with anticipation. The vessel drew close enough for us to make out human figures standing along its sides. The men looked slight in stature with tufts of black hair. As if they might hear us, we whispered to one another, "They look Asian."

About fifty feet away, our captain yelled out to them, "Are you Vietnamese?"

"Yes, we are Vietnamese refugees," they answered in our language.

We sighed in relief. Pirates, many of them from Thailand, had invaded boats traveling the South China Sea. They beat, robbed, kidnapped, or even murdered Vietnamese escapees. We weren't sure who was sailing in the other boat, but we figured they probably weren't another group of pirates.

"Can you help us?" the captain asked.

If we didn't get gasoline and tools to fix the engine soon, we all would drown. Leaders in the other boat agreed to help, but with certain conditions.

They didn't want to get right beside our boat because they feared one of us might try to jump into theirs. Their vessel, about forty feet long, had already crammed two hundred people onboard. We decided that a good swimmer from our boat would retrieve tools and a gasoline tank, then bring them to us.

One young man volunteered, diving into the ocean. As he swam back to our boat with the needed tools, a shark's fin peeked out of the water nearby. We screamed for him to swim faster. When he reached us, everyone scurried to pull him up as fast as we could, just before the shark's wide-open mouth threatened to chomp his leg.

After refueling, the crew was able to start the engine, and the boat moved forward again under its own power. The other Vietnamese boat sailed alongside our boat. We floated together for a few more hours while fixing the engine. It finally purred to life, and we were able to journey onward together to Pulau Bidong.

Our captain asked them to sail alongside us to Pulau Bidong, since we had a chart that gave us the direct route. Also, our boat continued taking in water from the flooding, so their boat might help us if we ran into more problems. For the next two days, our boats sailed side by side, now progressing steadily across the quiet, shark-filled waters of the sea.

My stomach churned from hunger. My dry tongue stuck to the roof of my mouth. We had only about a gallon of water left, and our food supply was gone. The leaders of our group doled out a daily ration of water to each of us—just one capful. My cousin Tuyen was so sick from dehydration and hunger that I thought he might die. I couldn't let that happen, especially after losing contact with my father and my other family members.

I crawled around the boat, picking up grains of rice that had fallen out of bags in our food supply during the rainstorm on the night my father had disappeared. Tuyen was so weak that he couldn't chew anymore. So, I chewed the raw grains to soften them. Then I put the mush into his mouth to swallow. I felt strong enough to give him my capful of water, too.

Far in the distance, the captain noticed something that was perhaps a larger vessel. We sailed toward it, taking the chance that they might have food and fresh water. We hoped they would be willing to help the "boat people," as the thousands who fled Vietnam had come to be known.

As we approached, I could barely believe the sight—a ship so big and tall, it looked like a small city. Those onboard eyed us coming closer and closer. Their faces did not look Asian, and we couldn't tell their nationality. When we got close enough to hear clearly, someone on the big boat grabbed what looked like a megaphone and called out to us. They spoke English, and I could make out much of what they said because I had studied the language in high school.

"Are you some of the boat people who escaped from Vietnam?"

"Yes!" we yelled back.

"Don't worry," one of them said. "We will help you."

Theirs was an oil-drilling ship stationed in that area for years. Many boats like ours had passed their way. Our boat continued slowly taking in water since we hadn't fully repaired the holes. But the people on the other boat assured us we didn't have much farther to go, about one more day's journey. They had enough food, water, and gasoline to help us make it to Pulau Bidong.

They threw food down for us, including crackers and different fruits. I caught a pear. It tasted sweet, juicy, and cold against my tongue—the best pear I'd ever tasted. I chewed a bit of it and put it into Tuyen's mouth, but his eyes stayed shut.

"We are going to be okay," I whispered in his ear.

He opened his eyes and smiled a little.

"We are almost there."

We had been in a holding pattern, waiting for a breakthrough that would usher us safely to the next chapter of our lives. Now with the help of food and a working engine, we regained hope for what was to come. I assured Tuyen that he would be just fine.

"You can make it if you don't give up. I promise."

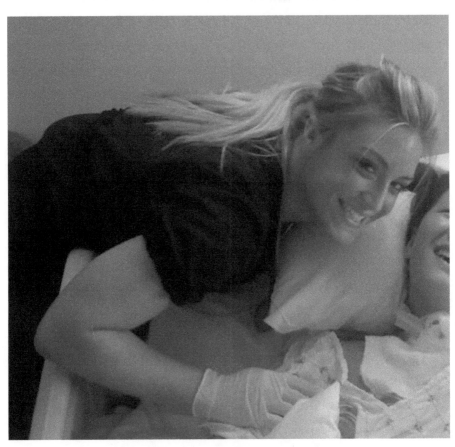

Nurse Tiffany with Queena - Recovery Floor,
Tampa General Hospital, 2008

CHAPTER 9

SHE'S RESPONDING!

"YOU WILL BE ALL RIGHT," I assured Queena, just as I had assured Tuyen all those years earlier when he was lifeless and weak during our escape on the boat. I didn't know if Queena could hear or understand my words, but just in case she could, I wanted her to know I was with her. No matter what the doctors said, I needed to think positively. They might be giving up on her, but I would not! More importantly, I wanted my daughter to believe she could recover.

"Everything will be just fine," I often told her.

I lived by her bedside, disconnected from the world beyond the walls of Tampa General Hospital. Day and night, my thoughts centered on Queena's condition, researching information about her injuries, finding methods to care for her, rubbing her muscles, making her as comfortable as possible. I didn't watch the TV news or check my email or take phone calls—not even from my mother, brother, or sister, who all lived in California. I left it to Robert and Anna to keep them updated on Queena's condition. Everyone understood. It took too much energy to talk to everyone and repeat all that happened—or didn't happen.

My mother and siblings decided to fly to Florida to visit Queena and support our whole family. They stayed at our house, which had plenty of room since I spent my days and nights at the hospital.

One day, my sister was on the phone with her husband, who had remained behind in San Diego, when I saw her face go white. When she hung up, she told me her husband had learned some disturbing information from news reports about Queena's attacker. She took a breath.

"Police," she said, "suspect Kendrick Morris of having raped another woman the year before."

I could barely believe it. I didn't want to believe it. If this was true, his first attack had occurred in 2007, when he was just fifteen years old. Soon, more details filtered in from family members who had read or heard various reports. His other victim had been a sixty-two-year-old woman working at a daycare center. She had been opening the center one morning in June 2007 when a man wearing a ski mask came up behind her, forced her into a back room, and raped her. He got away. The woman never saw his face, so she couldn't identify him. Police had collected DNA evidence but had no further leads to find the attacker.

Ten months later, when detectives collected DNA evidence at the scene of Queena's rape, they realized it matched the DNA already in their database from the other woman's attack. They had identified Morris as Queena's attacker, based on a combination of evidence. Now, the DNA linked him to the first rape, too. When I heard the news, I could think of nothing else to do but pray.

Please, God, help this sinful world!

Then came another blow. The neurologist who had cared for Queena while she was in a coma told us Queena would be discharged soon. He said she would probably live out the rest of her life in a vegetative state. He told me I should look for a nursing home.

I don't remember what I said to him, if anything, but I screamed inside. I kept looking at my daughter lying in bed and surrounded by stuffed animals from friends. Just a few weeks earlier, she had been part of her graduating class. She had a full scholarship to the University of Florida and a promising future. But just twenty-five minutes on April 24 had changed all of that.

While alone with Queena, I kept repeating, "No, no, no." No, I wouldn't accept the doctor's prognosis. How could I accept it and still believe in miracles? My daughter's hopes and dreams were not dead. Her mind, her soul still lived. Anna even saw her smile one day while playing Queena's favorite music.

"You will prove the doctor wrong," I whispered to Queena, believing against the odds that she could hear me. "You will get well soon."

From then on, hospital staff pressed me to find another place for her. I kept telling them no. Robert and I didn't think Queena should leave the hospital and the top-notch equipment they had to care for her. The neurologist and nurses took such good care of her. Yet my resistance to moving her led the doctor to call a meeting. He wanted to assure us that she needed to transition. The hospital was not the place for a long-term stay, he said. At a nursing home, she could receive adequate care, as well as daily therapy that might help her chances for recovery.

Wait.

The doctor had used words such as *therapy* and *recovery*. These were terms he hadn't mentioned before. "There is hope? A chance for recovery?" I asked.

He encouraged me. He told me there was always hope, even though life offers no guarantees. Each person's brain responds and recovers differently. He asked about Queena's grades in school. I told him she was an honor student who had earned straight A's, and he smiled.

"She has a better chance," he said. "She has a lot going for her. She is smart; she is young; and she is a fighter."

Anna, sitting beside me, finally spoke. "The doctor is right. A discharge from the hospital is great news. That means Queena is improving and ready to move forward. You must think in a positive way, Mom."

I wanted to be optimistic, but at that point, I felt more mentally exhausted than anything else. The experts said my girl had to leave, and I really had no choice but to comply.

A social worker stopped by daily, clipboard in hand, to check for progress in finding Queena a nursing home. She even provided me with a list of places. I had no idea where to start in my search, so I called Cheryl, Kristen's mom, who was an occupational therapist and had experience helping patients in Queena's condition. She agreed to help by offering to visit several facilities with Robert and me.

The following week, we met Cheryl and drove for hours, touring nursing homes, talking with employees, and listening to executives say how much they cared about the disabled or elderly clients in their care. Those facilities starkly contrasted with Queena's private room in the ICU, however. Two or more patients shared large, bland-looking rooms with only a curtain to separate their beds from the hallways. Some of the buildings were messy and unkempt. In one facility, one nurse had to cover twelve rooms. She visited each room only once every four hours. These places seemed more like warehouses than homes for the sick.

Back at the hospital, a nurse overheard Robert and me discussing our concerns. She recommended a facility in Sarasota, about sixty miles away. The next day, we drove about an hour to a place called HealthSouth Rehabilitation Hospital. The facility looked relatively new with clean rooms and a staff who greeted us warmly. On the way out from the main facility, we saw another building with the sign: HealthSouth Inpatient Rehabilitation. Robert and I stopped to take a look. The nurse gave us a tour and explained that their facility was designed to bridge the gap between hospital and home. I noticed their patients' rooms were large and had private bathrooms. Two gymnasiums, a library, and a cafeteria with a varied menu attracted us as well. It seemed ideal for Queena, and it would allow me to stay with her for long stints.

One problem stood in our way. The facility served short-term patients with at least a little brain function—not those like Queena, who had none. According to doctors, she needed a long-term or permanent place to live out the rest of her days.

How would they accept Queena in her condition? I didn't know the answer to that, but I truly believed God would help us make it happen. God was the One in control—not me.

After twenty-one days in the ICU, the hospital moved Queena to another room on the recovery floor. It was a transitional step toward her release to a nursing home or rehabilitation center. Instead of my recliner, I slept on a cot in this room while Robert continued to sleep in the van in the parking lot most nights. With both of us at the hospital day and night, however, the nail salon I owned suffered for lack of management. Customers decreased, and so did my income. We held on emotionally and financially, telling ourselves that things would change soon, that our lives would be "normal" again.

A window in Queena's hospital recovery room overlooked Tampa Bay. On our first day there, I spotted a tall church with a distinctive shape. I placed pictures on the windowsill showing Queena before the attack. The pictures and the church would remind me daily of the miracle of healing that I prayed for—the miracle we all needed.

Nurses arrived in the morning to give Queena her first bed bath after being in the ICU. It took three hours to untangle her hair because of the sticky glue-like substance used to attach the electrodes and wires that tracked activity in her brain. I imagined how fresh and clean Queena felt after being in the ICU for so long. Still, she didn't respond to their touches.

Later, when the physical therapist and occupational therapist came for her first therapy session, I held my breath. Yes, the doctors told me she had no brain function, but I hoped therapy would trigger something. After all, the doctor said there was always a chance.

The therapists pulled her up and supported her back so that she sat on the edge of the bed. They placed her arms on the table in front of her. They gave out simple commands to see if the stimulation of movement triggered her muscle memory. One therapist encouraged her to hold herself steady to the table. No response. After a few moments, they determined that Queena had no muscle function at all. Another therapist didn't say anything with her mouth, but her eyes reddened. As she tried to work with Queena, tears fell down her cheeks.

As much as I wanted to focus on my daughter, I couldn't help but think about her attacker in that moment. I wanted to hurt that beast as much as he'd hurt my child. For so long, I'd avoided thoughts of him, but now I couldn't. I blamed him for all of our family's pain. I screamed at him on the inside. *Kendrick Morris, you are a monster! You did this to her!* I wanted to scream these things, to open the window on the ninth floor of that hospital room and shout them loud enough so he could hear me from inside his jail cell.

But I couldn't.

The walls of my throat had closed in, and when I opened my mouth, nothing came out.

The hospital staff settled into a new routine. After Queena's bath each morning, the physical therapy team came in to exercise her limbs. She did not respond to them. A lift team then used a machine to transfer her body to the recliner. She would sit there and sleep all day long. Nurses showed me how to watch her monitor. I had to make sure her oxygen and her heart rate didn't fall below certain readings. I kept hoping to see some sign—a huge smile, a word escaping from her lips, the slightest movement of her hand. No such sign came.

Cheryl visited alone one time, without Kristen. She did some exercises with Queena's arms. The effort touched me. I welcomed anyone who genuinely wanted to help—be it through prayers for healing, suggestions, or taking time to help Queena work her muscles. As it turned out, Cheryl had even more to offer. She recommended we open an account at the local bank to aid in paying for Queena's treatment. Many future expenses for rehab would not be covered by whatever insurance we secured for Queena after the Medicaid ended. Cheryl suggested asking for donations from people in the community who were following the news reports.

I had no idea how much money we might need, but I didn't have the time or the presence of mind to organize a fundraiser and establish a bank account to collect donations. Cheryl said not to worry. One week later, she returned to the hospital with information on a bank account she'd set up. I was the trustee, and the first donation of one hundred dollars had come from Cheryl herself.

Then came our first miracle. A nurse named Tiffany started working with Queena. She bathed her while playing my daughter's favorite music—the Foo Fighters and Taylor Swift's first album. She talked to Queena, as if expecting her to answer.

"Queena, do you like shopping?" she asked one morning.

No response.

"Do you have any favorite stores?"

Still no response.

Tiffany named a few stores in the mall, but Queena's face revealed nothing.

"Do you like Juicy Couture?"

Suddenly, Queena's face brightened, and her lips curled into a smile. It was just a slight smile, but in that moment, it was everything. It was a miracle, and I saw the whole thing.

I ran around the hospital telling anyone who would listen, "She is here! There is hope."

Tiffany went to the doctor and told him what she'd seen. The next day, he visited Queena's room to evaluate her. He asked a few simple questions, instructing her to smile to indicate yes or remain expressionless for no. With every question he asked, she responded with either a smile or an expressionless face. Clearly, she understood what he had asked her to do. She could respond to the world around her!

Yes, inside that motionless shell of a body, my girl still existed. Relief and hope washed over me like a flood. I felt light as a feather—like my worries and fears of Queena being in a vegetative state had instantly disappeared. I remembered the short-term rehab facility we liked in Sarasota, the one that didn't take patients with no brain function. Now, Queena might be eligible.

I asked the doctor if she could go to inpatient rehab instead of a nursing home. Could Queena start therapy right away?

"Yes," he said, clearly moved by this sudden change in her condition. He later filled out the appropriate paperwork, approving Queena for treatment at HealthSouth in Sarasota.

We called the rehab center to discuss proper care, therapy, and accommodations. I explained Queena's transition, that her condition had improved, and that she needed help to recover fully. They explained that she would share a room with another patient, but I told them no. She needed a private room, so I could sleep there every night. I wanted to be at her side twenty-four hours a day. A few days later, the center approved a private room for Queena, equipped with a sleeping sofa for me.

After we realized Queena could respond to us, I talked to her more often. I made sure to explain her surroundings. I told her we would miss her fall college preview, but we could reschedule for the spring.

On June 16, paramedics came to Queena's room and transferred her to a stretcher for transport to the rehab facility. As her stretcher rolled through the hallway, the nurses all took turns saying their goodbyes. Queena's face appeared excited and emotional at the same time. Her expression indicated to us that she was missing someone. Other nurses noticed, too. Tiffany wasn't there. One of the nurses ran to find her.

Finally, Tiffany arrived at Queena's side and held her hands. Tears welled up in Tiffany's eyes. "Queena, I will see you again soon, but not on a stretcher.

I want you to walk in here and look for me, and we will go shopping together at Juicy Couture."

The scene overwhelmed me. I wanted so deeply to make their wish for a shopping excursion come true. I cherish Tiffany and the other wonderful nurses.

"Queena will never forget you, Tiffany," I said. "She will come back for that shopping trip."

Queena beamed when she heard the promise of the shopping trip. She had always been my little fashionista. In that short goodbye, I witnessed just how compassion and care can breathe life into someone. It was truly the love of God.

Vanna's father safely back in Saigon - Summer, 1981

CHAPTER 10
ARRIVING ALIVE

(1981)

The water still seeping into our damaged boat, we sailed through the night to Pulau Bidong. Tuyen was still alive, but barely. Our ship had gotten off-course, and we were forced to stop at a small fishing village. Lights beamed against the black water and the even-darker sky, making the village look like a small city settled on top of the sea. Our captain asked for directions to the island of Pulau Bidong. The fishermen looked at us and smiled but offered no information to help. The captain held out a twenty-four-karat gold ring to encourage them. They took it and suddenly remembered the way. One of them pointed us in a different direction than we had assumed we should travel.

I hoped the man was right. My body, covered in damp clothes, shivered in the night air. My cousin Tuan let me borrow his t-shirt to wear outside. I admit that I closed my eyes and thought about death that night. I figured we had a ninety-nine percent chance of dying if we didn't reach the island soon. The other one percent, I left open for a miracle. Where were those God-sent whales that had pushed us along?

At some point, I had stopped caring about my destiny or whether I lived at all. I still had no idea what had happened to my father. I imagined Mom's sadness if she lost both of us. Yes, she would cry and grieve for a long time, but she still had my brother and sisters. Eventually, she would recover. Life would move on for them in Vietnam, just as it had after all the other devastations we'd suffered during the past decade. With those hopeless thoughts in mind, I soon fell asleep beneath the vast darkness above, unsure of whether I would see that sky again.

The songs of birds awakened me the next morning. I opened my eyes to a bright, clear sky—clearer than any sky I could remember—and the sight of birds flying gracefully overhead. They sang the most peaceful melody, as if holding a classical concert just for me. For a moment, I thought I had died indeed. *Is this Heaven?* A beautiful mountain range dotted with tall trees and flowers in a variety of vibrant colors surrounded us—a white sand beach in the distance. On the shore, I made out ghostlike figures moving through the dense morning fog. I realized that we'd reached the island. A few smaller boats carrying Vietnamese and Americans circled our boat and helped push it onto the shoreline.

"Welcome to Pulau Bidong," someone shouted.

On the island of Pulau Bidong, off the coast of Malaysia, a refugee camp had been established. It was one of the happiest moments of my life. We would never forget this day—a day written onto the lining of our hearts. It was the beginning of a new journey for us. We'd arrived with the clothes on our backs and nothing else. But we held the promise of a better life!

On the island, smiling faces greeted us and welcomed us to our new future. People lined the shore, other refugees looking for friends, parents, brothers, sisters, sons, daughters—anyone they knew. Workers for the American Red Cross wheeled over stretchers for those who couldn't walk. I pointed to Tuyen and let them know his dire situation. They rushed him to the island hospital. The rest of us got off the boat one by one.

When my feet touched land, I felt like I was walking on air. The earth actually seemed to move beneath my feet after so many days at sea. After everyone disembarked, we all stood together to watch the boat that had carried us to this new world sink into the sea. Only a few minutes passed before the water overcame it. We'd made it just in time.

Leaders on the island later told us that ours was boat No. 46 to dock on the shores of Pulau Bidong. It was February 17, 1981. We had been floating on the open sea for almost five days. We were lucky to have arrived alive. Some of the boats that left Vietnam were lost at sea for months while searching for an open port. Other boats simply disappeared.

The leaders guided us to an office, where we met workers who were with the United Nations. I was surprised that they all spoke Vietnamese very well. I showed them my necklace that my father had given me. I gave them the information about his service record and my aunt's whereabouts in the United States. We filled out paperwork. We were told that we would be able to receive mail and phone calls. The workers gave us clothes and food and assigned us to a makeshift hut that four people shared. I was so grateful for the shelter, still better than a cracked boat with no future. My body stank, so I couldn't wait to bathe, change into clean clothes, and rest.

The refugees, thankful to have survived, jokingly referred to Pulau Bidong as "Buon lau, Bi dat," meaning "a sad place." It was a stepping stone for everyone to reach their desired destinations. The island was probably less than a mile square and divided into sections labeled A through G. The refugees lived in makeshift huts made of wood from the forests and sailing fabric, tarps, or whatever washed up on the beach. They built beds from flotsam, bamboo, or salvaged timber from wrecked boats.

After settling in, I walked around the island to see the other "boat people" and how they lived. Despite the island's small size, it looked like a little Saigon to me with a hospital, school, church, food markets, a jewelry store, café, and even a tailor. In time, I ran into old friends and classmates from Vietnam who had escaped on one of the forty-five other boats to arrive before ours. I was told that some people created businesses on the island because they had no one in America to sponsor them. They planned to make new lives for themselves in this location.

I set my hopes on a more stable life on the other side of the Pacific on the West Coast of the United States. Representatives from Western countries including the United States, Germany, France, Norway, Sweden, Australia, England, Denmark, and others came and interviewed people. Those who were lucky received an offer to settle in one of those countries. Others remained on Pulau Bidong for years because no country wanted them.

At night, most of the shelters glowed with candlelight, except for the longhouse section, which had neon lights. My first night on the island, and on many occasions in the weeks to come, I stopped at a Vietnamese sandwich shop, just to look at the food I longed for from back home. Some of the sandwiches, sweets, and drinks I hadn't tasted since before the war ended and Communism left us poor and eating cassava and cheap barley. I had no money to buy anything in the shop, but just the sight of it all satisfied me, reminding me of another way of living that wasn't all about struggle, danger, and survival. One day, I would have that kind of security again with a family of my own. In America.

I spent most of my days exploring, watching other people. There were English classes to prepare people for resettlement that were taught by Vietnamese volunteers who knew some basic English. I never bothered to attend those, having known some English from back home.

I made some friends on the island, and we shared stories about our journey to Pulau Bidong. I heard many tales of people dying from starvation and dehydration when their boats were stranded on the ocean for many weeks. I was astonished over just how fortunate we were.

My cousins and I sent a telegram to our family back in Vietnam to let them know we had arrived. A few weeks later, my name sounded over a loudspeaker on the island. I had received mail. It was a letter from Mom. I cried as I opened it. I was afraid of learning how my family fared and whether or not they had heard from Dad. As I read, my trembles turned to shouts of joy. My father lived! His small boat got lost in the storm, but he'd made it back to Saigon. I could barely contain myself. I missed my father so.

His survival strengthened my determination to do what he had said: *Never give up.*

I didn't know how to make it on my own, but I knew I had to try.

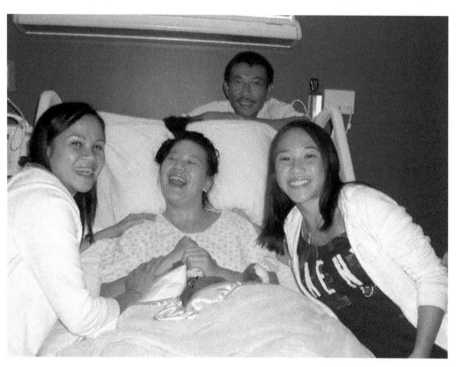

Vanna's sister Tina (left), her husband Hoang, and her daughter Amy visiting
Queena at HealthSouth Rehabilitation - Sarasota, FL, 2008

CHAPTER 11

REHAB—A FIGHTING CHANCE

WHO WOULD BELIEVE SOMETHING SO horrible could happen to a good girl, innocently returning library books in the United States of America? I couldn't get that thought out of my head. On the news, I had often seen stories of innocent people who had become victims of terrible crimes. I just never thought it would happen to my family.

Now, in the nearly two months since Queena's attack, I cried out to God more than I could ever remember—even more than on my near-death voyage from Vietnam. Before this tragedy, I didn't think faith played much of a role in life's circumstances. Yet, as I rode with Queena in the ambulance that took us from the hospital to HealthSouth Rehabilitation, I hoped that my pleas to God would change what I saw in front of me.

"God, if You are real, please heal my daughter," I pleaded. "Mend our broken hearts."

From somewhere inside me, I sensed God's Divine voice speaking. *The evil that wanted to take Queena's life did not escape My eye,* the Voice whispered. It settled me, reassured me that better things would come. All that had happened to our family seemed so unfair, but God had not turned away from us. All was seen and known. God would make it all right.

Some might think it crazy, but for the first time, I began to see the potential for purpose in our tragedy. Had God allowed this to happen in order to stop Kendrick Morris from hurting other women? Did God have a Divine hand on Queena all along—even throughout the brutal attack—saving her life? I know that others, especially those who don't believe in God, would find my thoughts illogical. Still, I held onto them. I wanted to believe my daughter's pain was not in vain. God had a reason. I had to believe that.

I sat in that ambulance, holding a bag with Queena's clothes and a folder filled with her medical history. The paperwork described my daughter in the clinical, matter-of-fact terms that doctors use. Queena is eighteen years old. She was sexually assaulted on April 24, 2008. She sustained a "traumatic brain injury, anoxic brain injury, ocular infarction, and retinal hemorrhages . . . " I couldn't keep reading. Instead, I concentrated on sending positive thoughts and hope to my daughter.

"This is the biggest challenge you will ever face," I told her. "But you will do fine. I will be right next to you to protect and help you."

I didn't know much about the rehabilitation process to come, and I don't know how much Queena understood, either. Yet I think we both saw rehab as our only chance to fight for her future—*our* future.

Queena's new room featured high windows that overlooked the parking lot, built-in red-wood dressers with a big-screen television, and a sofa bed that welcomed me for rest each night. During the day, I transformed a cot into my personal desk by placing it in front of the sofa and positioning my computer and other work items on top of it. The room had its own private bathroom, too, which meant I no longer had to travel home for a shower.

Directly across the hall, the nurses' station, along with their kitchen, gave me a sense of security. The nurses sat just feet away in the event Queena needed quick attention. At the time, Queena was the youngest patient there. Nurses enjoyed caring for someone her age for a change and gave her special attention.

Queena and I lived at HealthSouth for almost five months. We met many other families caring for their loved ones during this time. Queena's friends often stopped by for visits, and Anna traveled frequently from college in Lakeland, despite her hectic schedule. The facility allowed dogs, so Robert even washed Gracy, Queena's fluffy twelve-year-old, one-eyed Bichon Frise, and brought her to visit. Gracy had cancer in one eye, so it had been removed, but Queena still loved her dearly. Gracy loved and missed Queena, too, since she'd been in the hospital for so many weeks. I lifted Gracy onto the bed, and she kissed Queena all over. Then they snuggled with Gracy's white fur against Queena's skin.

The room at HealthSouth looked somewhat like a college dorm room, decorated with flowers, teddy bears, and family portraits. One day, when I went home to get some of her comfortable clothes, I happened to notice the weekly planner Queena kept inside her book bag. There it was, sitting with books and papers that a high school senior would have. The last note inside the planner was on April 24.

Books due, it read.

I burst into sobs. Even after all the praying and peace I had felt, at times, I couldn't help but break down. I composed myself after a while. My tears and questions served no purpose now. I went around the house, gathering pictures of my daughters and me laughing together, pictures of Queena in goofy poses, pictures of her on the soccer and volleyball teams, photos of her friends—all symbolizing the life she once had, the life I prayed she would have again.

We'd received numerous prayer cards during Queena's recovery process. One came from members of St. Peter's Episcopal Cathedral, where they had heard about the attack. *Beautiful angel of God's own creation, you are in our hearts and minds*, the card read. *We pray that the Spirit of the Living God will enter your body, mind, and spirit, and heal you of all that harms you. Blessed mother, who stays by her angel's side, you are also on our hearts. We give thanks that God has given you strength and courage. May God's healing Spirit give you peace. We pray for you both every day!* Members from the cathedral signed it.

More prayer cards and well-wishes arrived from other church groups throughout our stay at HealthSouth. Family friends, coworkers, and high school classmates visited often. They sent cards and encouraging words that always lifted my spirits. In the aftermath of this tragedy, the community embraced us. Even strangers who heard our story in the news wanted to help. They donated to the fund that Cheryl had established on behalf of Queena. Visitors stopped by on weekends and sometimes weekdays, too. At times, I worried that Queena may not get enough rest, but the smile on her face told me she loved the company.

Of course, Queena's friends from East Bay High visited frequently, including Priscilla and Rachel, who wrote on a poster that hung on Queena's wall, *I miss not seeing you every day. This place is amazing, though. I can't wait till we can be together every day again! I love U!*

Our old neighbor, Robbie, from Glen Burnie, Maryland, flew in for a visit. Robbie and Queena had attended the same private Christian school in Maryland. His mother had watched my girls while I worked. Anna, Queena, Robbie, and his sister treated each other like siblings. Robbie reminded Queena of some sweet memories they'd shared while in Bible class together.

"Remember, Queena?" he said, telling of a time when the teacher asked them to write something on the chalkboard related to faith. Robbie had written, *I give my head, my heart, and my life to my God and one nation, indivisible with justice for all.* Queena had written, *But those who trust in the LORD will find new strength. They will soar high on wings like eagles. They will run and not grow weary. They will walk and not faint* (Isa. 40:31).

Robbie encouraged Queena to draw on that faith for her strength. "I know God has big, big plans for you," he said. "But be patient, Queena."

One day, the first firefighters to arrive at the scene of the attack showed up wearing their uniforms. We talked a lot about what happened that night. Some were volunteers from Bloomingdale Fire Station No. 27. They'd been preparing to eat a late dinner when they'd gotten the call of an attack at the library. The senseless violence and Queena's injuries touched them deeply.

They wished they could have done more for her, they said. Some felt the attack represented a failure for the entire community. They failed to stop such evil against an eighteen-year-old girl returning her library books.

Their words gave voice to thoughts I had mulled over in the past months. How could this happen in our quiet American suburb, where neighbors waved to one another in their subdivisions, where video cameras watched over public buildings, where security guards and police responded within minutes to cries for help? My daughter's story, they said, inspired them.

"Queena, you are not forgotten," one of them said to her. "Keep fighting."

Specialists guided Queena through therapeutic exercises each day, stretching her arms and legs, talking to her, and telling jokes that caused her to smile, at least on one side of her face. The muscles on the left side still couldn't move.

The speech therapist came into her room at ten o'clock in the morning for half an hour. At eleven o'clock, Queena went to the gym for physical therapy. After an hour-long break, she went back to the gym to meet the occupational therapist for another hour. In the afternoon, the speech therapist came back to Queena's room.

Each therapist worked diligently yet gently to teach Queena how to move again—her vocal cords, her arms, her legs. They dressed her in clothes I'd brought from home. They brushed her teeth and braided her hair, just the way she used to like it. The speech therapist stimulated her oral muscles using lemon juice, then root beer because she liked the taste better than lemons. She used VitalStim equipment to apply electrical impulses to the swallowing muscles in Queena's throat. Through electrodes attached to the skin overlaying the musculature, the impulses stimulated the motor nerves.

Physical therapists transferred Queena from her bed to a "tilt table" to prepare her for standing in an upright position. They pushed her in a wheelchair from her room to the gym or to the occupational therapist's room and back to Queena's private room again. They eased her on to floor mats and helped her to sit upright.

I watched over it all, making sure the caregivers got to know my Queena. I made sure no important details about her condition fell through the cracks. At night, nurses came in and wrapped her in big bath towels and took her to the shower room, where they shampooed her hair and soaped and rinsed her body, as if cleaning a baby. By nine o'clock, they put her to bed. I turned off all the lights and warmed my food in the microwave, hoping the strong smells of homemade Vietnamese dishes wouldn't arouse her. I turned on the nightlight I'd brought from home, set my laptop on my makeshift desk, and researched everything I could concerning brain injuries and Queena's symptoms. I constantly asked doctors and therapists about the new information I learned.

I asked Queena's caregivers to follow certain practices that had helped others with similar conditions. I requested that nurses turn my daughter every three hours to prevent bedsores. I asked that they enter and leave her room very quietly without turning on the light at night. Queena had become hypersensitive to noise, and her body tended to tense up easily.

A website, KidsHealth.org, mentioned that the brain is like a computer that controls the body's functions, and the nervous system is like a network that relays messages to parts of the body. So, the damage from Queena's lobes (the frontal, parietal, temporal, and occipital) blocked the messages coming into her brain from anywhere in her body, where the brain tells the body how to react.

That's why Queena couldn't move her arms or legs or the rest of her body or follow commands because signals were getting mixed up, or left out, before being carried away from the brain through neurons to the body. I read about methods to treat her condition through therapy and rehabilitation. One article said that people like Queena must learn how to move a finger, swallow, breathe without assistance, utter a few words, and start living a "second life."

I didn't understand what the author meant by a "second life." Queena has only one life—the life she'd been living for eighteen years. Soon, that life would include a full recovery from a vicious attack. Soon, that life would include her calling me from the University of Florida. I could hear her, just like Anna during her early college days a few years before.

"Mom," she would say, "you don't need to visit me; just send money."

I usually fell asleep around midnight each night, only to wake up three hours later when the nurse came in to turn Queena and give her medicine. After more than a month at HealthSouth, Queena made progress. The atrophied muscles in her arms still caused them to curl by her chest. The doctor explained that the spasticity was the result of uncontrolled tightening (increased muscle tone) caused by disrupted signals from the brain. But other parts of her body were more responsive than before.

She not only used her facial muscles and smiles to communicate yes and no, but she also responded to us by squeezing our hands, blinking her eyes, or raising her foot. She could hold her head up for about ten seconds. Even these small movements thrilled me. The former Queena, *my* Queena, still existed, alert and aware.

I conducted my own test one day to be sure. I held her hand.

"Is your name Daisy?" I asked.

She laughed but did not squeeze my hand.

"Is your name Diana?"

She laughed again, but no squeeze.

"Is your name . . . Queena?"

She squeezed. *Yes.*

The patients and family members I met at the rehab facility had more hope than those I'd met at the hospital. Understanding and compassion, rather than despair, filled their eyes. One man who had broken both legs during a car crash assured me that my daughter would walk again. She would go through the various treatments, just as he had, and just like him, she would walk again.

An older woman stopped us on the way to the gym for therapy and gave Queena a fluffy stuffed polar bear. She'd had it for a while and explained that she wanted to give it to the right person. Daily, she'd watched me and the nurses wheel Queena to her therapy sessions. The woman noticed the half-smile on my daughter's face and deemed her the perfect recipient. I took the bear and put it on Queena's lap, wrapping her left arm around it. The bear hid the feeding tube that ran to her stomach.

Somehow, these small gestures made me feel like our lives might be bearable, even as a patient in a nursing facility with inpatient rehabilitation. I had fought for Queena to stay in the hospital, but now I saw the benefits of being away from the constant life-or-death emergencies that passed regularly through the intensive care unit. Here, we didn't see the helicopter landing frequently with critically injured patients. We didn't see people lying on stretchers rushed into operating rooms. We didn't see groups of loved ones clustered in the waiting room with tears drying on their cheeks.

We did, however, see patients hooked up to life-saving equipment, as if they were half-human, half-machine. Yet I felt that we existed on the same ground to some degree. Rehabilitation was the great equalizer. No one cared about what you did or who you were before you arrived. Everyone just focused on what you could do now and how you could learn to live independently again. They cared about how you might make life purposeful again by overcoming whatever brought you to this place. They cared about how you might maintain hope and a dream in the meantime.

I stepped outside of Queena's room briefly one day to talk on the phone. When I returned, I realized that the nurse had allowed an unknown woman to enter. The woman sat in a chair next to Queena's bed, watching as tears streaked my daughter's face.

"Who are you?" I asked. "Why is Queena crying? What did you tell her?"

She introduced herself as Dr. Sears, a psychologist. She had come to work with Queena and the rest of our family to help us deal with anxiety, stress, and grief. She had introduced herself to Queena and explained why she'd come. According to Dr. Sears, before she got a chance to say much else, my daughter had started crying. I couldn't stand to see Queena cry, so I didn't like Dr. Sears in that moment. She had made Queena sad.

"No, thank you," I told the doctor. "We don't need that service. We're doing fine. Besides, no human could heal the kind of pain we've suffered. Only God."

"I understand why you feel that way," she said gently.

She went on to tell me that I was in mourning, that I had experienced a crushing loss. My hopes and dreams for my daughter had vanished. She told me that I had a right to feel sad. If I ever needed someone to talk to, she would listen.

I couldn't get over how she'd read my mind—no, how she'd read my *heart*. I had cried out to God, but I hadn't allowed myself to truly mourn the future that I'd envisioned for Queena. A future that, even if she did recover, would still be much different. The anger that I felt for Dr. Sears faded as I realized how much she understood me. She got it. The tears that Queena cried represented my daughter's release. All this time, she had held those tears back, and one visit from Dr. Sears now opened the dam for them to flow.

After that day, I called Dr. Sears almost daily. God had sent her to help me—to help *us*—deal with the sadness, the doubts, the regrets buried deep inside. One day, I told her how tired I was. Anna had been a huge help. She came on weekends to care for her sister and to give me a break. She told Queena funny stories and inside jokes that only the two of them understood. It gave me a chance to go home, do laundry, and bring Queena a fresh set of clothes. Anna allowed me to escape the rehab center and take a "real" shower. Still, the constant caregiving wore me down.

Vanna in Chinatown - Los Angeles, 1985

CHAPTER 12

ONWARD AND UPWARD

(1981-1989)

Authorities in Pulau Bidong contacted my aunt in California. From then on, time passed quickly. Each day, I stood on the island's shoreline to meet passengers on incoming boats and to wave goodbye to those who left for the "promised land" of freedom. Unlike my latter years in Vietnam, a certain energy filled the air, an expectation of good to come.

Just two months after I had arrived on the island, my aunt called me. We talked on the phone in the island office. Don't worry, she told me; she had made the necessary arrangements for my arrival in California. First, she sent me twenty dollars—a lot of money for an eighteen-year-old in Malaysia in 1981. I went straight to the sandwich shop and bought a loaf of Vietnamese bread.

Soon, my turn came to leave the island. From Pulau Bidong, our group of former boat people journeyed to Kuala Lumpur, the capital of Malaysia, and stayed there for a few weeks. By June, I boarded a plane for the long flight to San Francisco. I couldn't believe the next phase of my journey had finally begun. Other refugees stayed on the island much longer than I did, including my two cousins, Tuan and Tuyen. They had to wait for another American organization to sponsor their trip before they could leave Pulau Bidong. That meant that I had to travel this leg of the journey without any family members with me.

This was my first time flying outside of Vietnam. Somehow, excitement and the promise of a better future overpowered any feelings of loneliness I had. When the plane finally landed, I looked out of the window at a beautiful landscape, just like the America in the movies we'd watched back home. We waited for a few hours, then transferred to another plane bound for Los Angeles. I recalled the name from my high school studies: Los Angeles, California—one of the most famous cities in the world.

I deplaned and walked into a huge airport, where thousands of people loaded down with luggage moved swiftly to their destinations. I walked slowly, uncertainly, wearing a large name tag on my chest and hoping to spot my aunt through the chaos. She saw me first and ran over to give me a big hug. Soon, sponsors from United States Catholic Charities stood with us and welcomed me, too.

From then on, it seemed everywhere I turned, people wanted to help me. The Americans who had rescued me from Vietnam made sure I transitioned smoothly to my new country. They generously helped pay my way to their country and even accepted my cultural differences. On the drive to my aunt's house in Anaheim, we passed through Chinatown. Asians bustled about freely—talking, bargaining, and selling. My aunt explained that vendors sold authentic Vietnamese food and seasonings, including fish sauce.

I began to see America as more than a land faraway to be studied in my school books. It could be my home. Yes, my father had fought on the right side in the Vietnam War, on the side of the United States—I *knew* this now. I promised myself that I would get a good job, start a family, and bring my parents and siblings here, so it could be their home, too.

My aunt lived in a four-bedroom house with her husband and their seven children, six boys and one girl. Her husband worked for the aerospace company Boeing during the daytime, and she worked the night shift for another company on an assembly line. In the morning, after she got off work, my aunt went straight to the market to buy ingredients to make homemade food to sell to her friends. In this way, my aunt earned a little extra income. I helped out in any way I could. At night, I slept in a bunkbed in her two older boys' bedroom.

With help from United States Catholic Charities (USCC) and the US Citizenship and Immigration Services (USCIS), I was issued a Green Card (officially known as a Lawful Permanent Resident Card). My Green Card allowed me to live and work permanently in the United States. I also received five hundred dollars from USCC as a gift for me to start a new life.

Some said I shouldn't have done it, but I used the money to buy essentials and treats for my parents and siblings still in Vietnam. I went to the market and ordered fifty pounds of school supplies, soaps, and toiletries, as well as candies and cookies. It took months to ship the care package by boat. When it arrived, my family was just as proud as they were surprised. They could only wish for those items in the previous six years. Mine was the first and biggest box sent home in their whole neighborhood.

Soon, I applied for welfare and started receiving two hundred dollars, plus food stamps each month. I didn't like depending on the government for my income, but I figured independence would come in time. I practiced driving and got my first car, an old Datsun that overheated daily. I began to meet people and make friends. Eventually, I met a young man named Robert. He was eight years older than I, and he treated me like a younger sister. He was sweet, kind, and very private. He played the organ and sang. We became like brother and sister to each other, but soon, our lives took different paths.

My first job was for a company that turned pig hearts into heart valve replacements for humans and paid three dollars an hour. My coworkers and I sat behind a long metal table in a freezing, sanitized room made of glass. We wore lab coats, hats, and gloves. For hours, we picked bloody pig hearts from an ice-filled bucket and used long, sharp knives to trim the tough meat around each valve, so the company could prepare and sell them to hospitals.

I earned enough money to move out of my aunt's house and rent a room from a family who lived in Santa Ana. I attended community college, taking computer science classes after work. College wasn't the route for me, however, and I dropped out after one year. I wanted to focus on getting a higher-paying job, so I could support my family and afford to sponsor them in the United States.

My cousin Tuyen recovered on the island of Pulau Bidong after almost dying on the boat trip from Vietnam. He made it to the United States and majored in electrical engineering at the University of San Diego, California. We were so proud of him. Meanwhile, I went to beauty school, where I earned a manicurist license. I took a job at a salon in Azusa and became known among clients as the best manicurist in the city. Later, I went back to school to train as an aesthetician.

At twenty-four, I earned my citizenship in the United States. I cannot fully describe that day. I felt so excited. I had studied hard and taken the test about American history. As a new citizen, I could sponsor my family to immigrate to America, my new home.

For a time, I lived freely as a young, single woman. I went to work during the week, then spent weekends socializing and dancing with friends at a local nightclub. I met a young man in my dancing circles. Minh was Chinese but raised in Vietnam like me. He was my first love. We married and had our daughter, Anna, in 1987. In Vietnamese, the name *Anna* is *Van An*, which means "peaceful cloud." My life had been so hard up to that point that I hoped her name would bring my firstborn child good luck and success.

I loved my daughter, and I so enjoyed being her mother. Her presence forced me to put her needs above my own. I stopped socializing and going out all the time. But Minh still wanted to party. I later discovered he cheated on me with my best friend. I had no patience for anyone who was not faithful to me, or my daughter. I respected myself too much to allow myself to be disrespected. I had too many other options. So, I left the relationship in favor of becoming a single mother.

With a baby in tow, I explored Disneyland, Hollywood, and Redondo Beach. Instead of nightclubs, Anna and I went to Chuck E. Cheese's every weekend. We practiced learning shapes, sounds, and the numbers on her toys. I saved every penny I could and eventually bought a brand-new Honda Prelude.

Despite my new life, I missed my parents and siblings in Vietnam, especially after having Anna and separating from her father. I didn't want to move back to Vietnam, but I yearned to visit loved ones. My mother had not yet seen my beautiful baby girl. But when I suggested a visit to Vietnam, my father told me not to fly back to the country.

"Too risky," he said.

The government might put me in jail because I'd escaped illegally. Later, I wished I had taken that risk. It would have been worth it to see him one more time. On October 16, 1988—seven years after my journey to the United States—I received a telegram: *Your dad passed away Oct. 10, 1988.*

That is all it said. No details, nothing more. I called my aunt, who insisted I bring the short note to her house, so she could read it for herself. I put Anna in her car seat and headed for Anaheim.

"Is this real?" my aunt said, reasoning that my mother may have meant something else. Perhaps, she'd sent a coded message to prevent Vietnamese authorities from knowing what she really meant. Perhaps, my father had escaped and made his way to the United States, too. I hoped she was right, but we could only wait for more information.

Months later, a letter came. There had been no misunderstanding, no coded message in the telegram's words. The story shocked me. It snatched my breath away. My father had gone to a restaurant that day in October. When he'd gone back outside to leave on his motorcycle, a sixteen-year-old boy approached him from behind. The teen mistook my father for someone else—someone he wanted to kill. He stabbed my father with a scimitar, slicing through his body near the spinal cord.

My father, a soldier, survived years of battle during war. He'd endured a harsh, cold prison. He'd overcome the disappointment of defeat. Yet he died a senseless death at the hands of a sixteen-year-old boy. Innocently, he'd driven his motorcycle to a restaurant to grab a bite to eat, only to have the life he'd fought so hard to preserve stolen by a teenager, someone who didn't even know my father. The attacker was someone who was seeking revenge, and we were not surprised by his age. Violence raged throughout Vietnam, and criminals started young.

But back in 1988, my father's murder simply proved that I needed to get the rest of my family out of that country before it was too late. I looked at Anna and thought about how lucky she was to be born in America.

I thought about my father years later, after Queena also fell victim to a sixteen-year-old attacker. Maybe my feelings of grief and disbelief after Queena's attack mirrored the sadness I'd felt after my father's death because they'd both fallen prey to a terribly misguided sixteen-year-old boy. I remember confessing these private feelings to the psychologist, Dr. Sears.

"I feel exactly like I felt after my father died," I said. "I know that sounds silly because Queena didn't die."

Yet the Queena I had previously known and loved *had* been taken from me.

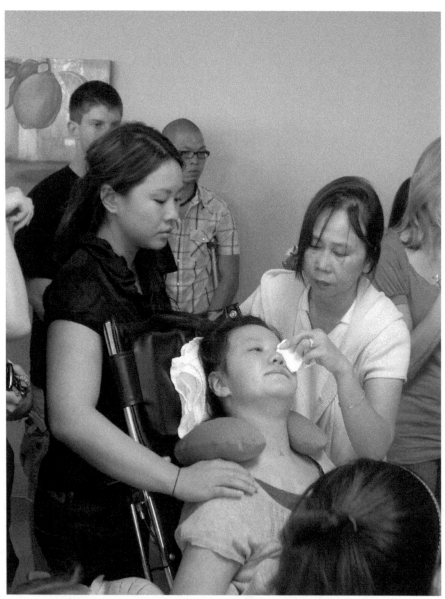

Healing Prayer Service held for Queena at HealthSouth Rehabilitation cafeteria - July 27, 2008

CHAPTER 13
PURGING THE BITTERNESS

THE MANY PRAYER CARDS AND spiritual encounters I'd experienced since the attack boosted my confidence in the power of prayer. Up to this point in time, my exchanges with God had strengthened me. I had been given hope and faith to keep going. I was able to encourage my family and live out those words my father had taught me when I was Queena's age.

Never give up.

Now, as her condition slowly improved, I sensed we needed a different experience, one that would move God from helping us to cope and survive to prayers that would move God's heart to help us heal physically, emotionally, and financially. Queena's Medicaid benefits would soon expire, and we had not secured an alternate provider.

One day, Cheryl told me the story of her son's friend, who had survived a car accident just two months before the attack on Queena. He, too, suffered from a brain injury. I logged onto a website that his family had created to document his journey to recovery. I related deeply to their story. Like me, their first two months had gone by in a blur. Like me, tears and disbelief filled their days. Like me, they clung to hope. After reading their story, I learned so much about patience and waiting in faith. They didn't know me, and I didn't know them; but through their writing, I knew I could keep hanging on and fighting for Queena's recovery.

Other people also encouraged me without even knowing me. For instance, Emanuel, the man who worked the reception desk at HealthSouth, always smiled, and peace seemed to ooze out of him. One day, I asked if he went to church. He attended Bahia Vista Mennonite Church, not far from the rehabilitation center. I had never heard of it, but I felt compelled to ask if one of the pastors might come and pray for Queena.

Emanuel passed along my request, and a short time later, Pastor Dave Kniss stood in my daughter's room. He listened as I told him about the attack, Queena's dashed dreams, and her injuries. I told him how my daughter prayed to God and clung to her Christian faith from an early age. During the visit, he prayed for Queena to be healed and for God to watch over us.

Then, to my surprise, he started asking questions about my beliefs. I told him that my parents had raised me in the Buddhist faith. As an adult, I didn't practice Buddhism, and I respected many different religions. I told the pastor how often I prayed for strength, courage, and healing since the attack. He asked if I believed in Jesus Christ. I wasn't sure. He talked about Jesus' love and how He died on a cross for us—for *me*. I had heard about Jesus from my daughters during their childhood education at the Baptist school. I had heard about Jesus from the prayer group at the hospital who ended their prayers with His name. I had also heard about Jesus from other Christians who reached out to our family. Yet I had not quite heard about Him in the terms Pastor Dave described.

The more I listened, the more I understood the spiritual experiences I'd had since Queena's attack. I began to understand the reason behind my cries to God and the peace I felt while on my knees, the new strength I sensed within, and the growing faith that I had in the idea that God could change things. I learned that all of that grew out of Jesus' love for me. That love had drawn me closer and closer to this moment with Pastor Dave.

"Do you believe the things I said about Jesus Christ?" Pastor Dave asked.

"Yes," I responded.

"Do you want to let the love of Jesus fill your heart?" he continued.

I did.

More than allowing Jesus' love to enter me in some tangible way, I wanted to purge the bitterness I felt toward the senseless violence and evil of this world. I wanted to rid myself of the bitterness I felt toward Kendrick Morris. Did those two desires go hand in hand?

Pastor Dave encouraged me to focus on the story of Jesus' willingness to give up His life for me. Focus on that unconditional love. If I truly believed these things in my heart, I would become a follower of Christ's love—a Christian. Tears trickled down my cheeks, and peace enveloped me. The same kind of peace I experienced while crying out to God and praying at the hospital, but more intense this time.

He led me in a prayer where I acknowledged my belief in Jesus and His love for me. I realized that I had yearned for this moment. This was the salvation, the saving grace, other believers described. Now it would be part of my story, too.

The day after Pastor Dave's visit, doctors said Queena had advanced enough to remove her tracheostomy tube. For nearly a month, she had breathed through this tube, carrying around an oxygen tank wherever she went. Finally, she could breathe on her own. The tube left a penny-size hole in her neck, but the doctor expected it to heal.

Other blessings followed. A member of Pastor Dave's church visited weekly to pray for Queena. Soon, I suggested that the church hold a special prayer service. I had never attended such an event, so I didn't know what to expect; but I would do anything to feel closer to God and to help Queena in the process. I asked for permission to use HealthSouth's cafeteria for the service to be held in late July. I ordered food, after Pastor Dave confirmed that Vietnamese fried rice and egg rolls would be appropriate for the mostly American crowd we expected. I sent invitations to everyone who knew Queena personally or who knew about her, including the people who had sent cards.

Queena wore an outfit from Abercrombie & Fitch, where she used to work. I combed her dark hair into a neat ponytail. We rolled her wheelchair into a packed cafeteria. So many people had come, including Queena's high school friends and members of Pastor Dave's congregation. The firefighters who had visited us earlier brought bouquets of colorful flowers and teddy bears.

Queena sat limply and stared blankly at no one in particular. She smiled from cheek to cheek at one point while surrounded by a circle of girlfriends. They all squealed with joy around her. Then the church band started to play, and their singers sang. The heartfelt music drew the tears out of us, especially Queena's friends. Above the quiet sniffles, Pastor Dave spoke a comforting message based on verses from Psalm 23:4:

> Even when I walk through the darkest valley, I will not be afraid, for you are close beside me. Your rod and your staff protect and comfort me.

At a time like this, he said, we all have questions. Still, God can "make order out of chaos, a blessing out of tragedy." He talked about forgiveness, too, compelling me to let go of the bitterness I felt for Kendrick Morris, or at least to begin the process. Then he asked everyone to circle Queena's chair and to lay their hands on her. We all crowded around my daughter. Her girlfriends knelt in front of her. Anna and I stood to the side.

Pastor Dave rested a hand on her shoulder and said, "Queena, there's a lot of love for you right now."

That's when Queena started crying loudly, the moans drowning out his voice. Anna and I cried with her. Then, everyone else cried, too. Even the firefighters brushed away tears. Queena did not miraculously walk or talk that evening; but when we left, we felt just a little better, with a little more hope guiding us back to her room.

Later, on September 8, 2008, Pastor Dave baptized Anna, Queena, and me. A medical van transported us to the church that morning, and we wheeled Queena to the front entrance. She loved the music and expressed her emotions both by weeping and smiling. We wiped away her tears. Emanuel assisted Pastor Dave in baptizing each of us during the service. Since Queena could not see the audience, Pastor Dave asked everyone to clap their hands as a show of affirmation. When Queena heard the clapping, she burst out with sobs of joy. She knew what was happening.

The church displayed a photo of her on big screens, so everyone could see her up close. One of the church women had knit beautiful white prayer shawls for each of us, and the church also gave us a large bouquet of roses. After the service, people came forward to encourage us.

"It was a wonderful morning of celebration," Pastor Dave said.

Prior to the prayer vigil, a reporter wrote an article about our family for one of the local newspapers, *The St. Petersburg Times* (later renamed *The Tampa Bay Times*). After avoiding the media for so long, I finally had the desire to reach out. Weeks before Pastor Dave's visit and the healing service, I sifted through the business cards left at the hospital. I found one card with the name of a Vietnamese reporter, Dong-Phuong Nguyen.[2]

The idea of talking with someone who might understand my broken English appealed to me. She would be able to relate to me and my daughters. I called her and introduced myself as the "Bloomingdale Library attack victim's mom." She answered in a gentle voice. Her words were a mix of Vietnamese and English. Our names had not been released publicly, but many people in the Vietnamese community had contacted her because she'd written previous stories about the attack. They wanted to help. Some in the religious community wanted to visit and pray for us.

I hadn't planned on crying during our phone conversation, but I couldn't help it. Emotion flowed out of me, as I told Phuong what a good girl Queena was, how she always brought me gifts for Mother's Day and Father's Day, how she made the honor roll and accepted a full scholarship to the University of Florida. For the first time, I released the details of Queena's condition to the media. Many in the public knew she still suffered from her injuries; but the degree of brain damage, the blindness, and the lack of mobility was not known.

I agreed to a face-to-face interview, which was a major step for me. For months, Anna and our family friends had dealt with the public, even updating my mother. Now, I would do the talking. I didn't know if I'd made the right decision or not. I just wanted more people to join me in prayer at the vigil we were planning.

The day of the interview got off to an excellent start in rehab. Queena stood up for the longest period since the attack—forty-five minutes. The progress put me in a great mood. I told Queena that a reporter was coming to speak with us. I put on soft music to relax her. Phuong soon arrived but seemed a little shocked to see Queena's condition. Queena lay on the bed surrounded by stuffed animals, communicating only by smiles. Phuong asked a lot of questions, including whether I wanted to say anything to the public.

"I want to request that the community pray for my daughter," I said. "I want every pastor to please pray during their service for my daughter's one hundred percent recovery."

After she left us, she wrote an article that ran on the paper's website that same evening. It was then published on the front page of the newspaper the next morning. It touched me so deeply. The headline read, "'My Soul Is Broken,' Mother of Beaten Teen Says."[3]

The article did not include Queena's name or mine, but it did have information about donating to our fund. This was a godsend, since my business continued to deteriorate because I spent all my time at the rehab center. At that point in time, we could barely pay our bills. The article ran just before the scheduled prayer service, so some of the people who attended the event at HealthSouth came from the community to support us.

In the follow-up story that Phuong wrote about the service itself, she interviewed several of the people who attended. She quoted Kristen's mother, Cheryl: "The crime that shattered the innocence of this one family has also shattered the innocence of all her girlfriends. Their lives have been changed. She is the embodiment of happiness, goodness, and innocence. I don't think she believed there was this type of evil in this world."[4]

After both articles, people commented online and sent emails of support from around the country. Diana, the president of the Vietnamese Student Organization at the University of Florida, wrote:

First off, let me start by saying that you and your daughter are a great inspiration to everybody. You are very strong and kind-hearted. I knew that VSO should do something to help you out, especially since your daughter was supposed to attend UF. Please email me a picture of you and your daughter and maybe some information so I can get donations for you and your daughter.

A neurologist named Jimmy in Chicago wrote:

I want to send my regards so that you know there are people out there who care. As a neurologist, I know how tough things can be for you, both emotionally and financially. I would like to send a card or gift to your daughter and yourself, as well as a small check to help out. You and your daughter are in my thoughts. I wish you both the best and hope the both of you can find the strength to keep progressing forward.

The response from readers across the country bolstered what Cheryl and others had told me. People wanted to help. They'd been waiting for me to let them. Soon after the articles, Queena's high school friends put together a car wash fundraiser. One of the TV news stations previewed the event a few days early. Unfortunately, the weather didn't cooperate. It poured the whole day of the car wash. I felt badly as I thought about the teenagers washing cars in the rain—if any cars bothered to stop at all. After a while, I called Anna, who had participated in the fundraiser. To my shock, she said many cars stopped and that they had already raised $475. She told me that many drivers didn't even want their cars washed. They just stopped by to drop off a check and show their support.

I told Queena everything about the fundraiser. By now, we gauged her awareness by her smiles, hand squeezes, and facial expressions. We could tell that she did not recall details of her attack, even though she knew about her injuries. She knew we needed to save money for future expenses that wouldn't be covered when her Medicaid coverage ended.

"Queena, promise me that you won't worry about anything," I told her. "I will take care of everything, and your job is to continue to recover. We all love you so much. We just want you to focus on getting better and on your bright future ahead."

A second fundraiser, a spaghetti dinner event, was scheduled to take place in a couple of days. Strangers from various parts of the community put it together. Beanie's Bar & Sports Grill prepared and served the spaghetti. A local restaurant donated salad. Mango Jo's South Shore provided ice and beverages. A woman named Melanie from the Ruskin Chamber of Commerce and a group of others organized everything. Local businesses and residents donated money and then came to enjoy the food.

Several networks covered the story for their local news broadcasts. I watched the event unfold on TV at the rehab center's nurse's station, since I didn't want to leave Queena alone that evening. I didn't want to watch the event in her room because I didn't want Queena to become stressed by details about her attack that she hadn't remembered. On the news, a long line of cars crawled slowly along US Highway 41 in Ruskin, heading for the VFW post, where the fundraiser took place. Many drivers parked in the overflow lot and rode a shuttle to the fundraiser, even before the doors opened at four o'clock. Some didn't stay for the dinner, silent auction, and music. They simply dropped off their checks and left.

Queena's name still hadn't been released to the public, so these people had no idea who we were. They just wanted to support us. After the event ended, Anna and Jenny Phuong—Robert's niece, who was like a sister to my girls—brought a purple and pink banner to the rehab center. More than one thousand people who stopped by the fundraiser had signed it.

"They say you are a miracle child," Anna exclaimed proudly.

These strangers could not have known the full truth of that statement. Around this time, Queena would go into fits of crying and loud screaming for no apparent reason. Nurses seemed unfazed by these occurrences, often not even getting up from their seats at the desk across the hall to calm her. Such cries from brain injury patients must have sounded routine to them, but not to me. I researched the matter online. From what I could tell, Queena suffered from "neuro storms," or excessive activity in the brain that creates a "storm" of electrical activity. The neuro storms and the ups and downs of

Queena's recovery constantly reminded me that her life did indeed fit the definition of a miracle, just as those donors said.

At the fundraiser, players for the Tampa Bay Lightning hockey team signed a pink hat slated to be auctioned. However, rather than take home his prize, the high bidder left it for Queena.

Anna told her sister the story later, then asked, "Queena, do you know how special you are?"

Another man gave Queena a music box that he'd given to his sister while she'd battled cancer. The sweet melody had brought her joy in his sister's final days. Now, he surrendered it to a young girl he didn't even know because he knew Queena had suffered so much.

Weeks later, Phuong, the reporter, forwarded another email that she'd received from Michelle Phan, a young Vietnamese-American woman who made a name for herself on the internet. Michelle had gained attention from people worldwide through her YouTube videos, where she demonstrated how to apply makeup to enhance beauty. She had an inspiring story about pursuing her dreams despite financial setbacks. She and a group of her friends wanted to host a fashion show fundraiser called "Fashion for Compassion" for Queena at the Tampa Convention Center. It would be dedicated to raising awareness about "a sexual assault case in Tampa."

The sacrifices that others wanted to make for my daughter touched me deeply. I called Michelle, heard her speak in broken Vietnamese like my daughters Anna and Queena, and immediately felt comfortable talking with her. She asked if she and her friends could visit Queena. I agreed to let them come.

The girls came on a Saturday, but they arrived after I went home to wash and pack fresh clothes for the following week. Anna had stayed at the rehab center to watch over Queena, so she was able to greet them. Michelle drew a picture of a beautiful girl on the poster in Queena's room. Still excited long after the girls' visit, Anna told me that Michelle's drawing took her less than two minutes to complete. What a memorable afternoon!

Queena's birthday at two years old - 1992
Seated from left: Vanna's sister Tina, Queena, Vanna's mom,
Standing from left: Vanna's sister Tam, Anna, Vanna, Quang, Uncle Cao
(Vanna's mom's brother), and his daughter.

CHAPTER 14

A LONG-AWAITED REUNION

(1989-1992)

Change is never easy. My daughters and I had a comfortable life in America, but we weren't a wealthy family. We had financial struggles, yet we always seemed to have enough, even in lean times. I hadn't told the girls many details about my life when I'd first immigrated to the United States. I'd forgotten some of those struggles by the time the girls were old enough to understand my past circumstances and the choices I'd made.

After learning of my father's murder, I didn't want my mother and my siblings staying in Vietnam. Thankfully, my first job at a nail salon in California paid me enough money to hire a lawyer to speed up the legal process of moving them to the United States. By 1989—eight years after I'd first arrived in the United States—the U.S. Immigration and Naturalization Service approved my family's relocation to America. I felt relieved after waiting such a long time without much progress. Of course, the process would still take time, but now I could see the end.

As a next step, I needed to save five thousand dollars for four airline tickets for my three siblings and my mother. That meant working long hours. Anna stayed with a babysitter at least ten hours a day, six days a week because I worked so late. I felt so lucky that Anna was a good baby. She behaved well, listened, and never complained or cried for her mom. Of course, I did feel guilty when I dropped her off every morning and picked her up at night. I beat myself up many times about my work/life balance. But I had to trust that I was making the choices that were right for us and our family.

I would tell Anna that when my mother was here, she didn't need to go to the babysitter anymore. "Grandma will take good care of you. But she's stricter than I am. She will make you have your meals and nap on time. She will not allow you to eat your favorite ice cream too late at night."

We would giggle about that. I couldn't wait for those days to come.

At the time, I had a boyfriend, Quang, who helped me in many ways after I separated from Anna's father. He was from Rach Gia, about 155 miles southwest of Saigon. Rach Gia sits on the eastern coast of the Gulf of Thailand, part of the South China Sea. He and his younger brothers had escaped in 1977 when he was nineteen.

He told me how they'd boarded a small fishing boat in the middle of the night with about three hundred others. The idea had been to make their way to a refugee camp in Thailand. By that time, his family had to liquidate all their assets, but they had pieces of gold to bribe officials to pay their way out of the country. They sailed into the Gulf of Thailand without life vests or extra clothes, only the t-shirts, shorts, and sandals they wore. No one knew what their future would bring.

Quang said Thai pirates attacked their boat several times during the journey. They were always armed, so he and his brothers did their best to cause no trouble. Finally, they landed at Pattani, Thailand.

At the refugee camp, they were told that there was no more room. They would have to refuel and leave. Indonesia was an option, but the captain thought the voyage would be too perilous. He had an idea. That night, after steering the boat far enough away to be clear from the view of Thai officials, he instructed the others to destroy the vessel and swim back to shore. Everyone jumped, taking slabs of wood to help keep them afloat as they swam.

The refugee camp had no choice then but to accept them. Like Tuan, Tuyen, and me, they somehow had arrived on the shores of Thailand with nothing but the clothes they wore.

"It was a miracle that we survived," Quang told me.

He and his brothers endured nine months in the refugee camp before they learned they would be traveling to America. His older sister had been in the United States since 1976 and got her church to help sponsor them. They settled in a two-bedroom apartment near Los Angeles to begin their new life.

"We were thankful we were given refuge and a hope of survival," he said.

Quang had co-signed for the loan on my Honda Prelude. He also picked Anna up from the babysitter each day. He treated her like his own child. I appreciated the way he loved my baby. We married in 1989. I was twenty-seven years old.

We rented an old, two-bedroom house with a big yard that had a small cottage in the back. We rented that to his older brother. I was happy for the extra money to help with our rent.

The following year, on April 22, 1990, Quang and I welcomed our newborn daughter into our lives with excitement. I wanted her name to start with a Q, after the first letter of her father's name. I flipped through a dictionary of names and found *Queena*.

Years later, as a little girl, Queena complained about her name. "Mom, I don't like being a queen. I want to be a princess."

Anna was four years old, and Queena was nine months old when my family arrived from Vietnam without Dad on January 31, 1991. Quang and I, our girls, and my aunt's family went to the airport to meet them. Emotions flowed heavily during the reunion. My sister, Tina, fainted in my arms. My aunt cried nonstop. She asked so many questions about my father.

"He was supposed to be here," she kept saying.

My mother cried as well. "His destiny was to die in his own country," she said.

My siblings looked thin and malnourished. Mother looked tired from the long trip, and they all suffered from airsickness. I hugged them and told them not to worry. I would take care of everything. We drove back to our house, where I had winter clothes, including coats and socks, ready for them.

Everything I had hoped for seemed fulfilled. I had a job that paid well enough to bring my family to a safe place and get them settled. I had two lovely daughters of my own who were both healthy. Promising futures awaited everyone. This was *my* American dream.

Mom stayed home to take care of Queena while Quang and I worked during the day. We needed the extra help because Queena often came down with fevers. Mom and I took turns holding her throughout the night. Meanwhile, Tina went to cosmetics school and eventually earned her manicurist license. Within three months, she had a job where she could walk to work. My brother, Dung, went to college to become a civil engineer, and my youngest sister, Tam, attended a local high school. She and my brother took the city bus to school and to the jobs they had on the side. Our days were hectic and tiring. Everyone worked very hard, but I encouraged my family to adjust. In America, their hard work would pay off with a better life.

But like many refugees from Vietnam learned, life in the United States proved much harder than we imagined. We were resilient and certainly worked hard, but even today, I can't imagine how so many people could find the courage to come to a new country with no money, no jobs, and the inability to speak the language.

My cousin Tuyen wrote to me regularly about his and Tuan's struggles. "Life was tough as we had little money, but we were full of hope and determination," he said in his letter of November, 1990.

In October of 1981, four months after I'd arrived in the United States, Tuan and Tuyen had boarded a charter plane to San Francisco. Just before Halloween, they arrived in Pasadena, where they met up with a number of people who had been on the same boat and rented an apartment together to share the cost. About seven of them lived in a one-bedroom apartment, sleeping on the floor in sleeping bags.

Tuan was eager to earn money to help his family back in Vietnam. He purchased a used motorbike to commute to work. His first job was working on an assembly line at a ramen noodle factory. Every day, he would come back to the apartment smelling like ramen noodles from the seasoning powder that saturated his clothes.

Tuan also took night classes at a community college to pursue a degree in automobile technology. Throughout his early years in America, Tuan held various odd jobs to support himself while sending money to his family back home.

Tuyen attended Pasadena High School but also would do odd jobs such as cleaning neighbors' yards to make extra money. He graduated in 1983. He wasn't sure what to do next because he wasn't fluent in English, but he found a summer job working at a newspaper, earning minimum wage. When summer was over, he enrolled in Pasadena City College and took a few classes for about five dollars a unit. There, he met other students, discussed possible career paths, and learned of possible scholarships and grants.

Before the first semester ended, Tuyen applied to and was accepted at the University of California, San Diego, to study electrical engineering. The university offered him various aid packages, including federal grants, California grants, and work study to cover college expenses.

Tuan was very happy for his younger brother. He purchased an old, run-down car, fixed it up, and drove it from Oakland to San Diego, where Tuyen had moved, so he could commute to school. Every holiday and spring break, Tuyen would drive to visit Tuan, his only immediate family member in the United States.

Tuyen graduated from college with honors in 1988 and continued on to graduate school. I attended his graduation. I was so proud and happy for him.

Tuan eventually was able to sponsor the rest of his family to come to the United States, and they reunited in 1990. He opened his home to his family and supported his younger brother and sister until they were able to live on their own.

So, no, America did not make it easy, but only here could we have accomplished this degree of success. Even now, I realize how many privileges our children take for granted every day. They are so lucky to be born and raised in a country with so many opportunities and to lead such comfortable lives.

Queena's high school graduation at HealthSouth Rehabilitation cafeteria -

August 2, 2008

CHAPTER 15

GRADUATION DREAMS

BY MIDSUMMER 2008, QUEENA'S FRIENDS prepared to leave for their respective universities. My daughter, on the other hand, had not been able to attend her high school graduation ceremony. I had to do something about that. I called Sharon Morris, the principal of East Bay High School. Queena had always had a good relationship with her. Principal Morris even visited Queena in the ICU. Queena had cried out when she heard her principal's voice. Now I had an idea, and the principal agreed to make my dream become a reality.

It was one o'clock in the afternoon on August 2, 2008. Anna had already done Queena's makeup, curled her hair, and helped me dress her in the traditional red cap and gown for East Bay High graduates. Various honor cords and sashes decorated the gown, symbolizing Queena's accomplishments, including her place on the honor roll and as a member of the National Honor Society. The nurse helped Queena into her wheelchair.

We rolled her through the hallway at HealthSouth, into the elevator, then down another hallway. Queena's friends lined both sides of the corridor leading into the rehabilitation center's cafeteria. They wore their red graduation gowns, too. The school board chair, the superintendent of schools, the school administration, and the principal all wore black gowns. Teachers, coaches, parents, family, friends, and Assistant State Attorney Rita Peters also joined in the special graduation ceremony on Queena's behalf.

East Bay High students walked into the cafeteria one by one to the sounds of "Pomp and Circumstance," as if experiencing their graduation ceremony all over again. Anna and I pushed Queena's wheelchair in last. We were too overcome with emotion to focus on the cameras zooming in on us from the *St. Petersburg Times* and *ABC Action News*. I had talked with the TV reporter by phone and asked their crew to come. I hoped more media coverage would influence state administrators and help extend Queena's Medicaid, since the cancellation of her coverage was still pending.

Queena's friend Kristen, the class valedictorian, gave a speech, just as she had during the school's official graduation ceremony nearly two months earlier in front of 296 peers.

"Good afternoon, and welcome to the celebration of East Bay High School's fiftieth graduating class, the class of 2008," she said in the quaint cafeteria. As she continued, she tweaked a portion of her speech for this special occasion:

> Thanks to the support of all of our teachers, parents, and other important people in our lives, we have gained a lot of knowledge and, hopefully, wisdom as well. Of course, those things are important, but as I've learned in these past few months, what is more important than knowledge and wisdom is compassion and friendship. When I am gone, I want to leave the world a better place. However, knowledge and wisdom alone do not accomplish such a task. It is the love and care towards others that truly makes a positive impact on the world.
>
> I once thought that success was measured by a person's possessions or accomplishments. I realize now that success is so much more than that. Wealth, prestige, status—all things that people generally associate with success—are, in reality, superficial and not the true definition of what matters in life. I now know that to be truly successful, one must not seek to satisfy themselves but rather reach out to others around them. When the desire to help other people overtakes the desire of self-gratification, success has been accomplished. It is that level of love and compassion that makes the world a better place to live in.

Some people spend their entire lives striving to feel the level of love that I feel from and for all of you. Although our lives have taken an unexpected turn, the compassion that we have all felt is more than enough to last a lifetime. It is something that we will cherish forever. And that is truly the measure of success. Sitting in this room today, we can feel the love for each other. As we head off in different directions, we will always have a connection to one another.

These past four years have shaped us into the compassionate young people we are today, and no matter where life takes us, we have an unbreakable bond. I am so thankful for having known all of you, and each of you has had a lasting impact on my life. I love you so much. And, Queena, you are my hero. I love you more than I can say. Keep fighting, and I'll see you at UF.

When Kristen said, "Queena, you are my hero. I love you more than I can say," Queena started crying aloud, and the whole room cried with her, including me, of course. A few other speakers took to the microphone. Then the entire class sang the song "Hero" by Mariah Carey. Certain lyrics were particularly poignant: "Lord knows . . . Dreams are hard to follow . . ."

Principal Morris congratulated Queena on making the honor roll and placing among the Top Ten students of the Class of 2008. She then handed her an honorary diploma. Technically, Queena still needed to make up a half credit in English to graduate because she'd missed too much of her final coursework due to the attack.

My heart swelled with emotion. I had envisioned the typical graduation scenario. I had imagined Queena sitting in the first row with her honor roll friends, walking across the stage to shake the principal's hand, and throwing her hat into the air with a huge smile. I had imagined myself running to her, hugging her tightly, and telling her, "I am so very proud of you," then hosting a graduation party for her and her friends, just as I had done for Anna.

Instead, tears ran down my face as I listened to so many others express profound love and respect for my daughter, who now needed a wheelchair inside a rehab center. This had not been a good year for East Bay High. Two students had died in a fatal car accident; one student had committed suicide; and another popular graduate died after dancing with friends in Orlando. Two more students had been shot during a drive-by at a bus stop, and a classmate had been charged with the shooting. Finally, just days before graduation, the school's personable quarterback had died in a tragic car accident. I got goose bumps thinking about these tragedies, sensing the unfairness of life—realizing the fact that good people die, and personal safety can be an illusion.[5] Now, at this special graduation ceremony for Queena, everyone—men and women, alike—wept quietly.

Part Two

COURAGE AND THE COMMITMENT TO LOVE

Queena's nineteenth birthday, surrounded by her high school friends at

our home - 2009

CHAPTER 16

THE BLOOMINGDALE LIBRARY
ATTACK VICTIM COMES HOME

THE GRADUATION CEREMONY, ALONG WITH those first fundraisers, showed me how much other people could care about someone who wasn't even a part of their family. I learned this through the worst tragedy of my life. The entire Tampa Bay region reached out to us, doing what they could to piece together our broken dreams and plans for the future. From then on, friends—and strangers, too—organized countless fundraisers. Everyone wanted to help us pay for medical bills and therapy sessions not covered by Medicaid or insurance. Even as the months and years ticked by, they did not forget Queena.

Another deadline loomed heavy on our hearts. Queena's Medicaid coverage for rehabilitation services at HealthSouth had been extended only to August 15, 2008. One day, we received an envelope that looked official from the office of U.S. Senator Bill Nelson. I had written to him earlier, asking for help with Queena's medical bills. Queena still hadn't been approved for the Supplemental Security Income, or SSI, even though I had applied for these benefits while Queena was still in the hospital. So, I wrote to Senator Nelson's office, telling him about the slow progress and our urgent financial need.

He had previously pushed for Queena to receive Medicaid through SSI, rather than through the Department of Children and Families, from which she had previously received health care. The letter stated SSI Medicaid had been approved. Senator Nelson later sent us a personal letter that read:

Dear Ms. Nguyen,

Several weeks ago, you made me aware of the difficulties your daughter was experiencing with the Supplemental Security Income determination progress. Knowing of your patience and our mutual efforts to monitor developments throughout this lengthy process, I was pleased to learn that a favorable decision was ultimately reached on her behalf. You are to be commended for your persistence in this matter.

As your United States Senator, it has been a pleasure to assist you.

Sincerely,

Bill Nelson

I read the letter to Queena.

"Isn't that nice?" I asked.

She just smiled, but I marveled at how far her story had reached. Other government officials, state leaders, and medical doctors worked behind the scenes, including Governor Charlie Crist, the Agency for Health Care Administration, and Dr. Emese Simon, who wrote a letter of appeal to Medicaid. The push by reporters who kept Queena's story in the media, along with the efforts of our local community, helped as well.

I read from the Bible about a man named Gideon who didn't think he measured up. He called himself the "least of the least" among the tribes of Israel. Yet God had selected him to lead His chosen people to victory in a battle against their enemies. I believed God had great plans for my daughter, just like Gideon, and I told her so.

"Never give up," I said, repeating our family's battle cry. Then I read a verse from Hebrews 10:34-35 (NLT): "You knew there were better things waiting for you that will last forever. So do not throw away this confident trust in the Lord. Remember the great reward it brings you!" With all my heart, I prayed for better things to come in Queena's life—a great reward for all that she had gone through.

As a little girl coming home from her private Christian school, Queena had talked to me about God and her faith. At the time, I hadn't accepted the truth her young mind offered. Now I had come to accept her truth as my truth. I read Bible passages to keep *her* spirit strong, even when parts of her body remained so weak. Perhaps, I also needed to read them to keep my own spirit strong.

Unfortunately, the relief we felt after receiving Senator Nelson's letter didn't last long. Within a month, Queena began suffering from severe muscle spasms, especially in her legs—common among brain injury patients. The spasms hindered her therapy and recovery. She cried and cried in pain every time the therapists tried to stand her up.

I asked Dr. Simon to order acupuncture for Queena every morning, thinking this might help her relax. Also, I asked the massage therapist to come more often. Meanwhile, Anna and I kept rotating her body throughout the day. Her list of medications increased, including drugs for seizures, as well as strong pain pills such as oxycodone every two to four hours. The medicine kept her drowsy to the point that she slept all day, even during therapy sessions. I tried to dwell on the positive. Recovering from a brain injury is a long process, I reminded myself. It is bound to have its highs and lows. I prayed for a high point to come soon.

Instead, our low point deepened. On September 25, 2008, Medicaid notified us that Queena's stay at HealthSouth would no longer be covered. She needed to leave the rehab center by the end of October. Medicaid had agreed to extend coverage beyond August 15 only if her progress showed continual improvement. According to Medicaid's evaluation, Queena had reached a plateau. She still couldn't move most of her body. She still required a feeding tube. She could not talk. For these reasons, her slow progress did not justify spending the sixty thousand dollars per month it cost to keep her there. Medicaid would pay only for physical therapy three days a week while she lived at home, rather than living at the residential rehab center.

At this point, Queena was deemed totally disabled and dependent. She could continue receiving some Medicaid benefits, but I had to choose supplemental insurance from an HMO representative. Because I didn't have any idea which insurance company to choose, Queena was automatically enrolled in Amerigroup.

I fought for Queena to stay at the facility and keep getting therapy five days a week. No matter how much I insisted, the decision stayed the same. I had to accept it. Queena needed to move home, and I would need to be her primary caretaker. The caretaker part worried me most. I had spent the past six months by her side, talking to her and studying her condition. But I had never been in charge. A nurse or some other trained personnel always did the major work while I assisted. Now, I would have to operate the equipment she needed to stay alive. What if I messed up? What if something happened to my daughter while in my care?

During a meeting with Queena's rehab doctors, therapists, and a Medicaid administrator from Amerigroup, Robert became so frustrated that he lashed out at one of Queena's doctors, accusing him of taking the insurer's side rather than looking out for Queena's best interests. The doctor denied it. Queena's well-being was his priority, he said, but Medicaid was right—her progress had plateaued. Others spoke up during the meeting, including Cheryl, who came to support me. The thick cloud of tension in the room had me in tears. Everyone's face looked sad and full of regret. In the end, the doctor gathered paperwork for the appropriate equipment, medical supplies, and prescriptions Queena needed to survive at home.

Solemnly, I prepared myself for the huge task ahead. Our entire house would need to be renovated. Health care workers visited to assess the layout and recommend ways to modify the rooms. Queena's upstairs bedroom could not accommodate her without installing an elevator, which wasn't an option. My master bedroom downstairs would need to be redone and the master bathroom enlarged to accommodate her equipment. We needed to make more space in the shower to fit her roll-in seat while being bathed. We needed to install a wheelchair ramp, as well as an electronic Hoyer Lift to help her transfer in and out of bed. We had to remove carpeting and install tile for easy movement of her wheelchair.

Word spread throughout the community that Queena was moving home. To my surprise, people still cared after six months' time had passed. Journalists found fresh angles for new articles that kept Queena's story in the public eye. One reporter from Fox 13 Tampa Bay, a local TV station, asked to do a story about the changes to come for our family. As usual, Cheryl agreed to act as my spokeswoman. I so appreciated her unwavering support. When the reporter arrived at our door, Robert and Cheryl gave him and the camera crew a tour of the house, commenting about the doors and hallways that would have to be widened and the twenty-four-hour care Queena would need. Soon, the reporter's story aired on the evening news, and a flood of responses came in from strangers who wanted to help, including builders and contractors.

We waited to hear how much of the renovation costs Medicaid would cover and whether we were bound to use contractors that they provided. Later, on October 22, 2008, the *St. Petersburg Times* ran an editorial headlined, "Victim Deserves Help to Recover."[6] The editorial revealed that Queena was being forced to move out of the rehabilitation hospital and into home care. The writer pointed out that if the state succeeded in convicting the teenager charged with assaulting Queena, taxpayers would likely pay for his imprisonment for decades to come. Yet the government insisted on pushing the victim out of rehab after only a few months of care. The opinion column called for the governor to step in to ensure Queena received the best medical treatment she deserved.

On October 23, the day after the editorial column appeared, I learned that not only would Medicaid stop paying for Queena's care at the rehabilitation center, but the insurance also would not cover any of the necessary renovations to accommodate her care at our house either. Also, I learned that chances were slim for her physical, occupational, and speech therapy to be covered.

I didn't know what to do or where to turn. I had no money left of my own. I was broke. In the six months that I lived by Queena's side, my salon, Elegant Nail Spa, went into decline without my supervision. Regular clients found other salons. I could barely pay my bills, let alone afford renovations on the house. I was frustrated, weary, and tired—a crippling kind of tired that made it hard for me to even think. My heart felt heavy enough to weigh down my chest. Now that I had lost this latest battle, my faith was weakening, too.

Then just days before Queena's HealthSouth release date, I received a call from Brenda, the associate director for Self Reliance, Inc., a nonprofit organization that helped people who have disabilities live independently. A slew of people in the community—contractors, builders, and high school students—had called her office. Queena's name had still not been released to the public, so they'd called Brenda's agency, hoping Self Reliance could connect with the media and find a way to reach us.

"Apparently, there was an article in the paper," she said.

As news of our situation spread throughout the area, Cheryl's husband, John, had already started on the renovations, along with Robert and a contractor. They started with the smaller, least-expensive jobs, such as breaking down my bedroom to bring in Queena's equipment, making room for her pink wheelchair and necessary medical equipment, and widening the doorframe and inserting a new door. John had even asked what color Queena wanted her room to be.

Of course, she liked pink, but which particular shade? I remembered a set of sunglasses inside a pink case from Queena's favorite Juicy Couture store. A woman from the community had bought them and sent the glasses to Queena after hearing in one of the media stories how she liked the color and the store. I took the glasses case to Home Depot and matched it to a bubblegum pink shade of paint there. I knew Queena would love it once she regained her full sight and saw clearly again.

Over the next seven days, good Samaritans flooded our property. Some reached us through Brenda; others came from various emails and phone calls to people who knew us. Jonathan, chairman of the Remodelers Council of the Tampa Bay Builders Association at the time, offered up the services of affiliated contractors and subcontractors around the Tampa Bay area. A man named Jim from Brate Built Construction in Ruskin also wanted to help.

Reverend Sabrina Tu of St. John's United Methodist Church in Tampa assembled an army of plumbers, carpenters, and other volunteers. A designer for the large homebuilder Taylor Morrison Homes also inquired about our needs. Jose, executive director for a nonprofit called Rebuilding Together Tampa Bay, also offered to help.

We didn't have much time. Queena initially had to be out of the rehabilitation center by October 31, but we managed to get the date extended to November 5, 2008. People in the community hosted several more fundraisers in the days before her return home, including a doo-wop dance, a 5K run, and a car wash.

Cheryl continued to represent us by talking with the media and various donors. Her help took a lot of the stress off me while I focused on helping Queena. Also, because of my broken English, I felt uncomfortable speaking in front of crowds. To whomever she spoke, Cheryl always expressed our gratitude and asked for continued prayers.

On top of all that generosity, two health care agencies offered to provide therapy for Queena at no charge. An administrator for one of them even said she could stay at the facility temporarily if we couldn't finish renovations before she had to leave HealthSouth. As a personal gesture of kindness, three different people gave Queena sets of real pearls after learning that she had lost hers during the attack.

All the love we received from complete strangers reignited our hope. We began to feel that leaving the rehab center might be for the best for Queena. Despite the hardships, other human beings showed me that God's love still existed in America and in the world.

I knew the healing process would take a long time and that finding good caretakers to help around the clock might be tough emotionally—and financially, if insurers didn't help. Yet, after holding onto my faith for the past six months, I couldn't let go of it now. Queena needed to relearn how to live, just like a newborn baby. Even her laugh now sounded more like the tender giggles of an infant, rather than an eighteen-year-old. Healing would take time, and maybe Queena needed to get out of that medical facility in order to grow again in the warmth and love of her own home.

"Miracles do happen," Cheryl said one day while we discussed Queena's prognosis.

"I can see clearly in my mind, like it was yesterday," I told her. "I see Queena coming home from school, getting out of her car, her backpack over her shoulder, and saying, 'Hi, Mom!'

"I want that miracle."

We prepared Queena for the transition back home on Wednesday, November 5, 2008. We dressed her in a pink shirt and pink sweatpants. Nurses and therapists came into her room to say tearful goodbyes, just as the staff had done at the hospital. An ambulance drove the hour-long trip from Sarasota to Tampa. Along the way, I told Queena, "You are in God's heart today. Your life is in His hands." I held her hand, closed my eyes, and asked her to pray with me.

"I'm praying for rapid healing for her body and her mind," I said to God, as paramedics watched. "For relaxation and peace, for relief from the pain, for restoration of speech . . . Thank You for placing Your hands on Queena's life. In Christ, Amen."

During Queena's recovery—first at the hospital, then at the rehabilitation center—I often thought of my cousin Tuyen's weakened condition as we'd floated for days on the South China Sea. Now, here I was by my daughter's side, willing her not to give up on life, just as I had willed Tuyen to hang on decades earlier. After our escape, we'd become closer than cousins. We became like brother and sister. Since the attack on Queena, he was one of the few people I talked to frequently—sharing my feelings and the details of Queena's condition. In one of his emails to me, Tuyen responded:

Dear sister Vanna,

I'm quite thankful to be a part of this healing process. Most people don't come close to understanding what you have been through and are still going through! This crime was unspeakable. It shows us the evil, dark side in our world. These criminals aren't human, since even animals don't do this to their own kind. But this tragic incident also shows us that there are so many other good people among us who want to help a stranger they have never met.

Many, many people have been touched by what happened because they see that you and Queena represent the brighter side of human nature. It's what they wish every mother and daughter could be! Through it all, you have also shown the world that there is no boundary to a mother's love for her children and that love will enable Queena to overcome whatever evil has been done to her. In all cases of "good vs. evil," good always triumphs!

Love,

Tuyen

When the paramedics opened the ambulance doors and maneuvered Queena's gurney to the ground, somehow, she must have seen or sensed something. Was it the light from the outdoors? Was it the comforting atmosphere of home? My daughter raised her face toward the sky and smiled wide. In my heart, I knew what she wanted to say if she could only speak the words:

"Thank God, I'm finally home!"

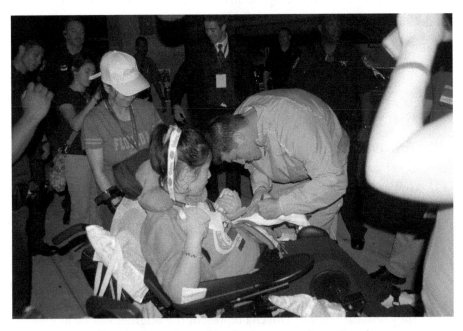

Tim Tebow signing a Gator shirt for Queena at Gator Growl event -

October 16, 2009

CHAPTER 17

A NEW NORMAL

QUEENA'S HOMECOMING HELD ITS JOYS and sorrows. She entered the front door without a backpack hanging over her shoulder. I didn't hear her usual "Hi, Mom" or see her sparkling smile as she breezed by. She wasn't able to nuzzle up to her furry friend, Gracy, before sauntering upstairs to the privacy of her own bedroom, where she finished homework and giggled on the phone with friends. On the days when I wasn't at the nail salon, Queena would hold off calling her friends. Instead, she'd run into the downstairs master bedroom and snuggle with me while I took a nap.

My former bedroom was now her room, equipped with a medical bed. My joy in her homecoming came from sensing that Queena felt more comfortable here than in the sterile environment of hospitals and rehabilitation facilities. The thought of bringing her comfort after all she'd endured made me happy. Still, after she settled into her bed that first day, I ran upstairs, peeked in on what had been her *real* bedroom, and burst into tears.

Our new normal brought many new challenges. I had to learn how to use the feeding tube, the Hoyer Lift, the wheelchair, the shower chair—every piece of equipment she needed—without the presence or assistance of trained medical personnel. I had to monitor physical and emotional needs and look out for any changes in her cognition that could lead to possible seizures.

I bathed her, dressed her, and administered her medications on time. I took her to appointments at rehab centers, picked up her prescriptions, and read and signed all necessary paperwork. Whenever I could grab a few minutes between these activities, I browsed brain-injury websites to look up the neurological terms her doctors used. I desperately wanted to increase my knowledge and understanding of my daughter's conditions.

Her pills presented the most frustrating challenge by far. Queena had so many pills to take at precise intervals of time. Every four hours, she had to take one medication or another, and it took me almost an hour to prepare and crush them because she couldn't swallow them whole. I used a manual tablet-crusher on four pills at a time to transform them into powder—not an easy task for me. I'd had problems with my wrist for years after falling in a snowy parking lot while working at a nail salon in Maryland. Still, I could not let that discomfort stop me.

Then one day, I reached my breaking point. My frustration over the caretaking and pill-crushing overwhelmed me. I couldn't hold my emotions in anymore. I ran to the bathroom, turned the shower all the way up, and yelled, "Dear God, I don't want to give up! What can I do now? Show me, God!"

I cried until no more tears came. I don't know how much time passed before I composed myself and walked downstairs. There, I saw Anna perched at the dining room table, crushing the tablets herself. I was so grateful. Yet sadness came, too, watching one daughter sacrificing her time for my other daughter.

After nearly an hour, Anna was still crushing the pills with all her might. By that time, Queena needed her meds. Desperate for a solution, I walked into the kitchen, hoping to find anything that could help. I spotted my Vietnamese pounding pestle on my countertop. *That's it!* I took all of Queena's meds, placed them in a plastic baggie, and used the pestle to crush the tablets. Within two minutes, it turned the pills into powder. In that moment, I distinctly felt God's presence for the first time since bringing Queena home. I had not been forgotten. God had not left me alone in my hour of need. He still had plans for me! Through tears mixed with humility and joy, I felt God's Spirit saying, "I am with you, close to your broken heart, in touch with your shattered soul."

My situation improved immensely a few days later when Anna found a battery-powered pill-grinder online for only twenty dollars. With the simple press of a button, my biggest obstacle disintegrated into dust—gone! It may seem like a minor problem, but it represented a major turning point for me. From that day forward, I never felt alone. I never felt ignored. I knew God paid close attention to everything that concerned me, even something as little as crushing pills.

Money problems persisted, but my options were few. I had little time or brain power left at the end of each day. No time for my own personal care—such as cooking, cleaning, and laundry—let alone the time to boost my nail business in order to make more money. I didn't feel comfortable leaving Queena alone in the house.

Again, consistent media coverage was helpful. Donations kept pouring in from multiple sources: strangers who'd heard Queena's story, her former employer Abercrombie & Fitch, and fundraisers local groups held. Even out-of-state companies wanted to donate during the upcoming holiday season. A local civic group, the Rough Riders of Tampa, went above and beyond to purchase a used van to transport Queena to her numerous therapy appointments. Volunteers donated their time, providing various therapies and other services, as well as encouragement, to help Queena on her journey to recovery.

Two weeks after Queena came home, we received an email from Eric, an executive with Abercrombie & Fitch. Each year, the company took donations from customers willing to help a designated charity. This year, executives chose Queena as their cause. On Black Friday, Eric explained, Abercrombie & Fitch would hang posters and put out donation boxes in all company stores, including Hollister, Ruehl, and Gilly Hicks. Throughout the holiday season, the boxes would raise awareness and funds for the tragic incident affecting an Abercrombie associate. They called it "2008 Holiday Donation: Helping One of Our Own." Queena had loved working for the store, so the company's generosity meant so much.

After the holiday season, the company invited us to a ceremony at the Abercrombie Kids store in the local mall. I told Queena about the invitation and saw the excitement in her expression. I thought the event might stimulate her long-term memory. Even the smell of the store's signature cologne lingering in the air might bring back good thoughts of a place she once loved.

On the flip side, the event also highlighted a new concern. Because Queena had been raped, media outlets had not released her identity to the public. Most referred to her simply as "the Bloomingdale Library attack victim." Every time she appeared on the news, photos and video showed her from the neck down, sitting in her unique pink wheelchair.

Now I worried that people would recognize her pink wheelchair as we wheeled it through the mall on our way to the Abercrombie Kids store. I didn't want people staring and whispering about her. I didn't want Queena to know that strangers might point at her. I contacted Assistant State Attorney Rita Peters for help. She had a relatively simple but perfect solution. She arranged for Queena to enter through the store's rear door.

I invited Dong-Phuong Nguyen, the *Tampa Bay Times* staff writer, to witness Queena's reunion with her former Abercrombie & Fitch coworkers. She wrote, "Along the empty hallway, the familiar scent of the store's cologne flooded our nostrils while music pounded through speakers, vibrating in our ears. Queena moved her head around slowly, trying to take in the sounds and the smell. Then, as if the realization came all at once, she began to cry."[7]

I couldn't help it. I cried, too. The store stimulated memories for me that I didn't know still existed. I used to visit Queena at work sometimes. I'd come in quietly without telling her. I would spot her standing behind a clothes rack, folding collared shirts and dancing to the music. Finally, she'd notice me, and a look of surprise would show on her face.

"Mom, what are you doing here?"

"Just doing some shopping, and I thought I'd stop by to say hi."

Now, those memories seemed so distant. She would never fold clothes or dance the way she used to—at least, not outwardly. I had to believe that inside, she was dancing to the music that filled her ears. Nevertheless, the moment turned bittersweet for me.

Queena's coworkers and managers greeted her warmly. They remembered her as the young, vibrant girl she had been—the team player who always looked forward to going to work. The one who was eager to help or volunteer to fill in for a sick employee.

As the ceremony began, Amy, a district manager, read a letter to Queena from corporate officials that praised her strength and courage. All across the country, employees for Abercrombie & Fitch, from the stores to the corporate offices, donated money to a fund for Queena during the annual charity drive. The response was overwhelming! The company raised eighty-five thousand dollars. From a written statement, Amy read, "We hope the money raised will help with your recovery and will, in the future, help you pursue your dreams."

I was shocked, choked with emotion, and filled with gratitude all at the same time. I knew that the company employed a lot of teenagers like Queena, who worked part-time and did not make huge amounts of money. To have this come from her peers meant so much to me. The store also presented Queena with several outfits her girlfriends had selected, which included sparkly tops, trendy shorts, and a striped bag. They knew exactly what Queena liked. Anna and Queena's friends draped the items over Queena and posed for pictures.

"Okay, now you're getting really spoiled," Rachel said, as she giggled and Queena grinned. In that moment, I remembered that I used to tease them both by calling them "BSFFs"—best *shopping* friends forever! Later, just before we left, I asked everyone for continued prayers that someday Queena could walk, talk, and see again.

"Someday," I said, "Queena will get better and come back to work for the company."

The trip to Abercrombie & Fitch gave us renewed strength. Queena came out of her plateau and started improving again at a faster pace. She still used a feeding tube and wheelchair, and she couldn't talk or see clearly, but she began to laugh audibly, which was music to my ears. She also started to track people with her eyes as they walked by her bed. Her muscles strengthened and responded better during therapy. She swallowed better, which pushed her that much closer to tasting food again. I longed for the day when I could give her applesauce and pureed foods by mouth. I couldn't imagine what it was like to not taste food for almost a year.

Queena eventually began to communicate by spelling out words, one letter at a time. Anna would stand by Queena's bedside and ask a question. She would then recite the alphabet one letter at a time until Queena stopped her by smiling or raising both hands. Eventually, Queena would spell out a word. The process was slow, but it was wonderful to be able to interact with her in this way. Her accomplishment was even reported in the *Tampa Bay Times*.[8]

One night, Anna asked, "Who is your best friend?" Queena stopped Anna on the letters M-O-M.

Anna ran to me in the kitchen. "Guess what, Mom? Queena said her best friend is M-O-M."

I ran to Queena, hugged her, and gave her a big kiss. "Really, Queena? Your best friend is not one of your nine girlfriends?"

Queena smiled. Her answer resonated in my soul.

Queena's nineteenth birthday came on April 22, six months after her return home and two days prior to the anniversary of the attack. An article appeared in *The Tampa Tribune* to mark the celebration of her birth.[9] Yet for me, it marked the remembrance of what I refer to as her *second birth* after emerging from the coma following the traumatic seizures and lost brain function. My heart broke as I recalled that dark day. I didn't believe that my daughter's disabilities made her less of a person, but I really missed *my* Queena—the person she was *before* her severe injuries.

I wanted to remember her as that happy, cheerful, and positive young woman. Still, the new Queena impressed me, too. She defied doctors' predictions, not only because she'd survived but also because she'd improved beyond their expectations. No, she couldn't walk, speak, or see; but when she smiled, everything around her brightened.

To celebrate, we gathered around her and sang "Happy Birthday" at a sushi restaurant. As she tried to blow out the candle on her banana bombe dessert, I held up the cake, and Anna took a picture. Even the birthday candle on her cake seemed to signify a blessing. In the photograph, the candle's flame flickers near Queena's face. Later, when I took a closer look, I saw the distinct image of an angel. It was as if the light of God's own Divine presence was in the flicker in the smallest but in the most impactful way.

The image prepared me emotionally for the call that came later that night from Rita Peters. The prosecutor and I had developed a relationship over the past year. She was not just an attorney but also a woman with the heart of a mother. She knew the first anniversary of the attack and Queena's birthday would cause unfathomable events to replay in my mind, like scenes in a horror movie.

When I answered the phone, she asked if I was doing okay.

"I am trying my best," I said, stifling the flow of tears.

She went on to describe Queena as her hero. If it had been her, Rita said, she would have given up or died that night. But Queena fought the attacker with all she had in her. Queena left her blood at different parts of the crime scene, which led authorities to important clues in her case. She had fought hard. She did not let the attacker push her down. I told Rita that I was proud of my daughter, but I also knew that God's loving Spirit was surely the unseen Force that had kept her alive. Her Creator kept her alive long enough for us to find her and get her the help she needed.

Then Rita told me the specific reason for her call. The accused attacker had pleaded "not guilty" and had a public defender. During a status hearing scheduled for June, a judge would decide if the case was ready for trial. At the time, I didn't want to be involved with the trial at all. I wanted to focus on taking care of my daughter.

"We will just leave it in the hands of the court system and God," I said.

Rita agreed to speak on Queena's behalf during court proceedings and told me not to worry. Then, she mentioned that the daycare worker—the other woman Morris was accused of attacking—had asked to meet my daughter. She had lived in fear before the DNA found at the library linked Morris to both crimes. At that time, we had explained to Queena that her attacker would go to trial one day, but I didn't think she was ready to know about the details of the attack or to meet the other victim.

"Not yet," I said.

We weren't sure if Queena even remembered what happened on April 24, 2008. I told Rita that we might be able to meet the other woman at a later time. We still had so much emotion to work through.

"Please tell her we will pray for her to be strong and have faith," I said. "Pray for us, too."

After I hung up, it occurred to me that at least Queena's attack had led to something good for this poor woman. She no longer lived in fear, not knowing who had attacked her and if she would be attacked again. She now had answers.

Journeys away from home took so long in the new normal. My new life circumstances surprised me in many ways. I had grown accustomed to having many aides help me while Queena lived in the rehab facility. Now, with only one aide to help, preparing Queena for a trip outside the house turned into a major event. Things I had never thought about before became part of a cumbersome checklist that had to be double-checked every time we prepared to leave.

Still, some trips were worth the work, such as the one we took on May 5, 2009. It was Anna's day to graduate from Southeastern University—an occasion neither her mother nor her sister could miss. As I got myself ready for the ceremony, my mind raced through my new checklist of things to think about and do for Queena.

Will we be back in time for the next dose of her meds?

Perhaps I should take the dose with us to be safe. Is her water packed?

Food? Extra tubing, so she can "eat" and "drink"?

Sanitizing wipes to make sure the feeding tube is sterile?

Will there be a place for me to change her, if necessary?

Will her chair fit through the doorway?

Will we be able to sit where Queena can hear?

Will she be able to sense her sister walking across the stage to graduate?

Will her chair fit in the designated area for wheelchairs?

Will the facility be too cold or too hot?

Perhaps I need to pack an extra jacket, blanket, and a fan, just in case.

Is Queena dressed in an outfit she would like to wear?

Where are the special cones that she holds to help her hands contract?

I'd better grab a few of her favorite stuffed animals to keep under her arms, too.

Do I have enough napkins to keep her face dry?

Before I knew it, my checklist had consumed my preparation time, and we were nowhere near ready to leave. My heart hurt at the thought of being late for the ceremony. On one hand, I knew Queena needed me to be thorough on her behalf. I had to stand in the gap for her. On the other hand, I had never been late to any of my children's graduation ceremonies, not even kindergarten! I always arrived early to get a good seat and to set up my video camera. If we were late, I'd have videos of every graduation processional—except this one. For years, I had dreamed of watching Anna, draped in her college robe, walk down that aisle.

Despite the disappointment in myself, I pressed on, finally loading Queena into the van. My mother and our aide came with us. We headed toward Lakeland, about forty-five minutes away. We would miss Anna's entrance, but we arrived just in time to see Anna standing in line onstage to receive her diploma. Whew! As her name was called, Anna stepped forward, received her degree, and walked unpretentiously back to her seat. I looked at Queena and noticed that her eyes were red. Grandma and I cried, too. Anna had worked so hard to reach this goal. We were so proud of her. Yet my pride for Anna was mixed with grief for Queena. I tried so hard to stay positive. *One day*, I thought. *One day, Queena will fulfill this dream, too.*

By the end of that month, I enrolled Queena in a homebound school program so she could earn the remaining credits she needed in English and receive an official high school diploma. She would need that to attend college someday. Due to her vision loss, she would receive instruction through the visually impaired program. When I told Queena about homebound school, she looked at me with a puzzled expression, as if to say, "But, Mom, I already graduated!" She soon understood the plan of finalizing her credits and began a reading class. The move positioned Queena later for special college programs designed for students with physical disabilities or challenges.

My battles over insurance coverage waged on. The constant fighting with insurers over one thing or another was emotionally exhausting. This time, Medicaid reduced home health care from twenty-four hours a day to sixteen. The coverage would continue to decrease over time. This might not seem like a significant reduction, but to our family, eight hours of health care was huge. My body and spirit were weakening, and Anna worked a full-time job. It seemed extremely difficult, if not impossible, for me to care for my daughter single-handedly for an eight-hour stretch.

Queena couldn't move, talk, or see, which meant she couldn't call for help when she needed it. She had to be monitored around the clock. I feared she might have another seizure or stroke or throw up and choke on her own vomit. Bathing, dressing, transporting—all became complicated tasks, not to mention keeping all the medicines straight. I couldn't imagine what we would do when, or if, insurance stopped covering home health care altogether.

Trying to think of possible solutions, I remembered an email I'd received the prior year from Children's Medical Services (CMS). I made some calls and learned that CMS provided services for children with special needs. I cringed at the thought of labeling Queena a "special needs" child, but eventually, I enrolled her in the program. I had no choice.

Soon, she began receiving SSI Medicaid for home health care through CMS's provider, ending her enrollment with Amerigroup that had been established before leaving HealthSouth. As it turned out, CMS provided more coverage with fewer hassles. Once again, I found myself in the midst of God's silent grace and provision. Through struggles such as these, I learned that God's timing is perfect. Yes, her healing would come, I told myself. The Lord is good. God would provide for all of her needs.

In July 2009, I took Queena to a neuro-ophthalmologist specializing in vision problems related to the nervous system, including those caused by brain injury. A nurse showed her the pediatric eye chart with pictures. She asked Queena to identify the names of objects pictured. For instance, if the nurse showed a picture of an airplane, she asked Queena if it was a house. Queena would not respond. However, when the nurse asked if the picture displayed an airplane, Queena smiled in agreement. Also, Queena used gestures to indicate the color of the nurse's hair, among other tests she completed successfully.

Queena's performance showed a marked change from a previous examination in January. At that time, the doctor described her pupils as only slightly active. I could tell he didn't want to deliver the bad news. "Sorry" was all he had said.

Now, eight months after Queena had come home, he told me that her pupils were reactive again. Nervously, I asked him, "So, do you know how much she can see?"

He answered cautiously, saying that she might actually be seeing pictures and colors. "Her vision could be as good as 20/200," he indicated. The development meant a lot because doctors had told us repeatedly that most patients who suffer optic brain damage seldom regain their sight. The doctor held a look of awe on his face as he could not believe the improvement. (The *Tampa Bay Times* reported the good news in an article titled, "Teen victim in brutal 2008 Bloomingdale Library sex assault can suddenly see color and pictures, her mother says."[10])

My mind flashed back to April 2008 in the immediate days after the attack when Queena had sobbed and asked the police officer, "Why I can't I see?" before slipping into a coma. I remember praying that she would see again. I had begged and pleaded with the Lord to restore her sight. I wanted immediate answers and miracles. Each day brought devastation, as I woke up to find Queena seemingly in the same condition as the night before.

Now, I realized that sometimes miracles aren't immediate. Improvement may come in millimeters. But if you scrape together enough millimeters, you've got a mile.

When we left the doctor's office, I whispered, "You are still the God of miracles."

Queena grew accustomed to homebound school by the fall of 2009. Twice a week, her teacher came and read the newspaper for her. Her face brightened at articles about fashion, as well as inspirational stories. Always financially conscious, she also enjoyed hearing the current market prices for gas, milk, bread, and other everyday items. After reading the paper, the teacher played games with Queena to review her math skills. Then she read from the English textbook and asked questions to make sure Queena understood and could respond.

In addition to homebound school, Queena participated in a litany of therapies: vision, speech, occupational, aquatic, and physical. The schooling and therapy sessions became our routine, and I tried to settle into this flow of life—at least until God saw fit to change it. At the start of the school year, however, I couldn't help but reflect on the different life Queena would have been leading had the attack not happened. She would have returned to the University of Florida as a sophomore with her friends Kristen and Crystal.

Over the summer, several of her friends returned and spent some time with her. Queena had always admired college football player Tim Tebow, and Kristen giggled with her one afternoon, telling Queena that he attended the same church as she did in Gainesville. (At the time, Tebow still played for the Gators.) One day at church, Kristen said Tim Tebow had passed by her close enough for her to touch him. She admitted that her heart had jumped a little. How typical of a nineteen-year-old girl with a crush!

Anytime someone mentioned the Gators, Queena's eyes lit up, and she grinned a wide, toothy grin. She wore a tiny silver, orange, and blue Gator football around her neck, a gift from Alpha Delta Pi sorority. When the sorority heard about the attack and Queena's hope of attending college, they sent the pendant as a gift, although her chances of getting there seemed so remote.

In September 2009, however, God gave a wink and a nod to Queena's wish. It started when a reporter for *The Tampa Tribune* called to say that Steve Stock, the CEO for Guy Harvey, Inc., a company that typically focuses on ocean conservation, wanted to fulfill one of Queena's dreams.[11] Guy Harvey, Inc. was a major sponsor for the University of Florida's homecoming activities that year. Steve was a Tampa native and a UF graduate, whose daughter had followed his example to attend the school. A recent *Tribune* article mentioning Queena's love of UF had caught his attention.

Executives offered her a VIP trip to the university's infamous Gator Growl rally and homecoming in Gainesville. They also offered an autographed Gators national championship t-shirt and poster. The reporter would bring over the t-shirt and poster and connect me with company executives to arrange the trip. Of course, I accepted the offer, which included travel, hotel expenses, and tickets for Queena and five family members.

Steve called me personally with the invitation. He realized that his daughter could easily have been the victim of such a brutal attack. Reading the article in the *Tribune*, he said, "punched him in the gut." He would work with the campus student organization that organizes homecoming festivities to finalize details for our visit. I was so grateful for what he had already done, but I couldn't resist asking one more favor on Queena's behalf.

"Does she have a chance of meeting Tim Tebow?" I asked. "He is one of her role models."

To my surprise, Steve said the thought had already occurred to him. He wasn't sure, but he would work with the student organization to see what they could do.

I ran into Queena's room as if I'd won the lottery. When I told her about the trip, she screamed louder than I'd ever heard before. Later, her face lit up, and she smiled wide when we received the autographed t-shirt and poster.

"You are so special!" I told her.

Game day, Thursday, October 15, 2009, came quickly. Queena's world would broaden beyond our community on Florida's west coast. We left our home to spend the weekend 130 miles away at the University of Florida. Organizers reserved two hotel rooms for our family, including one for Queena that was wheelchair accessible and equipped with a rented hospital bed. Another big surprise inside Queena's room: blue and orange balloons had been hung everywhere. Two posters read, "Welcome to Gainesville, Queena!" and "We are so happy you're here."

The next day we waited to meet Steve in a park near the stadium. From far away, I saw a big guy walking alongside a smaller man and heading straight to Queena's wheelchair. I knew one of them had to be Steve. As it turned out, he was the big guy wearing a colorful shirt. His assistant, Dave, stood beside him. Steve gave Queena a big hug, then a kiss on her cheek. He had a warm voice and made small talk with Queena about the university and his daughter.

"Welcome," he said, "to Gator Nation!"

Queena offered a friendly smile, and I could tell she instantly loved Steve.

From there, we toured Florida Field, including our VIP seats for that night at the Gator Growl event. My mind skipped back to when I had brought Queena to the university for orientation. We had toured the whole school, from the bookstore to the cafeteria and the stadium. When we reached the stadium, I remembered Queena saying, "Mom, look at how amazing this stadium is! I absolutely want to be a part of Gator Nation." I looked at Queena now, and judging by her wistful expression, I think she might have remembered that trip, too.

Later, we ran into head coach Urban Meyer. After a short conversation between him and Steve, Coach Meyer escorted us to the locker room on an impromptu search for Tim Tebow. Soon, Tebow was kneeling beside Queena's wheelchair and welcoming her to homecoming. Steve pulled me aside, wrapped his arm around my shoulder, and said in a soft voice, "I think

Somebody up above was looking down on us today. It could not have gone more perfectly."

Coach Meyer gave Queena some Gator paraphernalia, and Tebow signed Gator gear for her to take home. Robert and Queena's aide, Ashley, took dozens of photographs as Tebow posed beside Queena. Coach Meyer, Steve, a Florida Key member, and other Gators, including teammates, posed with us for several photos.

I told Queena, "I can't believe your dream came true. You are so lucky to meet a Superman, a Heisman Trophy winner!"

Later that day, Marty Bladen, a Tampa memorabilia businessman, presented her with a donated helmet that Tebow had signed. Cameras flashed from various media outlets snapping photos of Queena, Bladen, and Tebow. I wasn't sure how Queena would ever get to sleep after seeing the camera lights flashing and the videos capturing this moment.

The next day, Steve took Queena and Ashley to watch the game from box seats in a luxury suite. Later he joined me, Robert, Anna, and the rest of our family to sit in reserved stadium seats. I asked to see where Queena was because I knew very little about football stadiums and box seats. Anna pointed upward.

"Look all the way up, Mom," she said. "Do you see the room with the glass window?" She explained that they had food, drinks, and air conditioning. "It's very fancy," she said.

We went home the following day. Queena immediately wanted her Gator gear placed in her room. We had received so many items, they covered nearly every surface. We hung the helmet Tim Tebow had signed on her wall and put the framed picture of the two of them together on her shelf. The bright orange and blue colors stood in sharp contrast to the pink bubblegum paint on the walls, but Queena wanted it this way.

The trip amazed us, especially Queena. The *Tampa Tribune* subsequently published a story about our trip.[12] Steve became a part of our family, treating

Anna and Queena like his own daughters. The memories he gave us were emblazoned on our hearts. To this day, whenever someone mentions the name of a certain former quarterback, Queena's cheeks turn an uncommon shade of scarlet.

Shopping for hand embroidery - Da Nang, 1992

CHAPTER 18

VIETNAM REVISITED

(1992)

Even more than a decade after leaving Vietnam, I could remember it vividly. I missed Saigon with its French colonial architecture, vibrant markets, and street food stalls. I missed my Da Nang, with its lovely sandy beach and beautiful scenery. I missed my high school besties. I ached to see what had happened there, what had changed and what remained the same.

In the early 1990s, I got the chance. Vietnam opened to foreign tourism, easing restrictions on travel. I talked to my mother about my memories and my curiosity, and she and I decided to return there together for a visit. Quang agreed to take care of Anna and Queena for me for three weeks. In March 1992, we traveled to Los Angeles International Airport, where we settled in for a twelve-hour flight to Seoul, Korea, and another five-hour flight to Saigon.

The last time my mother and I had been on a plane in Vietnam together, we had been grieving for her father. My maternal grandfather had taught us how to work hard in order to survive. I often heard how he had migrated south as a boy with his two younger brothers from China to Quang Tri, a province on the border that separated North and South Vietnam. He found work helping a Chinese merchant sell traditional Chinese herbal medicine and through the years became knowledgeable enough to open his own herbal medicine store. As a child, I visited my grandparents rarely. The twisting, narrow road from Da Nang to Quang

Tri wove through steep mountains and forests of evergreen trees, making travel difficult. The area also was not safe, its proximity to the border making it home to many Communist sympathizers before the war. I have scattered memories of my grandparents' house in winters rainy and cold, a coal-burning stove providing some warmth. On laundry days, my grandparents placed a large piece of metal mesh over the stove to spread wet clothes out to dry.

My grandparents had escaped the heavy fighting in Quang Tri in the summer of 1972 and moved to Da Nang to live with my uncle. On January 27, 1973, the day the Paris Peace Accords were signed, officially ending the war, my grandfather died. My grandparents and uncle had been gathered around the dining table, listening to the news on the BBC, and my grandfather became so excited that he talked about immediately going back to Quang Tri to check on what was left of his house and to rebuild his business. A few moments later, he collapsed from a heart attack. My mom and I had to take an emergency flight to Da Nang to bury him before the Vietnamese New Year arrived. That had been the last time I'd seen him or my grandmother before I'd left the country.

We landed at Tan Son Nhut airport, the same place where as an air base, my dad had refused to evacuate in 1975. I was in Saigon for the first time since my escape. Officially, Saigon now is called Ho Chi Minh City, but to me and others from South Vietnam, it is always Saigon.

At the gate, two lovely Vietnamese women greeted us wearing traditional ao dai—those sleek, flowing pantlike gowns. We cleared Immigration, claimed our bags, passed through Customs, and met my cousin and friends waiting just outside. They were looking for me but didn't recognize me. Soon, I stood right in front of them.

"Who are you all looking for?" I asked them in a joking voice in Vietnamese.

They were so surprised once they recognized me. After a few seconds, they joked back, "We are looking for a fat lady."

All of them looked much thinner since the last time we'd gathered. *They must experience a hard life here,* I thought.

I managed a laugh. "Yeah, I gained some weight because I eat too much cheese in America."

There we were—all five of us together again! We hugged and greeted each other. My first thought was, "Are we even going to like each other after all these years?" But it took just a few minutes to realize it was like we'd never been apart. It's a bond that we won't forget.

My cousin had driven his Mercedes to pick us up at the airport. He was a vice president for a famous bank in Saigon at that time. My friends rode their motorbikes and followed the car to my cousin's house. The car ride from the airport to his home proved to me that Vietnam had changed, as I had heard, but not for people like my friends. Only the people who had good connections got richer, though.

On the way to his home, I peeked through the window. Saigon looked the same as I remembered, with streetside stalls for pho (Vietnamese noodle soup), markets, and pagodas. My cousin told me Vietnam now welcomed tourists and investments from the capitalist world, which improved the lives of many urban Vietnamese. Life was better, and the government control was lighter.

After my mom settled in at my cousin's house, I asked my friend to take me by my old house. My mom had told me she hadn't been able to sell the house when she left Vietnam because the government said we didn't have proof that we owned the land. That was ridiculous.

I knocked on the door. A young boy with a North Vietnamese accent answered and told me his parents had bought the house from the government in 1991. Everything was so different here. I didn't hear the sounds of piano playing from my next-door neighbor's house, either.

I missed it. A lot.

The next day, I spent several hours in the morning on my friend's motorbike, traveling around Saigon. Traffic seemed much busier than when I'd left eleven years ago, more alive and bustling. Countless motorbikes, motor scooters, and motorcycles reminded me of mosquitoes, their little motors revved as high as possible.

Nowadays, the city was home to more than 8.6 million people. When I was younger, my friends and I used to take pedicabs through streets lined with acacia and flame trees—and that was fancy for us. I was amazed watching these neatly dressed young men and women zipping by, the women wearing white trousers and elbow-length sleeves to protect their skin from the sun.

My first stop was the former United States Embassy, which was an icon of the war. I never forgot seeing on the TV the last helicopters evacuating from its roof and the terrified surges of Vietnamese families, trying to secure passage from outside the compound gates before the Americans were gone. Standing at the entrance and seeing the roof once used as a heliport, I felt chills.

Then I visited the former president's palace, now called Reunification Hall. My eyes tearing, I remembered how, on April 30, 1975, North Vietnamese tanks broke down the gates, and the South Vietnamese government surrendered. It's preserved as it was on that day. Even now, I still don't understand why South Vietnam lost the war. Even without the support of the United States, South Vietnam had about the same military size as North Vietnam but with higher technology and it was more industrialized. Why did we lose?

The next day, I visited my favorite Vinh Nghiem Pagoda. My friends and I used to come here to study for our tests. This temple had become one of Vietnam's most popular destinations for Vietnamese "Viet Kieu," or "overseas Vietnamese," and foreign tourists. It sat next to the canal on Nam Ky Khoi Nghia Street, near my old house. When I visited there, the whole area was festively decorated with flags on the roof, on the stairs, and strung up over the courtyard. The temple was hosting a celebration with large bowls of incense that grew into glowing red piles of smoldering ash. The main hall filled with people praying to Buddha, and the street outside the gate became a mini market with vendors selling bushels of incense sticks. My favorite part of the day was waiting in the long line that formed to ring the pagoda's bell. When it was my turn, I swung the large piece of wood tied by a rope to the roof and rung that bell myself.

I spent a few days at a friend's house. As we walked around the city, I found myself feeling afraid—not of crime but because of all the traffic on the roads. If I can cross the roads here, I joked, I can cross them anywhere in the world. I finally would just get the nerve to step straight out into the streaming traffic, unharmed. I even helped a group of Westerners cross the street. Just follow me, I said.

The fourth day, my mother and I took a taxi to Ben Thanh Market. Such an amazing place, with an array of tropical fruits, Vietnamese vegetables, and best of all, stalls serving up food and coffee. I have developed a coffee addiction since arriving in America, but I am very picky about my coffee. The taste of Vietnamese coffee is out of this world. Never have I tasted such velvety smooth, rich, and bold yet creamy coffee like this in America.

One evening, my cousin took me to a rooftop cocktail bar at sunset. As we sipped on some delicious pink berry yumminess, I watched the expanse of city lights come on. It was a spectacular sight.

Not everything we saw was beautiful. During our stay in Saigon, I noticed many more street children than when I'd lived here. Generally bare-chested and barefoot, mostly about ten to fifteen years old, these children begged or scavenged during the day throughout the city, then gathered in the late evening to let off steam before sleeping on the streets. My friends told me they earned their livelihoods by cajoling foreigners into giving them money; some would pick pockets and steal valuables.

I wondered whether my children and I would be able to move back to live in Vietnam for good. The answer would be no. I had become much too accustomed to America's luxury, technology, and mentality. If I was unable to picture myself living in Vietnam, how could I ever picture my children there?

Visiting Vietnam, I felt tugged in two directions. On the one hand, I was happy to walk the tiny alleys and bustling streets of Saigon, reliving the fond memories of my childhood years. On the other hand, I was disappointed that I was singled out everywhere I went because I was a Viet Kieu—not a permanent resident of Vietnam. And because of disparities between Vietnam and Western countries, people in Vietnam automatically assume that everyone from America is super rich. All my friends thought that I was rich and expected me to treat them. Shop owners also often tried to charge me more for goods. Unbeknownst to them all, I, too, struggled to make ends meet in America. I had to put in many extra shifts just to save for this trip. I couldn't help but wonder if I would have acted the same way if I were in their shoes.

After a week in Saigon, we traveled to Da Nang to visit my grandma and my uncle. My mom said we could take a high-class train because it's clean, private, and easy to see the landscape. I couldn't agree more.

At the train station, I saw two separate lines at the counter, one for citizens and one for the Viet Kieu. I was outraged at the Vietnamese government implementing discriminatory policies toward the Viet Kieu. The train trip from Saigon to Da Nang costs sixty-six percent more for a Viet Kieu than a Vietnamese citizen. My mom bought us tickets for first-class sleepers; we had to share the cabin with two other people.

The train departed at 11:50 a.m. A few hours later, we stopped at a fishing village called Mui Ne. I slid open the window and bought the best hot vit lon, a fertilized duck egg. I remembered this being a hugely popular nighttime snack when I was younger, but it was too expensive for us back then. Longan, a fruit, here is also sweet. I bought some for my grandmother.

The next stop was Phan Rang train station, or Thap Cham, then Nha Trang. As we headed north, the railway line hugged the coast, and the landscape varied between rice fields, villages, and jagged limestone karsts jutting out from the fields, splinters of the mountainous ridge that delineates much of Vietnam's western border with Cambodia and Laos.

Eight hours later, we were at Nha Trang station. My mom bought some drinks, snacks, and banh mi, one of the most vibrant and delicious sandwiches in the world. It's loaded with fresh vegetables and grilled meat, piled high on a French baguette. A white American woman in our cabin bought the same thing, but the seller charged her triple. She didn't notice. I spoke up and told the vendor that she had overcharged and needed to give the passenger the proper change. The vendor refused. A Vietnamese-American in our cabin whispered to me not to bother because the other passenger was white. Some Vietnamese are taught that all their problems are caused by the West, especially France and the United States, and that Westerners "owe" the Vietnamese. They expect Westerners to spend money in Vietnam. I was happy to pay more myself, knowing a dollar went a lot farther for them than for me. I just wished they showed more respect to Westerners traveling in our country.

After an overnight ride, we arrived in Da Nang. I woke up at about 4:30 a.m. to photograph the sunrise and spent a good portion of the morning trying to convince the conductors to unlock the windows so I could get better shots without the glass.

Da Nang was the largest city in Central Vietnam and widely known as Vietnam's "most livable city," more peaceful than Saigon. My uncle and his wife drove two separate motorbikes to pick us up at the train station.

When we arrived at the house, I went straight to my grandmother's room. She was ninety now, lying in bed. I was crying. Her room was dark, but I saw my pictures from America hanging all over her walls. I was her oldest granddaughter; she must be so proud of me. The first thing she said to me was,

"Let's go eat your famous Da Nang food. You must be so lonely and hungry in America. My poor dear granddaughter."

Later, about midnight, when I walked past her room, she called to me and asked if I could give her some longan. Everyone else was asleep, so I couldn't ask them whether it would upset her. So I brought longan to her. The next day, she got diarrhea bad. My mom warned me to not listen to her. She can't eat that late.

We stayed with my grandmother for two weeks. My mom gave her showers, trimmed her nails, brushed her hair, dressed her in nice outfits, and helped her walk to the living room to hang out with the family. My mom cooked her favorite food every day. I didn't know whether I could do that for my mom when she grew older.

My grandmother spent several hours each day with me in the hot and sunny Vietnam afternoon. She told me about how my parents got to know each other, how my grandfather met her, and how he died. She showed me old photo albums, where I recognized the faces of my relatives.

During our stay, my uncle and his wife took us on their motorbikes to visit Hoi An. This magical little town lay just eighteen miles south of Da Nang, but it took us almost ninety minutes to get there because of traffic. I had never been there before.

Hoi An was a combination of Colonial French and Vietnamese—and by far, my favorite place in all of Vietnam. As I walked through the streets, I felt like I was walking in a fairytale. The Japanese bridge and old temples here were so amazing. The temples stood for centuries without using any form of mortar. They were heavily bombed during the Vietnam War, but to this day, scientists can't figure out how they remained standing. Hoi An also is an old trading port for silk, with hundreds of shops selling silk made to measure.

These three weeks had given me the joy of exploration of my own past as well as gaining respect and admiration for my parents. I realized more how much my parents had sacrificed in order to give me a hopeful future. I also realized how tragic their lives were under the influence of war, poverty, and Communism—and how while my father was in prison, my mother had given almost everything she had for the survival and well-being of her four children.

America is now my home, of course, but Vietnam will always have a special place in my heart. As a struggling refugee, I am proud of my Vietnamese heritage.

UF baseball team, Inaugural Florida Four tournament, Kneeling with Queena:
Pitcher Alex Panteliodis (left) and Florida coach Kevin O'Sullivan – George
Steinbrenner Field, FL, March 1, 2010

CHAPTER 19

HOLD MY HAND—I'LL WALK WITH YOU

I'M STANDING JUST OUTSIDE OF a long tunnel that is pitch-black on the inside. It's so long, I can't see where it ends. I tremble with fear. I don't want to go inside alone. Suddenly, a tall and slender man wearing a long, white garment approaches. He stands next to me. I look at him. His eyes are peaceful—more peaceful than any eyes I have ever seen.

"Do you know if there is another road that is better than this?" I ask. "This tunnel looks scary and dark. I can't go through this!"

The man responds calmly. "It is the only way. You need to go through the tunnel. There is no easy road."

He extends his hand. "If you hold my hand, I will take you through."

I trust the man immediately because I have no other choice. I hold his hand and walk slowly into the darkness of the tunnel. Suddenly, I feel a complete sense of peace.

When I awoke, I realized I'd been dreaming. Still, I couldn't shake the incredible feeling of peace I felt, despite being in the midst of chaos.

I went downstairs to Queena's room to greet her as I did at the start of each day. When I looked up, I noticed a framed print hanging on Queena's wall that had been given to me by a friend who knew of my struggle to hold on to something—*Someone*—stronger than myself. In the busyness of caring for Queena, I had forgotten to look at the image. Now, the picture of a gentle Shepherd standing among a flock of sheep, holding one little lamb in His arm, suddenly seemed so alive. The image of the Man stared back at me with those same peace-filled eyes I had seen in my dream. *He* was the Man Who had come to me. It was Jesus Who had called me to go forward into the tunnel while He held out His hand to guide me.

For the rest of the day, I wondered about the deeper meaning of the dream. I replayed it in my mind, as if it held some sort of lesson to be learned or something to be remembered. The dream raised questions that only I could answer.

What do I fear most?

What is in the long tunnel that causes me to be afraid?

Why is Jesus asking me to trust Him?

Then it hit me. My vision for Queena was to go to UF and graduate from college. This was my deepest desire for her.

"What if she is never able to accomplish this?" The question escaped my mouth before I could choke back the sheer thought. "No! No! Queena will graduate!" I insisted.

I spoke with a friend, confiding my frustrations over Queena's slow progress during the eighteen months since the attack. We had gone to myriad doctor appointments, rehab, therapy sessions, and occupational therapy. We had done it all. The doctors, therapists, nurses, and staff members seemed to genuinely care for and love Queena. Some even expressed hope, although most looked at her and admitted they could do little to help. Queena's brain injury caused her upper body muscles to be very tight. Her arms had contracted, and her hands were closed and unable to move. At this point in her recovery, we had hoped to see a greater degree of improvement.

I asked my friend if she thought I needed to change my prayer. I'd been asking Jesus to heal Queena.

"Should I pray for her life to serve some other purpose beyond my imagination?" I asked. "Maybe I should ask that Jesus do something for *me*."

"Vanna," she said gently, "are you willing to give up your dream for Queena's life in order to please God?"

"My dream?" I questioned.

"Yes, your dream of Queena's recovery and her ability to attend college someday," she replied.

The thought shook me to my core. At the time, I didn't realize that going to college was *my* dream. I always had thought it was *her* dream! Going to college was more than a dream—it had become a fact in my mind. It was an inevitable destiny! I thought, *No, I'm not going to give up that dream, and neither is Queena!*

Nevertheless, the question my friend so tenderly asked stuck with me. For many nights, I wrestled with the thoughts that she presented. To be completely honest, I wasn't just wrestling with my thoughts—I was wrestling with God, too. I asked the same questions over and over:

Why haven't You put Your hands on Queena?

Why haven't You healed her?

Do You really want us to give up on our dreams?

A few days after our conversation, my friend emailed me and said that she had been reading the daily devotional *Jesus Calling* by Sarah Young. The entry for that day reminded her of the dream I'd had about Jesus taking my hand. The devotional started with, "Keep walking with Me along the path I have chosen for you."[13] I was so confused. I couldn't see the way in which these words related to my dream or Queena's healing. Then, I remembered opening my Bible to the following verse: "Then, calling the crowd to join his disciples, he said, 'If any of you want to be my follower, you must give up your own way, take up your cross, and follow me'" (Mark 8:34).

For the first time since the attack on Queena, I sensed Jesus calling me to lay down my plans for Queena. *Yes, I should probably pray for something different,* I thought. *I should let go of the hope I had held onto for so long. I need to find new hope in Jesus Christ. I need to take His hand, trust Him, and walk through this dark tunnel that stretches out before me, even though I don't know where it will lead me or how I will ever reach the end.*

Later that day, my eyes straining through tears, I looked at my daughter lying peacefully in her medical bed. "Okay, Queena," I said. "I am not going to pray for you to go to UF anymore. Jesus is the One Who will decide your future. I trust in Him. I will follow His lead."

Queena's eyes turned sad. I couldn't tell her exact thoughts. I could imagine her saying, "Really, Mom? I couldn't wait to get there." Yet knowing how much Queena loved Jesus—even before I knew of such love—I trusted Queena enough to believe that she would want to walk in step with God, despite any disappointment.

I soon saw the benefits of my changed prayers. April 24, 2010, marked two years since the attack. We spent the day celebrating Queena's twentieth birthday. Over the previous two years, my house had become a welcoming center for staff writers of local newspapers and an increasing number of visitors, therapists, and homebound schoolteachers. Eight therapists came in and out for various treatments: rehabilitation, physical therapy, speech therapy, music therapy, chiropractic care, hyperbaric chamber sessions, acupuncture—and the list goes on. On an average day, she endured up to five therapy sessions, some inside our home, some outside. I often felt exhausted, but I believed the benefits were worth the effort.

By most standards, Queena's progress crept along because she still needed a feeding tube and a wheelchair. Yet she had begun to distinguish shadows and to speak the beginning sounds of a few words. When hungry, she said, "Hung." *Home* sounded like *ha. Hur* equaled *hurry*. She also learned to swallow and could eat food with the consistency of mashed potatoes. Another development, she kept her head above water without assistance. I credited any progress she achieved through therapy to the mighty work of God in her life.

Two years after Queena's brutal assault, the community still pulled together to help on her road to recovery, be it through events like her trip to UF, the aquarium, or through fundraisers to pay for the high costs of care that Medicaid didn't cover. As the hot and rainy summer of 2010 wore on, the Ruskin SouthShore Chamber of Commerce, the local electric company

(TECO), the county parks department, and other local businesses played a role in one fundraiser's success. A music festival was held in Queena's honor at E.G. Simmons Park in Ruskin. A local high school singing group and band provided entertainment, while festival-goers ate barbecue lunches, played in bounce houses, participated in other kids' activities, and took part in a silent auction, live raffles, and a bake sale. About two thousand people attended.

We took Queena to the fundraising event in her honor and were quickly overwhelmed by the outpouring of support. The event raised enough money to purchase a hyperbaric chamber for Queena to use at home. She had shown great improvement with this therapy over the previous five months, but we sacrificed greatly to take her to the treatments. Five days a week, I drove two hours round-trip to the facility in St. Petersburg. Having the hyperbaric chamber in our home meant less travel and more time to tend to other therapies and needs. With the money left over, we took Queena to a clinic in Tampa for neurotherapy. Each session cost about two hundred dollars, which Medicaid did not cover.

Perhaps trusting Jesus to walk me through the tunnel of darkness was the very thing I needed after all.

Queena's reserved parking spot at East Bay High School for her senior year -

Summer, 2007

CHAPTER 20
TIME FOR A CHANGE

(1993-2008)

Two years after my family arrived in the States, Quang and I separated. He wanted a housewife and enjoyed seclusion from the outside world. I wanted to work outside of the home and dreamed of managing my own business. I loved to socialize with friends. We just couldn't make our differences work, but we chose to remain friendly. I was thirty-one years old with two girls. Single motherhood had never been part of my American dream, but I accepted this new reality.

Without a husband to help pay bills, money became especially tight. I moved Anna, Queena, my mother, and siblings to a two-bedroom apartment. I sent Anna to preschool, which cost about three hundred dollars a month. I sacrificed because I knew starting her education early would pay off. I wanted my children to have the same opportunities that many other kids had in the United States. When the time came for Queena to go to preschool, however, she cried so much there that we finally gave in and allowed her to stay home with my mother.

We continued to struggle financially, so Mom rented out one of the rooms in our apartment to an older gentleman. That left one bedroom for everyone else. My mother and Queena shared a full-size bed; my youngest sister and Anna shared a set of bunkbeds; my brother slept in a small bed in the corner of the living room; and I slept on the living room floor.

My mother made sure my girls did exercises from children's workbooks each day. She also taught them to help her with laundry and cooking. They often tagged along when she went to the market for food. She gave them pocket change each afternoon for a snack from the ice cream truck. They got so excited when they heard the truck's jingle as it crept along the street.

Three years separated my daughters' ages, but I still found ways to dress them in similar outfits and colors every day. Despite how I dressed them on the outside, the differences in Anna's and Queena's personalities amazed me. Anna never complained or said much. She simply listened to what I told her. I could always count on her to admit when she misbehaved. Queena, on the other hand, cried a lot. She wanted things her way. Even when she complained, she had a cute, chubby face that no one could resist. My family spoiled her and obliged her every demand.

As time wore on, they grew into beautiful little girls with long and silky, dark hair. I typically combed their hair back and decorated it with headbands that showed their smart foreheads and healthy, pink skin. Their eyes glimmered like stars when they smiled. They played together, dancing and laughing. They were happy siblings. As a mother, all I wanted was to see my girls be happy. Sometimes when I watched them, emotions overwhelmed me. I saw our faces replacing the American actors in movies I watched as a child—movies showing families living in freedom and hope.

Anna's father, Minh, visited a couple of times. Once, he gave her a child-size motorcycle. She rode it around the neighborhood with a big smile on her face, as proud as she could be. Quang visited the girls quite often after our separation. As time wore on, however, he stopped coming around and then disappeared from Queena's life. The vision I had of a happy, traditional family—like the life I had known before the Vietnam War—escaped me, even in America.

By 1993, California's economy plummeted. Earning enough money to support our extended family grew even more difficult. I knew I had to do something.

I heard about many opportunities in Georgia, so I sketched a plan to move there temporarily, make a lot of money working, and give my girls the world. With the promise to send money back to California, I left Anna and Queena with my mother and drove to Georgia in the Honda Prelude I had paid off.

I knew I'd made a mistake shortly after arriving in Atlanta. I earned enough from the nail shop where I worked to send money back home, but drug dealers infested the neighborhood. I didn't feel safe. Plus, I missed my girls terribly. I felt so guilty for leaving them. I wanted them with me, but I couldn't bring them to my new neighborhood; and we really needed more money to support a family of seven. I felt stuck.

In October 1993, just a few months after I arrived in Atlanta, a friend who had moved to New York asked me to come and visit. I went there to explore whether better job opportunities existed in the Northeast. While I was in New York, the former owner of a nail shop in Los Angeles contacted me. He needed someone to manage a new shop he planned to open in Virginia. So, instead of returning to Atlanta, I went to Virginia. But, again, that venture never really paid off.

Soon thereafter, I found a job nearby at a nail shop in Silver Spring, Maryland. I became the top nail technician among the fifteen technicians in the shop. A few months later, the owner asked if I wanted to partner with her at another location she hoped to open in the local mall. I agreed. I didn't have the money to buy into the partnership, but the co-owner allowed me to pay my half of the business off with a monthly payment. Now, I not only had a job, but I'd become the business owner I'd always wanted to be!

I continued to miss my family, though—especially my daughters. After opening my first business, Nail 1st, at Marley Station Mall in Glen Burnie, Maryland, I continued to send money to California. Within a year's time, my siblings' situation changed. Tina got married. Tam graduated from high school and was accepted to the University of Southern California, where she wanted to major in finance.

After Anna and Queena finished their school year in California, I moved the girls to an apartment in Maryland to live with me. That fall, Anna started third grade, and Queena entered kindergarten. I hoped they wouldn't resent me for the year I'd spent apart from them. Gratefully, they didn't. In fact, we grew closer. Days could be hectic as a single mother, but with my business taking off, I began to feel financially successful.

I bought a single-family home and a piano. I hired a private instructor to teach Anna and Queena to play. I enrolled the girls in a private Christian school, where they soaked in the foundations of their faith and began to plant those seeds in their mother. Finally, my professional dreams were coming true.

A friend of mine gave me Robert's phone number, and we reconnected with each other. His voice sounded like the same sweet, kind big brother he'd always been. Our conversation went well. We both suffered much hurt regarding marriage. So, we understood each other and decided to grant our lives to each other.

By the summer of 1998, my business partner called me with the shocking news that he was not willing to renew the lease for the Nail 1st salon. He discovered that the landlord was raising our rent. Once again, my income was in jeopardy, but I found another shop for sale in Severna Park, south of Ritchie Highway, where Nail 1st was located.

The new shop, Jade Nails, was in a wealthy area, not too far from my home, my customer base, and the kids' school. Great! I purchased the shop and held a grand reopening on August 10, 1998. I had now launched my second business. By October of that year, Robert moved to Maryland to help me close down Nail 1st.

By June 1, 2000, we opened Riva Nails in Annapolis. Robert took care of Riva Nails, and I continued to work at Jade Nails. By that time, I had secured many clients. We worked by appointment only from ten a.m. to eight p.m., six days a week. We lived in the area until it was time for Anna to choose a college.

She settled on Southeastern University, a Christian college she had researched in Lakeland, Florida. I wanted her to attend the school of her choice. Still, I couldn't bear to be so far away from her. So, we decided if Anna moved to Florida, Queena, Robert, and I would move to Florida, as well.

By April 26, 2005, our new house in the Tampa Bay region of Florida was ready for closing. I was able to choose many of the interior options because the house was still in the construction phase when we made the purchase. We packed Robert's van with our belongings and made the first of several trips to move our family from Glen Burnie to Tampa. I looked into schools for Queena and a new business opportunity for me close by.

By August 12, 2005, I signed a ten-year lease for a nail salon located in a newly built shopping plaza. I chose a warm earth décor, dim lighting, a fancy ceiling with hanging Pendel lamps, and fans. My plan was to offer a midprice spa manicure, spa pedicure, gel nail and body treatment, and spa packages using only brand-name products. I named my new shop Elegant Nail Spa. I greeted my customers at the opening on October 22, 2005, with candles in every corner of the various rooms.

We eventually chose East Bay High School in Gibsonton, Florida, for Queena. She had always been a good student. She studied hard to earn good grades and build up her list of student activities to get accepted into the competitive school. Whenever she got less than an A on a test, she carefully reviewed the answers to learn—and to make sure the teacher had graded it correctly. When she found a teacher's error, she took her exam to the school counselor's office to protest the grade and won.

Queena wanted to round out her high school experience with sports, even though she wasn't the best athlete. She had previously joined the volleyball and soccer teams, knowing she would never be a star. I picked her up once from practice, and she wanted to throw up from having to run extra drills; some teammates had talked too much, and the coach had punished the whole team. When I got there, she carried two full buckets of ice and drinks after cleaning up the field by herself. When I said her friends should help, she said the coach had already told her the same thing. She didn't want them to help, however. They had played a good game, and they needed to rest.

"I'm not a very good player," Queena told me. "So, I'm doing something else."

Between her schoolwork, sports, and friends, Queena also volunteered for Life Path Hospice near her school. She sat behind the desk to greet people and answer phones. Whenever I picked her up at the end of her shift, she would be reading a textbook behind that desk. It was usually dark outside by then, and I questioned the safety of her working so late at night, but she deemed the job a perfect fit. None of her friends wanted to volunteer for hospice, she said—likely because hospice cared for the terminally ill. The agency struggled to find volunteers.

"They need help," Queena said. "I think this is a great job for me because they allow me to do my homework when I'm not busy."

Her time with hospice also gave Queena valuable life experiences others her age lacked. One evening, an elderly man waved as she passed his room, beckoning her to come inside to talk. She did. She sat with him for a long time. He told the stories of his journey through life. She laughed with him about the funny parts and listened through the sad ones. The next day, she stopped by the man's room again. This time, she found the door closed. The man had died the night before, not long after Queena had left him.

Throughout her high school years, Queena also mentored disabled students through a program called Best Buddies. She served in the Student Government Association and participated in Future Business Leaders of America, Students Against Destructive Decisions, the high school's yearbook and newspaper staff, the Fellowship of Christian Athletes, and the Mu Alpha Theta math honors society. On college applications, she proudly listed her honors and recognitions. She won the Brave Spirit award. Her varsity soccer team claimed district championship, winning the most games in the school district. She also made the principal's honor roll with straight *A*'s.

The University of Tampa and the University of Central Florida, both excellent schools, offered her full scholarships. Still, Queena had her heart set on being a Florida Gator. So, she waited to see if she'd be accepted there, too. On February 8, 2008, she got home from school and ran straight to her laptop. At four o'clock that afternoon, Queena logged in to the "Check Your Status" page of the University of Florida Admissions website to see their admission decision.

UF would electronically notify accepted applicants. A complication with logging onto the school's busy website slowed things down, and Queena tried anxiously to find out but couldn't. Two hours passed. Finally, one word flickered in front of her before she got an email from the school that began, "Congratulations!" A week later, she got an official letter by mail. She smelled it, kissed it, and skimmed the lines with her fingertips.

"Mom," she said, "this is my world, my future . . . I am going to sit at the top of a glass building in a high-rise." She giggled. "I will travel the world with the newest fashions. I am going to be a world-famous designer!"

I felt such pride. In Queena's college acceptance, my own journey came full-circle, too. It was the journey of a Vietnamese refugee who had survived her war-torn nation and fled to the United States. Despite my own struggles on the boat, the disappointments of life, and the senseless murder of my father, I had reached the point in life that every mother strives for. I could look back and honestly say, "I raised good children." I had equipped them to live out their own dreams.

Rachel Hall's testimony of the attack on Queena - 2010

CHAPTER 21

TRIALS, TESTIMONIES, AND QUESTIONS OF FORGIVENESS

ON AUGUST 31, 2010, KENDRICK Morris went on trial for attacking and raping a daycare worker ten months prior to attacking Queena. For me, the situation was hard to grasp. I learned from a news report that Morris had been charged as a juvenile with cruelty to animals, accused of killing a snowy egret and wounding a duck.[14] I read that children who abuse animals or wildlife often escalate such behaviors to include abusing people. Media reports cited detectives who said Morris' upper body displayed about forty marks, scabs, and scars.[15]

Morris had told child protection investigators that his mother, Lisa Stevens, and Steve White, a retired Tampa Bay Buccaneers defensive lineman whom psychologists described as Morris' stepfather, would whip him with a belt when he was about eleven years old. White and Stevens have a daughter together but were never married. On Twitter, White denied abusing Morris and said he was not part of the household when child protective investigators removed the boy.[16] Stevens was charged with aggravated child abuse but later pleaded guilty to contributing to the delinquency of a child, receiving a year's probation.[17]

If this information was true, I surmised he was an angry young man. Anger has an awful way of building up inside of a person over the years. Was it possible Kendrick Morris went from being a victim of abuse to abusing animals to ultimately abusing people? I remembered cases like that in Vietnam. I didn't want to believe these tragic stories happened in America, too.

His trial for the charges related to the attack on Queena was scheduled to begin several weeks after this first trial. He pleaded not guilty in both cases. When I had the chance, I followed the court proceedings by listening to news reports on the internet, away from Queena's room.

On the first day of the first trial, the daycare worker testified. Now in her mid-sixties, she broke down in tears while describing her attack on June 28, 2007. She recounted seeing a man outside the daycare center in the days prior. She then detailed the moment of the rape: how the masked man had grabbed the door while she'd been opening the business that day; how he'd wielded a knife, told her to disrobe, and covered her mouth in case she tried to scream. She hadn't known Morris, though they lived in the same neighborhood. Authorities captured his DNA after swabbing her. He was fifteen when he raped her.

My body trembled as I listened to her testimony. *Oh, God, please help this world!* I felt so horrible for her. She waited ten months without any leads or suspects—until the DNA from Queena's attack matched the DNA from hers, linking the investigations.

On September 2, 2010, the jury deliberated for four hours before finding Kendrick Morris guilty of raping her.[18] As the bailiffs handcuffed him, Morris turned to look back at his mother, the only member of his family who was present. His father hadn't been in his life.

I wanted to scream as I watched the video footage. I didn't want to believe he had done these same horrible things to Queena. Morris was so young. A part of me hoped for his innocence in both cases. As a mother myself, I felt so bad for his mom. Even if she did abuse her son, she must have felt so much pain watching the authorities take him away in handcuffs.

Yet the trial forced me to confront feelings about my daughter's case that I had ignored. Since the attack, I had put Kendrick Morris out of my mind. I focused instead on doing what I felt God wanted me to do—to take care of Queena. As my faith in Christ grew, I began to see Morris as I imagined God sees him. Early on, I viewed him as a monster, someone unworthy of my compassion. Yet when I understood Jesus' unconditional love for me, it became hard to deny that God loved Kendrick Morris, too.

Now that a jury had found him guilty of raping this daycare worker, I couldn't escape the idea that this same young man—really, still a boy—had hurt my daughter also. Prosecutors had announced that they would hold off on Morris' sentencing hearing in the daycare worker's rape until after Queena's trial ended. If convicted of the charges in Queena's case, Morris would then be sentenced for both crimes. He could possibly be sentenced to life imprisonment.

I wondered how I should feel about a life sentence. The more pressing question that could no longer be ignored was, "Should I forgive him?" More important, "Do I *want* to forgive him?" Uncertain of my own emotions, I asked a close friend to help me sort out my feelings. In an email she wrote:

> I feel for you as you have to go through this, too. He deserves life imprisonment, but for your sake and your family's, I hope you will forgive him as much as possible. Jesus' teaching is to forgive our enemies. In the model prayer which He taught to His disciples, He said, "Forgive us our debts, as we also have forgiven our debtors" (Matt. 6:12-14). Perhaps you already have done this.

Through tears, I thanked God for sending me a friend so sweet and with such a beautiful heart. She was the only one who talked about forgiving Queena's attacker. I struggled through so many emotions. I wondered how I would ever be able to let go of the immense anger I felt deep inside. The only thing I could think to do was to pray for help and guidance.

The very next day, another friend, whom I had met while living in Maryland, sent me the poem "When I Say I am a Christian," by Carol Wimmer.[19]

When I say, "I am a Christian"
I'm not shouting, "I've been saved!"

I'm whispering, "I get lost sometimes
That's why I chose this way"

When I say, "I am a Christian"
I don't speak with human pride
I'm confessing that I stumble -
Needing God to be my guide

When I say, "I am a Christian"
I'm not trying to be strong
I'm professing that I'm weak
and pray for strength to carry on.

As I read the opening words of the poem, I was reminded of whom I needed to be as a Christian. To forgive Queena's attacker, I had to truly understand the forgiveness of Jesus in my own heart. Once again, I turned to prayer. I prayed for the strength to forgive, as Jesus had forgiven His attackers. I believed that crossing this threshold of unconditional love in the Kingdom of Heaven would be worth all the pain my family had suffered while on earth. But if I couldn't find the strength to forgive the person who had committed such a horrible crime, would I be able to find the threshold of Heaven for myself? Is this what it means to love one's enemy?

Our day in court came on Monday, September 27, 2010. Kendrick Morris was to be tried on charges of kidnapping, aggravated battery with great bodily harm, and two counts of sexual battery with force causing injury in the attack on my beautiful Queena.

On that day, I felt a mixture of intense emotions—including dread, anxiety, grief, and despair. But I also had hope that God would take control. In order for that to happen, I needed to relinquish control, so I decided not to attend the proceedings. Another good reason not to attend was to avoid disrupting Queena's daily routine. I also wanted to protect myself from hearing the painful details of what Queena had endured. I stayed home and peeked in on the proceedings through media reports. This shielded me from bearing every hurt Queena had suffered. Instead, my brave, eldest daughter, Anna, attended the trial each day to represent our family.

We had recently taken Queena for a neurotherapy session, including a process called "brain mapping." The procedure revealed that she had activity in all nineteen areas where sensors were attached. The brain function rated low, but some activity and brainwaves did exist. This meant her brain was functioning, although at a reduced level. It meant her neurons were not dead. This small dose of encouragement helped me get through the very difficult days of the trial.

The first challenge for the attorneys was to find jurors who had avoided the intense media coverage of Queena's case over the past two years. Public defender Rocky Brancato requested to move the trial out of the area because of the publicity, but the request was denied.

Morris didn't testify, but friends and classmates had told reporters about how he'd been a lineman on the Bloomingdale High School football team until he'd needed tutoring to improve his grades. He and his mother lived with his grandmother, Lucina Stevens. He often hung out at the library after school and waited for hours for his mother to pick him up. The day after the attack, a sheriff's corporal saw him walking up to the library and stopped to talk to him because he matched the description of the "weird guy" Queena had told her friend she'd seen outside the building. He'd recently been listed as a runaway.

Anna also did not testify. My poor daughter listened as prosecutors held up her sister's torn clothes and displayed photos of her sister's skin covered in blood, grass, and bug bites. Chief Assistant State Attorney Michael Sinacore and Assistant State Attorney Rita Peters described the scene and Queena's condition when she was found. Her nose had been broken, and her forehead fractured. Rita told the jurors that Queena wore a gray sweater but had been naked from the waist down.

Queena had left a trail that led to her attacker: blood on the ground next to her car, her bloody handprint on a street sign, Sinacore said. But it didn't end there. Investigators found Queena's blood on Morris' sweatshirt, his semen inside her, his fingerprints on the bench outside the library, where others had seen him shortly before the attack.[20]

Anna relayed what happened in court to me over the phone. It was the first time I had heard the horrible details. I was glad I had made the decision not to go to the courtroom, but my blood boiled. No wonder Rita had told me she regarded Queena as her hero. My heart broke all over again, and my chest felt heavy. I wanted to beat the air and scream, but my body just shook instead. Unlike the first trial for the daycare worker, Queena could not tell the jury her story. Because my daughter could not speak, the prosecutors became her voice, threading the facts and details into a story for others to judge.

The trial lasted about eight days. Brancato argued that Morris wasn't the real attacker. Morris had told detectives that he left the library at about nine p.m. the night of the attack to walk to McDonald's and then a Walmart to call a cab. Four cameras over the Walmart doors showed Morris entering the store at 10:22 p.m. and exiting at 11:06 p.m., but all other store cameras showed him in the aisles after 11:34 p.m.[21] Brancato said that the time stamps on the door cameras showed that Morris didn't have enough time to attack Queena, move her behind the library, and then walk to the store.

But prosecutors said that witnesses and the DNA evidence proved Morris' guilt. They called Walmart loss prevention coordinator Roberto Soto to testify. He said power surges often cause the cameras to fall out of time.[22] The time stamps on the door cameras must be wrong, prosecutors said, because Walmart employees remembered Morris entering about 11:25 p.m. and saying he needed a cab. Someone at the customer service desk let him use the phone. The cab driver told investigators that he'd picked Morris up at the store at about 12:30 a.m. and took him home, but his family wasn't there. It turns out his mother had been in jail at the time, charged with violating probation by driving with a suspended license. Morris had borrowed money from a neighbor to pay the driver, then spent the night at the neighbor's house.[23]

His fingerprints were found on the library bench. Queena's blood was on his sweatshirt. More intimate evidence was swabbed from her body. The odds of Morris' exact DNA profile matching another person, Sinacore told the jury, were one in 320 quadrillion.[24]

Even though I wasn't in the courtroom, my thoughts turned to the ways in which my daughter had been forced to fight for her life. Queena was a true conqueror. My eyes stung as I tried to control my tears. As I'd drift off to sleep out of pure emotional and physical exhaustion, I thought of God. I knew God's Spirit was with me, watching over Queena, as well as the young man potentially facing a lifetime in prison. Whatever the outcome, I had to put my trust in God.

On Wednesday, October 6, 2010, I took Queena to SouthBay Rehab for her usual therapy sessions. While Queena participated in speech therapy, I went to the lobby to watch the news on TV for developments in our case. Surprisingly, the jury had reached a verdict after deliberating for less than an hour. I saw Queena's friends rush back into the courtroom. Rita Peters reached for Anna and held her hand. Then sobs erupted in the courtroom as the verdict was read aloud.

The jury found Kendrick Morris guilty of kidnapping, attacking, and raping my daughter.[25]

That night, I read more details about the trial in the *Tampa Bay Times*. I learned that Anna sat in the courtroom listening quietly as Morris stood without reaction to the verdict.[26] I regretted that Queena couldn't be in that courtroom to witness justice being served. She couldn't see her sister or the small army of her friends, who filled the benches to witness this day on her behalf, begin to cry. Queena still did not remember what happened. We spared her the most challenging aspects of the trial. We did not think it was fair to burden her with details, at least not at the time. Even if she had fully understood what happened to her at the library, she would have had no way to communicate her emotions or process her grief. She wasn't able to talk to a counselor or even express her thoughts to me or Anna concerning the trauma she experienced. We explained her disabilities to her by telling her simply that someone had hurt her. As for the trial, we told her about the court proceedings and that Rita Peters wore pink in her honor.

Still, standing there in the lobby of the rehab facility after hearing the verdict, I felt the biggest wave of peace wash over me. Finally, after two years, we had received some justice for Queena.

In the weeks after the trial, I asked Queena if she wanted to forgive the person who hurt her. I believe she understood me. She responded yes in the only way she could—with a smile.

Judge Chet Tharpe waited for more than seven months to sentence Morris. During that time, Michael Sinacore said a recent Supreme Court ruling prevented him from asking for a life sentence. So, Sinacore had to decide how many years he would request for Morris to spend in prison.

I was informed that I would have an opportunity to read a statement to Morris during the sentencing hearing. I didn't want to do it. How could I stand there and speak to him? Would he even listen to what I had to say? He had appeared cold and lacking in emotion at the trial, even when the verdict was read. It seemed as if he had built a wall around himself. I was both angry and sad for him, for me, for his mother, for Queena, and for Anna.

I eventually decided to write a letter to him for the sentencing. It was something I needed to do. I don't know how many different versions I wrote over the seven-month waiting period. My letters ranged from complete forgiveness to utter rage. At some point, I stopped writing and took some time to process my emotions. I prayed for him. I prayed for his mother. I asked God to strengthen me and to heal Queena.

One day, I opened the Bible and read the following passage: "'My thoughts are nothing like your thoughts,' says the LORD. 'And my ways are far beyond anything you could imagine'" (Isa. 55:8-9).

The words jumped off the page, beckoning me to fully forgive Kendrick Morris. I thought about how God loves even the most unlovable of people. Yes, when we do wrong, it hurts God's heart. Yes, the same God Who formed us and made us wants everyone to repent of wrongdoing and embrace Jesus as the world's Savior and Redeemer. Yet God doesn't remove unconditional love just because someone rejects the offer. God keeps loving us, even when we don't want it, can't accept it, or don't deserve it.

Now came my turn to practice the same kind of love that God had shown to me so many times in my life. I needed to represent God's love by forgiving someone who didn't deserve my forgiveness—someone who might not be able to receive it or accept it. The idea of forgiving Queena's attacker felt as easy as moving a mountain. It wasn't going to happen. I didn't have the strength.

I meditated on that passage in Isaiah, trying so hard to forgive, but my anger remained. I began to realize that I couldn't forgive Morris by my own power. I couldn't will it to happen. True forgiveness would only come as I slowly submitted this particular situation—and my whole life—to God. I was deep in the middle of my tunnel of darkness, and forgiveness would take time. I would need to release my desire for control over my own life and trust God more fully than I had allowed myself to do.

I believed that if my trust in God could grow, I could inch my way toward forgiving the young man who nearly killed my daughter, who ruined the future she had imagined for herself, and who destroyed my own dreams for her. Such forgiveness would not happen overnight. I realized forgiveness would be an ongoing process that might just take the rest of my life.

Title Boxing Club in Brandon hosted a "Fight for Queena" self-defense fundraiser

- April 12, 2014

CHAPTER 22
THE LOVE OF COMMUNITY

IN FEBRUARY 2011, ANOTHER CMS case manager called. Since Queena would be turning twenty-one the following April, her case would transition to the Adult Medicaid program. To receive around-the-clock care in the adult program, she would have to move into a nursing home. I nearly fainted.

"No way!" I said. "I can never let Queena stay in a nursing home. She would not be able to overcome that!" In my mind, the progress she'd made through therapy over the previous three years would be lost. "She is my baby! She belongs with me." I didn't understand why she should lose her benefits simply because she had aged. Her condition hadn't changed, and she still needed twenty-four-hour-a-day medical support.

The case manager told me that her care would have stayed the same if she had been seventeen when attacked. However, Queena had turned eighteen just two days beforehand. I shook my head in disbelief. How does this continue to happen? How could I pay for her health care when I already struggled to keep my nail salon afloat and my home out of foreclosure, while trying to tend to my own problems?

I prayed, "Where do I turn now, God?"

I felt the Lord urging me to reach out to the people in the media. So many times before, they had banded together as advocates for Queena. I texted, called, and emailed reporters I had dealt with over the years. As I shared our dilemma, people began searching for any kind of waiver for which Queena might qualify. The search revealed an exception in the guidelines for the Agency for Persons with Disabilities. This exception called for people with brain and spinal injuries who were younger than twenty-one to receive the level of home care Queena needed.

Next, friends helped me draft a letter to U.S. Representative Kathy Castor, and one of them even hand-delivered it to her on February 27, 2011. The next day, she responded, saying that she empathized with our situation. She sent a request for immediate review of Queena's care to Florida Governor Rick Scott, as well as the interim director for the Agency for Persons with Disabilities and several county and state elected officials.

From there, the story of Queena's needs spread through political channels like wildfire. State Senator Ronda Storms and her staff stepped in to help move things in the right direction. With the exception of the governor, each person contacted responded quickly, sending more information about other potential pools for resources and affirming our hope that Queena would receive the waiver for continued home care. Yet as time went on, the Agency for Health Care Administration (AHCA) and other officials denied us time and time again. Glimmers of hope faded.

Meanwhile, the media kept the community up-to-date with developments. Sarina Fazan from *ABC Action News* played a pivotal role in keeping the public informed of our situation. Countless news stories, articles, and additional coverage were broadcast in our surrounding area. Steve Otto, a columnist for the *Tampa Tribune,* articulated our plight better than I could have:

> I know there are rules and guidelines. But I have seen rules doom people with life-threatening disabilities. The rules also say we are going to have to feed, clothe, and house the creep who did this. His victim needs special help. It's not cheap. But I am willing to bet there is not a one of you out there who would deny her the care she needs, even if it meant denying her attacker that flat-screen TV in the prison dayroom.[27]

The community responded to our needs in so many ways. At one point, I had thirty offers for commode chairs. I chuckled with joy—of course, we needed only one. This community cared and supported us so much that I felt their love through these gestures of giving. Every penny donated, every letter written on our behalf, every fundraiser planned and held took my breath away.

Finally, on Friday, April 8, about twenty health care officials met to talk about Queena's health, her life, and, ultimately, the future of our family. Representatives from the Department of Children and Families, the Department of Health, and the ACHA attended. They made some headway. DCF agreed to a ninety-day reprieve to pay for at-home care, with Medicaid supplementing the funds. Great news, but it was just an extension, not a solution. They also talked about potential exceptions, but approval for a waiver like this was rare. Officials would have to wade through a lot of red tape. We left the meeting hopeful for a long-term solution and incredibly grateful that funding would extend beyond the coming two weeks when Queena turned twenty-one.

Her twenty-first birthday came with as much anticipation as dread for me. It signaled the need for celebration—*Yes, my daughter lived to see another year of life!*—but it also meant the clock kept ticking on that health care extension. We needed to get the waiver approved soon. That day, however, we tried to be joyful.

Indeed, we had so many things to celebrate. Through the past year of therapy, we'd discovered more information about how Queena's mind functioned. Her brain signaled correctly, but her muscles failed to interpret the signals. This gave us clearer direction on how to proceed with ongoing therapy sessions and continued hope for a miraculous recovery.

The community always came through at the perfect time for us. We received an email from Cindy, owner of Swim Spa Manufacturers in Clearwater, Florida, saying she'd read about Queena and wanted to offer a birthday gift. Cindy asked her daughter for ideas, and her daughter suggested giving Queena a swim spa so that she could use it as water therapy and relax her muscles. Not only did Cindy give Queena a beautiful swim spa in our backyard, but she also had an aboveground pool and a pool lift installed as well. This kind gesture reinforced our belief that we were doing the right thing by fighting to keep Queena home.

The gift boosted us emotionally, as the third anniversary of the attack loomed just days after Queena's birthday. My feelings spanned the spectrum—happy for her life one moment, then angry the next about how she had to live. Imagine you can hear those around you but can't speak. You can feel a touch but can't touch back. You can see a little bit, but you can't move, not even to wipe your eyes.

That had been my daughter's life for the three years since her attack—completely locked inside her body. She had some brain function but was paralyzed from the stroke and traumatic brain injury.

A few days before the anniversary, we held a prayer vigil in our house. On April 22, we held a small, private birthday party at a restaurant where family and friends showed Queena so much love and support. The third anniversary of the attack came on Easter Sunday, April 24, 2011. My mind flipped back to the days surrounding the tragedy three years earlier. Back then, Queena couldn't communicate at all with the outside world. But our family still believed we would get her back, that she would attend East Bay High School's prom, graduate, and go off to college at the University of Florida. She would get on with her life—we thought; we hoped. Back then, all I could do was cry out, "Why did this happen?"

For three years, Queena had relied on a feeding tube and a wheelchair. Anna and I, along with the help of a CNA, were caring for her. We took turns sleeping on a pullout sofa outside of her room while the CNA stayed at her bedside, turning her so she wouldn't slip off the bed, repositioning her if she started to choke, making sure she wasn't susceptible to injury from her seizures. I did a range of motion exercises with her every day. I listened to music with her. Talked to her. Read the Bible to her. Let her smell familiar scents. Put lotion on her. Held her hand.

Queena used to be the one who inspired us to go on in sad times. In her own way, she still did. Although she lay in bed, her body tight, we could tell her mind was very much alive. That gave us hope. She remembered who she was before the attack. She could understand. She could feel and react. We saw progress in her eyes, in her slight arm movements, in her wide smiles and giggles and infectious laugh. She went through intense therapies and treatments day by day but never gave up. She had such a love for life! And by God's grace, Queena made progress.

She learned to communicate through hand squeezes, grunts, and facial expressions. She appeared to listen now, and she smiled when we read stories to her. She could utter a few words and could see a little more than just shadows and colors. She took a few steps with two people supporting her and regained limited movement in her arms. And, somehow, her beautiful fighting spirit and her contagious smile kept everyone else going.

She kept us going, despite the unending fight for full health care benefits. She kept me going in spite of my emotional, physical, and mental exhaustion. I felt beyond tired, and sometimes, I cried out, "I can't do this anymore, Jesus! I'm too tired. I'm too overwhelmed." Yet day by day, she—and He—gave me strength.

In May 2011, Tom Orr, who sat on the board of directors at the Clearwater Marine Aquarium, invited Queena to celebrate her twenty-first birthday with Winter, the famous dolphin that had lost her tail in a fishing trap and became widely known for having a prosthetic tail. Tom and his team lowered Queena onto a platform in two feet of water so she could interact with Winter. As they did, I thought about the parallels between Queena's story and the dolphin's. Winter was a survivor, too. Like Queena, no one had expected Winter to live. She was the first dolphin to lose her tail and live.[28] Both Queena and Winter overcame amazing odds, demonstrating the power of an indomitable spirit.

Queena laughed excitedly throughout our visit to the aquarium. On the ride home, I sat in the back seat with her while her caregiver drove. She uttered the word *Winter* three times. I promptly called Tom with the good news. He later wrote to me:

> I had a dream in my heart that Queena would start talking more once she met Winter. I believe animals can break through to the soul when people can't. Winter had a tragic life event and survived, and Queena had the same thing. When they met that day face-to-face, their souls touched, and a bond was formed. God sent Winter down to help people find ways to heal themselves by looking at her reflection in themselves.

Often, God strengthened me through the living angels He sent our way. They didn't have wings. In fact, we simply called them friends and neighbors in the community. I realized that God put people in the right place at the right time to help us, to support us, to encourage us. I had to trust that eventually, everything would work out wonderfully. I decided then to develop a habit of saying, "I trust You, Jesus, in all circumstances." Instead of basing my prayer on "I hope so," my prayer would be, "God *says* so."

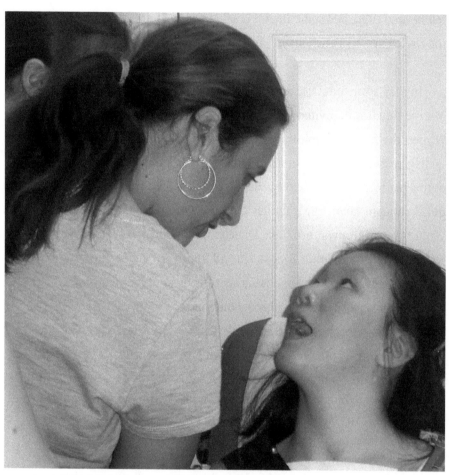

Assistant State Attorney Rita Peters talking to Queena on her nineteenth

birthday at our home - 2009

CHAPTER 23
A RAPIST SENTENCED

ON FRIDAY, MAY 20, 2011, I saw Kendrick Morris in person for the first time as he was escorted into the courtroom for sentencing. I had thoughts about forgiveness and mercy, but I admit that on that day, I stared at him with eyes that burned with contempt. Queena was serving a life sentence, trapped inside her broken body. Our family struggled, working daily to help her recover from the injuries he had caused, all while enduring our own emotional and financial strains.

For three years, I had left criminal matters to lawyers and investigators. I didn't need to know the details of that night outside the library in Bloomingdale. I focused, instead, on my daughter's little victories—recognizing light and shadows, holding her head up for a few seconds. But not that day. *That* day marked the end, the conclusion of the matter, at least legally speaking. Earlier, I had contemplated not going to the courtroom until Rita Peters sent me a message:

> I cannot predict what Judge Tharpe will sentence Kendrick Morris to, but suffice it to say, he cannot get life in prison because he was a juvenile at the time the crime was committed. I suspect Judge Tharpe will sentence him appropriately. He is a good and fair judge, and while Queena has been the focus of all the media attention, we must keep in mind that Kendrick Morris was also convicted of sexual battery of another victim. Know that she will be there at the sentencing, and I know that any words of encouragement from Queena's friends and family will go a long way with her. She is a dear elderly lady who is very kind.

In the months leading up to the sentencing, I had written, edited, and trashed more statements than I could count. I actually finished my final version at 1:30 a.m., just hours before the sentencing. Still, I struggled mightily over whether to attend. Thinking about the other victim settled it. This woman had sat through the entire trial alone. I knew little about her personal life and her family, but I felt I had to go to the sentencing and support her.

Minutes before the hearing, behind closed doors, I met and hugged the former daycare worker. I told her that I came because our lives had been destroyed by the same man. She cried.

Our family, along with many of Queena's friends, filled the courtroom. The sentencing lasted most of the day. Many people expressed their thoughts and feelings about the case—those who knew Morris, those who knew my daughter, and those who were state experts.

The former daycare worker spoke first. "When I see a light-skinned person, I start panicking," she said, referring to the fact that Morris is a light-skinned African American. Her quiet voice was barely audible through the sobs. "He had a knife. He made me get down on the floor . . . I don't have nightmares; but I think about it, and I just burst out crying." She said she wished Morris would never get out of prison.[29]

Queena's friend, Priscilla, who had discovered the bloody scene, said she was depressed, failing in school, and consumed with guilt, wondering if she could have done something to prevent the tragedy.

Anna cried as she read her statement:

> Kendrick Morris, you killed my little sister, my other half. You took away from me the most precious thing on this earth. She was my best friend, and the two of us were inseparable. I was her role model, her shelter. When we were young, I would hold her hand crossing the street. She would hide behind me when she was scared. I was there to protect her as best I could. But I was not able to protect her from you that night.
>
> What you did was horrific and evil; there is no doubt. You destroyed lives and dreams. It was an event that will haunt many for the rest of their lives. When I found out that law enforcement had caught you, the attacker, I had peace of mind knowing my sister was then safe. When you were found guilty, I had peace of mind knowing that justice would be served.

Nowadays, I sit and daydream about what could have been. The two of us being able to afford to take Mom on the vacation she always dreamed of. The two of us doing mission work together in a third-world country. Her walking down the aisle one day as my maid of honor. Her being able to proudly hold her sister's newborn baby. But those things will never happen. Because of you.

I now have to continue on with my life without the little sister I once knew. It is only by the grace of God that our family has been made whole again. I have a new sister, same physical body, different girl. Mom and I are raising her again, as if she were a toddler. She cannot walk, talk, eat, or see. She has *Sesame Street* on the TV, and she listens to kiddie music. I am encouraged by the fact that one day, after her earthly life is over, her body will be transformed into a new heavenly body, glorified and flawless, perfect in every way. She will spend an eternity of happiness with her Lord and Savior.

I pray for you often, Kendrick, and I want you to know that there is hope for your soul and your spirit. I would like to see you again, one day, in Heaven. Until then, my little sister will suffer. My family will suffer. But with God-given strength and support from the incredible community, we will continue to glorify God.

And you will suffer, rightly so. You can never have another opportunity to hurt another little girl, or another woman. You are accountable for your actions. But it is not I that decides what you deserve; it is God and the judicial system—and I have faith in both.

Your Honor, my hope and want is that you impose the maximum penalty on Kendrick Morris. Thank you.

Spectators wept as Anna expressed the suffering her sister lives with each day. I couldn't stand it anymore and burst out crying as she spoke. My precious Anna carried so much weight on her shoulders. Her pure heart and desire to change the world with her sister by her side had been dashed.

When it was my turn to speak, I just couldn't. My English was imperfect, my nerves on edge, and my emotions tearing through my body. Yet Queena's rapist would be sentenced, and he needed to hear what I had to say, too. On my behalf, Anna read the letter I wrote to Morris:

> Today, God gave me strength to write this letter to you. I don't want to see you walk back through that door never realizing what you did and what you will do with your life. Do you know that my soul is so broken from the night that you turned my daughter's life around?
>
> I am the oldest of four children who were raised in Communist Vietnam, where there was not much food, education, or opportunity. As I grew up, I did not know what freedom truly meant. Life was very hard. But God blessed me with parents who had the courage and love to risk getting me to America. They paid smugglers to sail me out of Vietnam across a dangerous ocean, and at eighteen years old, I found myself in a land of freedom all alone. When I arrived in America, I saw a country filled with hope and good people. I got a job and was able to bring my mom and siblings to America. Life was good.
>
> When I was twenty-eight, I had a little girl whom I named Queena. She was a happy, beautiful, and loving child who cared about her family. I watched my daughter grow up. She had long, silky, black hair and eyes that sparkled like stars when she smiled. She danced; she laughed; and she played the piano. She was so innocent. Queena had a pure and honest heart. She had many friends. She worked so hard in school and was one of the few seniors in her high school class to receive a full scholarship to the University of Florida. She participated in the student body council; she mentored handicapped students; and she volunteered at a hospice. I was so proud of her.
>
> Today, Queena only moans and utters sounds. She cannot see. She cannot walk. She cannot talk. I have not heard her voice in three years. She lies in a hospital bed and gets her food from a tube in her stomach. I live by her side, stroking her hair, massaging her face, cutting her toenails. I tell her I love her, and I try to bring her joy. I lift her to her wheelchair every day and wheel her outside and urge her to feel the wind in her face.
>
> I do not understand how a human being like you is capable of inflicting such brutality. My child was so loved; she knew no evil. I don't know what your sentence will be as I write. I do know of one person who

accepted Jesus while he was in jail. He studied the Bible and helped other people in jail become Christians. I am praying that this will be your experience. How that would bring glory to God and purpose for your life!

My daughter was in a coma as a result of what you did to her. The doctors kept shaking their heads and saying her brain would be destroyed forever. She was going to die. I ran to the church nearby. I kneeled down and used all the energy I had left. I cried out loud to God. "God, please save my daughter's life! I still want to have her, God. I don't want my daughter to die, God. Please help her!" Queena survived.

Why am I telling you this miraculous story about my daughter? Because I want to encourage you to recognize the power of God. We forgive you, Kendrick, for what you did to my daughter that horrible night—not because you deserve it, but because God deserves my forgiveness. I no longer have to carry the anger. We have no hatred. God will deal with the injustices. God will judge your life.

Any earthly sentence imposed on you is not enough to measure what was truly stolen from Queena. In whatever sentence is imposed upon you, you will continue to have the freedom to move about under your own power, to speak on your own, eat on your own, and do all of the daily activities of a normal human being. I hope and pray that you might one day spend eternity in Heaven, but I also hope and pray that you will serve your whole earthly life in prison. You imposed a sentence on Queena three years ago. The life sentence imposed on her is not in any way humane and never will be.

Queena may still be alive, but in a way, you took away her life, and mine, too.

Morris sat still, almost studious, while listening to my statement. He showed no reaction, and the hearing continued. I heard his public defenders tell the judge that Morris, too, had once been a victim. They told of beatings, neglect. They said his young brain was developing, not fully formed.

"It's easy for everyone to stand here and say he's evil," said Assistant Public Defender Maria Pavlidis. Yet the judge should consider other factors, she said.[30]

Sinacore countered, "Was he born this way or made this way? From our perspective, it really doesn't matter."[31]

The state wanted two sixty-year sentences for the daycare worker's assault and Queena's. Sinacore argued Morris should serve the sentences back-to-back, for a total of 120 years. The defense asked for less than forty-five years. Pavlidis spoke of a U.S. Supreme Court decision that forbade life sentences for juveniles who had not killed anyone. The decision deemed such a punishment "cruel and unusual" for youth.[32]

"You could have a good debate," the prosecutor told the judge, "about whether what happened at the library was better than homicide."[33]

The defense argued that Morris was a product of an abusive childhood and that he could be rehabilitated.

His mother spoke on his behalf. "I ask that the judge of this court show mercy, not, again, to minimize anything that's happened, but to maximize his opportunity to make amends."[34]

After a brief recess in the sentencing hearing, Judge Tharpe reemerged, and I braced myself for his ruling. He looked across the crowded courtroom wearing a somber expression.

"If ever there was a case that cried out for a life sentence," he said, "this is the case . . . A man has to pay for the wicked he's done. Kendrick Morris, you're a sexual predator. And you're going to be punished."[35]

Finally, he handed down a total sentence of sixty-five years for the two rapes. Morris, who had chosen not to speak during the hearing, showed no emotion. I looked at him and had no idea what he was thinking. He seemed unfazed. He shrugged his shoulders and rolled his eyes.

Quietly, I prayed. *Kendrick, our family has forgiven you. Our belief in a loving, forgiving God makes that possible. We would like if you also would seek God's forgiveness. He loves you and has forgiven you.*

Unlike the lawyers, I had not thought about a specific number of years. Nothing would have equaled the life sentence Morris inflicted on my daughter. The essence of who she was had been destroyed. While I continued to hope for a higher degree of recovery and continued to cherish her life, I had to accept that the Queena I once knew was never coming back.

When it was over, the former daycare worker reached over to me and pulled me close. We embraced for a moment before a crowd of supporters gathered, but I did not linger. I did not want to dwell in that moment of sorrow. I slipped away quietly and headed home to care for Queena.

On the way home, I thought about how the whole story looked from God's view. In the three years since the attack, my relationship with God had grown, and I could see things from a different perspective now. The One Who knows our comings and goings knew Queena would suffer a brutal attack. In fact, I now believed that God suffered with her on this road. God did not take this cup from her. Instead, God endured the pain of Queena's beating and rape just as God endured the pain of Jesus' beating and crucifixion at the hands of His human attackers.

I had come to understand that our loving Creator doesn't prevent suffering but is with us *in* and *through* our suffering. As a mother, I sought revenge. I wanted retributive justice to even the score—a life sentence for a life sentence. Yet God's justice is not "an eye for an eye or a tooth for a tooth" (Exod. 21:24). God's justice comes in a different form. It comes as a healing balm for all wounded souls—even Morris' soul. That was a lesson I was still learning. By God's guiding hand, Kendrick Morris was found, convicted by a jury of his peers, and sentenced to sixty-five years in prison. I felt satisfied with sixty-five years.

Once I pulled into my driveway, I forced myself to stop thinking about Morris and the sentencing. I went straight to Queena's room and turned my focus on her needs. She was hungry, waiting for me to feed her through the tube in her stomach. She looked at me with wonder. By now, I could interpret her unspoken questions by the look in her eyes or the frown of her mouth. She wanted to know what happened in the courtroom. I held her hand, took a deep breath, and told her the judge's decision.

"The attacker could not be sentenced to life because he wasn't eighteen when he committed the crimes," I said, explaining further about the Supreme Court decision cited in court. "But do not worry. He has been sentenced to sixty-five years. Even with any credits he might receive, Kendrick Morris will not see the outside of a prison cell until after his seventieth birthday."

Queena at "NIGHT to Shine," sponsored by the

Tim Tebow Foundation - 2017

CHAPTER 24
FROM VICTIMS TO SURVIVORS

THE CLOCK KEPT TICKING ON Queena's insurance extension. Despite support from elected officials and our best efforts to obtain a waiver for continued Medicaid coverage, we ran into a bureaucratic wall. Apparently, many people waited for waivers, just as we did. Yet the last one had been issued more than six years earlier. Time and again, officials and insurance executives told us nothing could be done.

Then, finally, a breakthrough came in June 2011. State Senator Ronda Storms and her staff spent countless hours challenging the bureaucracy in Tallahassee, trying to find a solution. To their credit, they refused to stop, even when their efforts seemed futile. Still, nothing changed, and we knew we needed a God-sized miracle. That miracle came when state legislators approved a thirty-six-million-dollar boost to a Medicaid waiver program.[36] We enrolled Queena in the program, which allowed her to remain at home and receive the twenty-four-hour care she needed. We were beyond grateful.

There were drawbacks, however. Some costs previously covered were no longer eligible. For instance, the insurance would not pay for anything deemed "medically unnecessary," and many of Queena's therapies fell under that category, regardless of whether we proved that the therapies led to progress. We would have to hold more fundraisers to continue those therapy sessions. From barbecues to fashion shows, golf tournaments, donated therapy sessions, and shopping fairs, our wonderful community had already banded together to help. Now, we prayed the generosity would keep flowing.

The outpouring of love constantly brought light to my dark days. On many occasions, I struggled to keep the faith. Despite the ups and downs, I remembered words from 1 Corinthians 13:13, a Scripture verse that says, "Three things will last forever—faith, hope, and love—and the greatest of these is love." The love from our community gave me strength.

One day, I received an email with a video link from a gentleman named Larry Ludwig. He sang a song called "Living Angel," which he wrote for Queena.

I read about you, and I started to cry
I don't even know you, but you showed me the light
I don't know how you went on after something like that
You could have gone away forever, but you came back

Maybe it's because there is still work to be done
And to let people know you have to stay strong
In the hardest of times, you can never give up
You find the strength in the love

You talk with your eyes
You say so much when you smile
I know a girl, and she touched my soul
I know a girl who's a living angel

And your spirit could not be broken
You united a family; a community came forward
The blessings rained down and fell from the sky
Strangers came to be by your side

To give support, to keep the faith
To show there's still good in this earthly place

In spite of the events that have transpired
You are and always will be a survivor

You talk with your eyes
You say so much when you smile
I know a girl, and she touched my soul
I know a girl who's a living angel

To overcome a tragedy is hard enough
But you overcame and spread love
To your family, friends, everyone
Like an angel, you rise above

You shine on

I think about you during the day
I send you love, prayers, and praise
You are a sign of hope; you've touched my soul
You are a living, breathing, beautiful angel

You're a living angel

Our insurance breakthrough, combined with the ongoing support from strangers, renewed my sense of hope. I thought about the injuries Queena had sustained, yet she survived. Yes, she survived a brutal attack, a bleak prognosis, and hours upon hours of therapies. But she also survived a completely changed life—one she did not choose. She survived. She overcame.

I tried to imagine her story from the community's perspective. Many had seen her at fundraising events, but Queena's name had not been revealed to the general public at that point. People connected with the family through reporters who knew how to reach me. In print or on the news, however, journalists referred to her as "the Bloomingdale Library attack victim." Media policies prevented reporters from publishing the names of rape victims, and initially, I had no problem with their alternative description.

Now, after listening to the lyrics of Mr. Ludwig's song, I saw Queena's story differently. So many who heard about the attack viewed Queena as someone who had "overcome." I wondered if the label "attack victim" might be casting a dark shadow over her. Did I want her labeled as a victim? Did I want people to feel sorry for her?

No. No, I didn't. Queena was always a positive person, and if she could speak, I believed she would want to be known as a survivor. A young woman who constantly beat the odds.

I talked to Anna about changing Queena's public name from "victim" to something more positive. We weren't ready to release her name, so we agreed on "the Bloomingdale Library survivor." We wrote a media release to that effect:

> Our family is requesting that in all future references to our daughter, you refer to her as the Bloomingdale Library survivor. Neither she nor our family look at ourselves as victims anymore. We are all survivors. Yes, we suffered a major physical blow to our daughter and our family, but our spirits were not broken. Indeed, the spirits in our family united with thousands in our community and brought us blessings beyond comprehension. To be a part of the love and the affection that has rained down upon us from people we never even knew before and to be an active part of a Christian community that has opened their arms, their hearts, and their prayers for us is a life-altering experience.
>
> God has blessed us in so many ways that it is impossible to name them all. Friends we knew before this incident rallied to our support immediately. Those of you in the news media did an honorable job in telling our story and respecting our angel's privacy. But nothing can compare to the way the Christian community and everyday wonderful strangers came to our assistance and have worked to ensure that we will receive the help that we need to continue our journey toward her full recovery. We are blessed! Our angel is alive

and well and healing more and more every day, and we give God all the glory.

Thank you for your cooperation. You in the news media have a difficult job. Reporting sensational stories while respecting the privacy of the parties involved is not easy. We want to thank you for your dedication to be considerate to those of us who have experienced tragedies in our lives; however, we no longer want to be labeled as victims. We are survivors!

Most reporters respected our wishes and referred to Queena as a survivor. In our minds, one word had such a great impact on how people saw my daughter and how I saw her, too.

Queena's twenty-third birthday, website launch, and prayer vigil - Keel and Curley Winery, 2013

CHAPTER 25

THE BLOOMINGDALE LIBRARY SURVIVOR CLAIMS HER NAME

APRIL 2012 MARKED FOUR YEARS since the attack. By this time, people in the Bloomingdale community and beyond knew Queena's story well. As with each anniversary, I thought about what might have been. If all had gone as planned, Queena would have been graduating from the University of Florida that spring.

Instead, she was making noticeable improvements. To the average person, these were small steps, but for those of us who knew and loved Queena, they seemed like enormous strides. Her spirits remained high, and somehow, she always managed to comfort those around her. She'd become very alert and responsive.

Instead of grieving, we celebrated Queena's survival as a second birthday from God. I thanked Him for medical developments. I thanked Him for the chance to have her with us. In her new life purpose, she served as an example to others who struggled in their own ways.

Anna often referred to the chaos theory, which says that something as small as the flutter of a butterfly's wing can ultimately cause a typhoon halfway around the world.[37] In our eyes, Queena is the little butterfly whose effect has inspired many, changed lives, given hope, and challenged limits. Despite heartbreak, her situation inspired her big sister, along with Mr. Ludwig and so many others who contacted us by email or online.

In May 2012, students from Queena's former high school contacted us. They wanted to organize an annual five-kilometer run in her honor and call it

"5K4Q." We were touched that they still held Queena dear in their hearts four years after the attack. Queena went back to her high school for the first time since the attack to meet with the students planning the event. She proudly wore her old student government association (SGA) shirt, sat at a long table, and joined the meeting.

Overall, the event raised forty-three hundred dollars. They donated the funds to our family, and we purchased a custom therapy bike for Queena. The school's SGA has held the fundraiser every year since. We also received a three-thousand-dollar donation from an organization that heard about Queena through the event.

The questions people asked me most often were, "How do you continue to press on?" and "How do you keep your head up after what you and your family have been through?" Then, whether friends or total strangers, they often commended me for my strong spirit and for Queena's inspirational fight. They said they couldn't fathom what it felt like to be in my place.

"You're handling everything so well," they said.

And, "I don't know how you do it."

Or, "You're superwoman!"

They didn't know that I hurt every day or that I thought about taking antidepressants to help me function but never followed through on my thoughts. They saw me wear my mask of bravery, which covered my inner struggle through the rough patches. I developed a script for responding to their questions and accolades. I simply listed any progress Queena had made, along with her daily schedules. I talked about her therapies. I stayed positive and intentionally ended on a high note. "She's doing great!"

Yet I fumbled when anyone asked for a more personal update: "How are *you* doing?" I never created the right script for that. If I answered truthfully, I would have had to admit I was weary. Bone-tired of seeing Queena face daunting challenges daily, challenges that none of us could battle for her. I was exhausted from a life with no pressure-release valve. Queena's life, my life, the life of everyone in my family revolved around her care. Naturally, I carried most of the weight. That is a mother's burden. If I didn't fight for her, who would? Of course, loved ones stepped up in my place if I asked. But they didn't know my child as well as I knew her. So, most times, I pressed through my fatigue. I kept going because Queena kept going.

At times, Queena's therapy schedule weighed us down like an anchor, tying us to a litany of therapeutic treatments. If we missed one day, Queena could suffer. Yes, it was that serious. Any amount of progress put wind in my sails and reawakened my senses, like a shot of espresso. For example, at first, Queena couldn't ride her therapy bike. But after a few months, with assistance, she could. Her growth—even small improvements like this—felt like coming up for air during a long swim. Breathe, exhale, breathe deeper.

By early 2013, nearly five years after the attack, my back began to give out from lifting and carrying my daughter every day. My immune system had become weakened from lack of sleep and constant stress. Yet I could not stop. It had taken me five years to get to this point. I kept telling myself, *We are tough. I am tough. Queena is tough. We will continue to run to the finish line!*

However, physical exhaustion wasn't my only form of weariness. I was emotionally spent, too. One night in February 2013, as I struggled with my emotions, I logged onto Queena's old Facebook page to look at photos and posts, hoping to lift my spirits. I clicked through her profile with tears in my eyes. Pictures of her before the attack sometimes triggered sharp pain, like salt on my wounds. I had looked at her profile hundreds of times since April 2008, grasping for any little bit of the daughter I once knew.

That night, I clicked on her "About me" section, where she listed her favorite quotes. Something jumped out at me—something I had read before but had never really hit me: "Life isn't ever fair. You'll cry because the time is passing too fast, or the timing was all wrong; but all that matters is being grateful for the moments you get and living them out to the fullest."

How could she be so wise at such a young age? I'm not sure if she wrote that quote or if it came from someone else, but it woke me up. *Be grateful for the moments you get.*

Something shifted inside of me. I began to feel that I was doing the community and Queena a disservice by not letting them know this beautiful, courageous, and wise young woman. It had been a year-and-a-half since we'd asked the community to refer to her not as a *victim* but as a *survivor*. Now, that change no longer seemed sufficient. She needed to regain her name, her identity, and her place in the community. She was no longer a "victim" or a "survivor." She was *Queena!*

At times, I wondered how five years had already passed. It felt like my life had always been this way. I never forgot who Queena was before the attack, but she was so different now that it almost felt like I had a third child. I still saw her spirit encapsulated in a body that didn't work for her, but I also had glimpses of the young woman she was becoming.

Anna agreed with me about making Queena's identity public. We discussed launching a website, too, where supporters could keep up with her progress. One evening, we were in Queena's room talking about what we should name the website. We did our best to include Queena in everything. Already, I had texted my friends and supporters for suggestions, and we read them to her aloud, one by one.

"Do you want the website to be called *My Angel* or *Living Angel?*" Anna asked.

Queena made a face with her mouth in the shape of an *O* to indicate no.

Anna kept going down the list of options, but Queena kept saying no. Anna came to the end of the list. Everything had been rejected.

Anna looked at Queena and simply asked, "So, do you just want *Queena. com?*" In a shock to both of us, Queena's face lit up with a smile. We asked her over and over, "Are you sure you want to use your real name?" The biggest smile framed her face. Yes, she was sure.

Anna felt that Queena.com might be too short, so she posed one last suggestion: "How about *JoinQueena.com?*" Another smile appeared on Queena's face. Queena wanted to share her personal journey with the public. She wanted the world to know her identity as they followed her to recovery. Soon, we launched www.JoinQueena.com and the Join Queena Facebook page.

From that point on, my daughter no longer lived in the darkness. We hid neither her name nor her face. She made the brave decision to show the world God's strength through her progress and continued healing. She wanted survivors of trauma to know that they don't need to hide behind the identity of "victim." They are bigger than the hurt others caused. They are more than their injuries or the crimes that visited harm upon them.

At the five-year anniversary of Queena's attack, we held a birthday party and prayer vigil at Keel and Curley Winery in Plant City, Florida. Anna made a presentation and introduced the attendees to Queena's website. A local pastor prayed over Queena. A friend gave an inspiring speech, and Queena's high school friends socialized with her. Queena commemorated the experience with a surprise to us. For the first time since the attack, she danced. A friend of ours, Phuong Duong, sang "I Won't Let Go" by Rascal Flatts, and Queena danced. Queena's trainer, Chris, helped her stand up, then slightly swayed Queena's body from side to side for a modest slow dance.

Afterward, our friend Rachel Brinton gave a moving interview to the media. Rachel is also a stroke survivor to whom doctors once gave a one percent chance of recovery. She went on to defy the odds and recovered fully. Rachel spoke to reporters about Queena.

"It's definitely *when,* not *if,* she'll be able to walk again," Rachel said. "And when she is able to walk, we are going to spread her story so far across the country."

Her words echoed within my soul. I dwelled on those words for many days. *When. Not if.*

Five to six days a week, the van that Rough Riders of Tampa had donated to us shortly after Queena's attack carried her back and forth to appointments, fundraisers, and therapies. By 2013, however, the 1997 Ford wheelchair-accessible chariot had begun to give out. I researched the cost of a new or used van. No matter where I looked, forty-five thousand dollars seemed to be the magic number. *Where am I going to get that money?* I already had to pay for some of Queena's therapies and other medical costs out-of-pocket, on top of our living expenses.

Once again, I needed to rely on the community's generosity. I brainstormed fundraising ideas, but God was already working behind the scenes. The River Hills Country Club contacted me, stating that the group wanted to host a golf fundraiser and that a local Zumba instructor wanted to host a Zumbathon for Queena. Although such things had happened many times before now, I never stopped being amazed each time God showed me that He knew my every need, even before I did.

In January 2014, a newspaper reporter called to say that a reader wanted to sell us a 2008 van at a bargain price. The van belonged to the reader's husband, Vincent Sussman, a popular high school football coach and principal who had died the previous October. Mr. Sussman lived for years as a paraplegic after falling from the roof of his home. After the accident, he went back to work, running his school from a wheelchair while using a voice-activated computer. His life inspired so many before he died.[38] His van, which cost sixty thousand dollars when originally purchased, had just forty-five hundred miles on it. I met Mrs. Sussman and took the conversion van for a test drive. It looked brand-new. She agreed to sell it to us for twenty-five thousand dollars.

So, by February, when the country club's golf fundraiser took place, we knew exactly what we needed to raise. We parked the van outside the country club, where donors could look at what their money would help buy. Queena spent the day roaming around the golf course with Anna and her boyfriend, Jonathan. She had the biggest smile on her face. She was out of her wheelchair, safely supported by her sister's arms, as they took a joyride in a golf cart to say hello to the golfers.

Meanwhile, a gentleman named Jim Ford, who had read about Queena in a small community monthly, arrived and waited to meet me. He'd sent an email a few days before through Queena's website. He spoke of her as an inspiration and said he wanted to help. We responded by encouraging him to attend the fundraiser. We talked for quite a while about Queena's progress through therapy, and I showed him the van. He talked about how Queena's story had touched him. Then, he announced that he had come to donate money.

He pulled out his checkbook and started writing. When he handed the check to me, I did a doubletake. We had already raised fifteen thousand dollars toward the van, and Mr. Ford's check was for ten thousand dollars! I felt overcome with shock, awe, and gratitude. I thanked him and called Anna over to show her the check. She then ran to Jonathan, who was sitting at the table selling t-shirts. Tears welled up in his eyes.

Through our talk, I learned that Mr. Ford did not live a life of luxury in nearby Brandon. He had such a big heart, and he sacrificed greatly for my daughter. I should not have been surprised. Similar experiences had happened to us countless times. We do not live in an overly affluent area, but the people who surrounded us often made the biggest donations and provided the most support.

*Family photo in front of The Crossing Church with Vanna's mom, Anna, and
Jonathan (now Anna's husband) - Tampa, 2014*

CHAPTER 26
TELLING QUEENA THE PAINFUL TRUTH

IN AUGUST 2014, WE BEGAN stem-cell therapy procedures in hopes of furthering Queena's progress. The process involves intrathecal injections of mesenchymal stem cells for Queena. The stem cells first are extracted and harvested from a small sample from the fatty layer of her belly area. The adult stem cells are prepared and "assigned" to be brain cells, then injected into the cells into the lower part of her back. This allows the cells to easily cross the blood-brain barrier. Once the cells enter the brain, they can reduce swelling and help heal damaged tissue. They may even remodel the scar tissue to replace it with normal functioning tissue, or at least partly heal the connections between the nerves and cells within the brain. The reinjected stem cells could also aid repairs to Queena's organs and neurological function in other areas of her body.

In conjunction with the stem cell therapy, I thought about connecting Queena with a counselor to help her work through the details of her attack. However, I needed to figure out how best to do this. Queena couldn't process her emotions. She had no outlet, no way of putting into words what she felt. Her thoughts were trapped. That's why we'd never told her exactly what happened to her. We'd told her that a "very bad person" hurt her. We'd said that he had been captured. We told her when a jury found her attacker guilty and when the judge sentenced him. But we did not tell her the ugly details. She did not know that she had been brutally beaten, raped, and, presumably, left for dead.

Anna worked with a professional counselor named Laura Curran, who helped us explain things to Queena in an appropriate way while also helping

Queena process the information as best as she could. As Queena continued to improve, I knew she deserved to know why her life had transformed so drastically. Laura asked Queena on several occasions if she would like to know the details, and each time Queena smiled, which was her yes response. Laura read some details from the journals and records that I had kept throughout this whole ordeal. She paused occasionally to ask Queena if it was okay to go on. Each time, Queena would respond with a positive yes expression. Queena impressed Laura with how well she expressed herself without using words.

Laura then prepared Queena's heart and mind for the possibility of remembering the details on her own. She read to Queena the beginning chapters of this memoir. We also engaged in several cognitive exercises intended to strengthen Queena's processing, memory, and communication skills. In time, Queena's unspoken reactions convinced Laura that Queena wanted to know what had happened. Queena was open to the readings and consistently responded positively when she was asked if she wanted Laura to continue.

Following Laura's lead, we decided that telling Queena more about what had happened to her would benefit her healing process. Of course, we did not want her to stay entrenched in the sorrow of this tragedy. We wanted her to heal from it and move forward, integrating this part of her story into a much bigger story of inspiration for others.

By the spring of 2015, nearly seven years since the attack, we decided it was time to give Queena the more difficult details. Laura, Anna, and I gathered in Queena's room. I was too scared to talk, so I just sat near Queena to support her. Laura took the lead and began telling Queena about the attack. Throughout the process, Queena's expressions showed us that she was nervous and scared but that she wanted to know more. Laura reminded her of the details she had already read to her from this memoir concerning her hospitalization and recovery.

Laura asked a series of questions to gauge Queena's reactions and how far we should go. "Use your arms for yes and eyes for no. Show me what you want to know more about," Laura instructed.

Queena's body clenched in her wheelchair, her legs shaking. "We need a moment to relax," Laura said, taking off Queena's foot strap. After a few moments, we continued.

We told her that Kendrick Morris was the person who had attacked and raped her. We reminded her that he had stood trial and a jury had convicted him. Anna talked with Queena slowly, calmly, to help Queena process what we presented. Then Laura went on.

"Do you want to know more about the medical decision to induce coma?"

No.

"More about your family's emotions during this time?"

No.

"More about Kendrick Morris?"

Queena grunted. Her whole body and face tensed. She clenched her fist.

"Okay, you want to know more about him. He was outside the library, waiting on a ride. His mom never showed up . . . "

Queena listened intently as Laura spoke, raising her fist with interest.

Finally, Laura asked, "Do you feel any relief knowing he was caught and is in jail?"

Queena raised her fist, clenched her body. *Yes.*

"Do you want to continue?"

Queena raised her fist again. *Yes.*

"Some items have been recovered from that night. Would you like to see or hold them?"

Yes.

Detectives had eventually returned Queena's book bag and everything in it to our family after the trial, but I had never had the courage to go through these belongings by myself. Now, Anna took out each item and showed Queena all of the things she'd had with her the night of her attack, including her makeup bag and cell phone. Queena rubbed her knuckles over the cell phone.

"Do you want to see what's inside the clutch?" Laura asked.

A raised fist. *Yes.*

Anna named the items as she showed them to Queena. There's an Abercrombie & Fitch employee discount card. Queena smiled, made joyful noises. A Busch Gardens pass. Insurance card. Student athlete card. Chick-Fil-A receipts. Queena smiled. A debit card. Ticket stub. Cancelled check. ATM receipts—so many receipts! UF Gator pens. A MAC compact. Lip balm. Five dollars in cash. A limo list for the prom of twelve girls. A playlist.

Anna read the titles: "Shawty Get Loose" by Lil' Mama.

Queena grunted happily.

"That's What You Get" by Paramour.

Queena smiled wide, grunted some more.

"More Chick-Fil-A receipts," Anna said, laughing. Queena grunted, laughing, too.

"You were a typical high school senior, eating out, shopping . . . Do you remember a lot of these items?" Laura asked.

Queena's body tensed. She grunted. *Yes.*

Finally, Queena had no more questions. She wanted to rest. I asked Queena if she wanted me to burn her belongings from that night. Her expression signaled that she did not want me to do that.

In the end, the counseling session went better than I'd imagined. Queena's smile helped me feel much lighter. She finally knew the most gruesome details of her story. She handled it well, and I hoped this would help her continue to move forward. I told her to keep the faith, and the Lord would carry her through. I am her mom, but I wish I had my daughter's strength. What a phenomenal young woman.

Queena's counseling sessions may have been a sign from God that none of us were quite finished with the details of that tragedy. The past returned with a vengeance in August 2015.

Kendrick Morris, we learned, had been granted an appeal to overturn his sentencing. An appeals court ruled it unconstitutional to impose lengthy prison terms on those who committed crimes as juveniles, with murder being the only exception. According to the court, lengthy sentences failed to provide the convicts with a chance for early release based on maturity and rehabilitation. The court granted Morris a hearing for resentencing.[39] This meant we needed to face him in court again. We would have to sit through another sentencing and relive details that we had worked hard to forgive and bury.

Grief washed over me. I felt that I'd forgiven him for hurting Queena, but that didn't mean I wanted him to be free. Every time some sort of setback occurred regarding Morris, I struggled all over again to truly forgive him, despite the hardship my family endured every day. I wanted to sit and be sad, to grieve over this new development. But I had no time for that. My daughter needed me nearly every minute of the day.

Queena's second round of stem cell therapy drew near. Since her first round in 2013, she'd been able to step with her right and left feet on command. After this second round in 2015, she took seven steps! Her strength and mobility also increased. Indeed, the momentum in her strength-building improved to the point that, for the first time, she attempted to roll out of bed in the middle of the night. Unfortunately, her head lodged in a small opening in the medical bed's guardrail. I sleep on the couch in front of her room, so I heard her moaning and ran to her immediately. Even so, it took emergency medical technicians two hours to free her. The experience scared her, but she chuckles at it now, even showing a sheepish grin when we talk about it.

As Morris' new hearing loomed and Queena's needs continued, people in the public regularly asked about her, about us.

"How are things going?"

"Is everything okay?"

A few close friends picked up on the distance I had put between myself and the outside world. They tried to delve deeper. I usually held my true feelings back, but one day, I decided to begin answering truthfully—at least with close friends and Queena's supporters. I began to say, "We're all still here, I guess." Or, "We're all healthy for the most part. Beyond that, no—not much seems okay lately."

And that was just the beginning. I began to tell people about the frustrations of running a floundering business due to the demanding schedule for Queena's numerous treatments. I talked about the disappointing meeting I'd had with the case manager from Medicaid's Long-term Care Waiver, who again wanted to reduce her allotments for therapy, medical supplies, and home health services.

To my surprise, unloading on a few willing recipients lightened my mood and provided relief. For most of my life, I preferred to be the one caring for the needs of others, not the one being cared for *by* others. I wanted to be the helper, not the one needing help. Now, I found myself in a position to lean on others, to depend on them. It was an uncomfortable space. Yet the more I yielded to my needs, the better I felt.

Still, I held back the more personal aspects of daily living. I denied my feeling empty inside—constantly reaching out to God to help keep my batteries charged and my heart overflowing with love and patience. I couldn't bring myself to tell people about the days when I hadn't found the time to eat or shower. I needed to keep pretending that my daily needs weren't as important as Queena's needs. I protected myself with the mask of my own pretense—convinced that no one saw my deepest vulnerabilities behind the mask.

When the attack occurred eight years earlier, I often asked God, "Why us?" I needed a reason for the suffering. After I joined a couple of brain injury groups, however, I found myself explaining the ways in which faith had held my family together. I believed that, if not for my daughter's injuries, I would never have met or spoken with many of the people I came to know. Nor would I have learned so much about love, patience, and forgiveness by talking to people and praying to God.

The privilege of leaning on God—and others—when I couldn't stand strong on my own may not have been the reasons tragedy and suffering had visited us. But these blessings would not have been experienced if tragedy and suffering had *not* visited us.

Queena as maid of honor for Anna's wedding - April 2, 2016

CHAPTER 27
MORE THAN SISTERS

SINCE THE ATTACK, ANNA HAD supported every endeavor and every effort to help Queena. She was the media contact, therapy assistant, fill-in aide, entertainer, and so much more. I grieved for the tragic impact on not just Queena's life and mine but on Anna's as well. She was an aspiring college student at the time, so filled with optimism for her future and Queena's. Then came Kendrick Morris, forcing this college student to trade in her rosy vision of life and, like me, replace it with the heaviness of grief.

Yet God still allowed an opportunity for Anna to experience happiness. One day in 2010, while looking in a grocery store for pie filling to make a raspberry pie crisp, she met a young man named Jonathan, who worked there. They became friends for several years before they finally started dating in 2014. Indeed, their love story is as beautiful and as sweet as raspberry pie, but it is not my story to tell. What I can say is that watching their story unfold was a blessing to me and to Queena. On April 2, 2016, Anna married Jonathan.

The wedding had been a little more than a year in the making. From the time Anna introduced Jonathan to us, it felt as though he had always been part of our family. When we learned of the engagement, Queena's face lit up, and she smiled every time we talked about it. Anna insisted that Queena be her maid of honor, and Queena enjoyed hearing about all of the plans to get dressed up and made up and to dance at the wedding reception. The other bridesmaids included Queena in planning the bridal shower and the bachelorette party. The girls often shared opinions and details through Facebook Messenger. I read the messages to Queena, and she offered input as best she could. We also helped her arrange a secret surprise for Anna to be revealed at the reception.

When the big day arrived, so did an unexpected Florida rainstorm. Rarely does it rain all day in April, but unfortunately, this was the exception. There was an utter downpour for most of the day. But we refused to let the weather dampen our excitement. Raindrops could not dull this important day.

I took Queena to Anna's house around noon to get dressed with the other bridesmaids. Queena was beaming from the moment she entered. She and Anna did what any sisters preparing for a wedding would do—they exchanged giggles and jokes while a makeup artist pampered them like princesses with hairspray, curling irons, and makeup brushes galore. Queena glowed. Watching Queena and the bridesmaids getting ready touched me almost as much as the wedding itself.

I cried, of course. My daughter was getting married! I witnessed my little girl step into the full bloom of her womanhood, watching her as she stood before me, ready to begin her own story. Where had the time gone? Wasn't it just yesterday that she took her first steps, then graduated from high school, then college? Now, she was getting married to a young man whom I adored. I was so happy for her!

Yet, as they often do, my thoughts inevitably turned to Queena. She probably would never have a wedding day. This made the moment bittersweet. I saw one daughter moving on in life while grieving the other daughter's pause in life. Then, I looked at Queena—*really* looked at her—and those sad emotions dissipated. Her face held no hint of envy. No, she was not thinking the way I did. She was radiant, so happy for her sister.

As the ceremony started, everyone scurried to their assigned positions and got ready to march out in a cavalcade of chiffon and roses. Robert walked me down the aisle, squeezing my hand all the while to remind me not to cry. The pianist began to play Yurima's "River Flows in You," and the bridesmaids marched out in perfect time. Each of them wore a dress unique in style but common in color. I loved that the dress styles seemed to match the young ladies' personalities.

Queena emerged last in the procession, with the best man pushing her in a wheelchair. She wore her signature ear-to-ear smile that lit up her entire face. She wore a beautiful rose gold sequined top with a matching blush chiffon ankle-length skirt that covered her feet but was sheer enough to show off her T-strap flat sandals with bold rhinestone accents. She also wore her favorite accessories, *pearls*—earrings, a necklace, and a bracelet. A beautiful bouquet sat on her lap.

My heart filled with joy as I watched Queena head for the altar. I knew it might be the only chance she'd get to come down a wedding aisle. Then, along with the rest of the crowd, I waited for the music to change and looked for Anna to come around the corner into the sanctuary. It touched me to see everything that she'd done for her sister and to see how beautiful Queena looked. Anna had never come to resent her sister's condition and the attention it required of us.

The change in music interrupted my thoughts. The pianist began to play Johann Pachelbel's "Canon in D," the melody Anna had dreamed of for her wedding march ever since childhood. Soon, the crowd stood, and in she walked with my mother as her escort. Wedding guests wiped tears from their eyes as my beautiful Anna paused at the end of the aisle. She wore a lace, v-neck, ivory gown in a fit-and-flare shape, with a sheer back that buttoned all the way down. A rhinestone headband rested atop her head, and a cathedral-length white veil cascaded behind her. Stunning!

We'd all waited for this moment since the engagement fourteen months earlier. After Anna walked down the aisle, a junior bridesmaid read from 1 Corinthians 13:1-13. Jonathan's uncle read a poem titled "An Uncommon Love," by Terah Cox. Anna and Jonathan lit their unity candle, while the pianist gently played Bob Dylan's "To Make You Feel My Love." They said their vows and exchanged rings before the pastor declared it time for Jonathan to kiss his bride.

At that moment, Queena let out a spirited laugh that sounded throughout the room. Everyone started laughing, including Anna and Jonathan, and it took a few moments for the guests to regain their composure. Then, Jonathan and Anna finally kissed. The pastor declared them husband and wife. The ceremony was perfect; the joy in the room was palpable; and Queena was radiant with pride.

Even on such a gorgeous occasion, I had to tend to Queena on schedule. Despite doing our best to work around the wedding agenda, we still got off-track. We had two outfits planned for Queena. She would need to change and freshen up between the ceremony and the reception. We hurried as fast as we could but were about twenty minutes late to the reception. I worried that Anna and Jonathan would be upset, but they weren't. Robert held an umbrella over Queena and me as we got out of the van.

And there was my new son-in-law, waiting for us with a smile.

"Sorry," I told him. "This is the first time in eight years that I've worn shoes with this high of a heel. They slowed me down."

Jonathan offered me his arm. "You're fine, Mom. We couldn't do anything without you."

Inside the clubhouse lobby, we lined up with the rest of the wedding party to be announced as we entered the reception. Amazingly, the plans carefully put together over the last year fell into place. Friends, family, and, most important, love packed the ballroom.

After dinner, we prepared for the toasts. Anna had asked a couple of her bridesmaids to help Queena put together a slideshow of pictures in place of the traditional maid-of-honor speech. She didn't know that the bridesmaids had also helped Queena put her feelings into words. They managed to sneak around and collaborate without Anna knowing. Pictures of my daughters sharing various memories together from childhood to adulthood flashed across the screen as voices told the story of their sisterhood. The voices belonged to Anna's friends, but the sentiment belonged to Queena. Here are some excerpts from the video:

> For those of you that don't know me, my name is Queena, and I have had the honor of being Anna's little sister my whole life. Today I have the privilege to be her maid of honor on one of the most important days of her life. I've heard that when two people get married, their marriage has a positive effect on those around them . . . Anna

often refers to the quote from the Chaos Theory: "It has been said that something as small as the flutter of a butterfly's wing can ultimately cause a typhoon halfway around the world." Anna has been fluttering her wings my whole life, and together, we have created a number of typhoons together.

Together, we taught Grandma how to line-dance, saved Mom from floating out to sea in the Bahamas, and have experienced many adventures. From Vancouver and Ocean City to Key Largo, Disneyland, and the Bahamas—we've had plenty of laughs together. Anna has always pushed me to be outgoing and try new things. Her encouragement has enriched my life with so many wonderful experiences. From family vacations, swimming with Winter the dolphin, the Luke Bryan concert, crazy experimental treatments, busy days at amusement parks—she has always been there, dragging me out of my shell, and I am forever grateful for her . . .

One of my favorite bittersweet memories is when she convinced me to accept the ice bucket challenge. At first, I was all for it. Then I realized how shockingly cold it was, but she was still there to protect me and shield me from the frigid temperatures.

I also remember when I got my first speeding ticket. Anna was home on winter break, and I got pulled over on the way home from Starbucks. I called her crying because I was so afraid to tell Mom. When Mom got home from work, Anna went downstairs first, and I hid behind her. Anna told Mom that I made a big mistake. Of course, Mom panicked and thought the worst. Anna told Mom about my ticket because I was so upset, I couldn't speak. When Anna nervously told Mom about my ticket, I thought she was so brave. We have always had each other's back. Thanks, Anna, for bailing me out of that one!

Over the years we have laughed, cried, dreamed, talked about our futures, celebrated new life, prayed with each other through the hard times, and rejoiced during the good times. I can easily call Anna my sister, but that title doesn't truly express how much she means to me. She is more than my sister; she is my best friend. I'm so glad I now get to share her with Jonathan.

Jonathan, I want you to know that the way you support and encourage my sister does not go unnoticed. Hearing your admiration for her in your voice is refreshing, and I know Anna will forever be loved and adored by you.

I remember the day Jonathan proposed to Anna. We were at Disney, and Jonathan kept checking with Mom, Grandma, and me for the perfect time and place. At first, he thought the restaurant would be best, but it was too crowded. The big windows were next on his list, but my chair was too big for a front-row seat. Then, he asked about proposing on the beach behind the resort; but Mom said he was crazy because it was February, and it was way too cold outside. Jonathan was so easygoing and patient through this whole ordeal.

Mom finally found an office with a window view downstairs, and Anna thought we were silly when we wanted to move the whole group. Reluctantly, she followed. Jonathan pretended to watch the fireworks, even though I know he must have been incredibly nervous about his master plan. Grandma wanted to have her picture taken with the fireworks but patiently stood ready with her camera for the moment that was coming. Finally, Jonathan got down on one knee, and Anna started screaming! If you look at my face in the video, I'm so happy for both of them.

Anna, thank you for always loving me, protecting me, and being my biggest supporter. Thanks for always holding my hand, even though Mom made you do it! Thank you for always letting me cut your birthday cake and blow out your candles. Thank you for being such an amazing big sister!

Since we were little, you have encouraged me and looked after me, always ensuring I am safe and happy. As you continue your life with Jonathan by your side, I know we will always share our special connection, but I want you to take this verse with you. "For I know the plans I have for you," declares the Lord, "plans to prosper you and not to harm you, plans to give you hope and a future," Jeremiah 29:11.

God's plans are always right, and it's God Who sent you on that raspberry pie mission way back when. Your new husband will encourage you, look after you, and ensure you are safe and happy from today forward.

I love you, Anna and Jonathan. Now, everyone, raise your glass to the bride and groom. May you forever cherish each other as much as you do today.

Cheers to the bride and groom!

Anna and Jonathan sat speechless, as did most guests in the room. I don't think a single person watched and listened without tears in their eyes. Queena smiled her classic smile, as if to say, "I've got your back, too, Anna!"

The rest of the night gave way to dancing. Queena and her date, a new friend named Derrick Perez, danced together. They'd met when his mother, who often treated Queena with aromatherapy, had brought him to our house. The two had instantly clicked, and a sweet friendship blossomed. Derrick often accompanies Queena to her fundraisers and hangs out at our house, bringing over scary movies to watch with her. At the wedding, they spent the evening on the dance floor with everyone else, Derrick swirling Queena's chair around to the beat of the music. For the first time in a very long time, I thought that somehow our family might find joy in this new definition of *normal*.

A few weeks after Anna's wedding, the eighth anniversary of the attack came around. Rather than dwell on it, I focused on the fact that Queena had defied the odds—that *we* had defied the odds. The anniversary reminded us of her fighting spirit. It reminded us of the preciousness of life. God worked through this tragedy, not just sparing Queena's life but also allowing her to make an impact for Him far bigger than she could have ever imagined. Through her story, I began to trust that God had a purpose for me—for everyone—and that He could, indeed, work all things together for our good, as the Bible says.

Still, despite my growing faith, sometimes I found God's methods and life plans hard to understand. Some days, I wondered, *Is God leading me to something great?* Other days, I thought, *Will I make it through another day? Why am I going through all of this?* I didn't like to admit it; but at times, especially on anniversaries of the attack, sadness weighed down my heart, and it ached. With each of Queena's accomplishments—the steps she could take, the babyish sounds she made, the smiles, the laughter from her heart—I remembered the pain she suffered, the struggles our family endured.

This particular year, I chose to think of her amazingly bright smile and infectious laugh. I thought of how she pushed past boundaries of modern medicine, onward for a better life. In my mind, I saw Queena as a fighter, the very definition of strength and perseverance, the meaning of joy.

I also saw how much we needed each other and the community around us. While reading the Bible one day, I came across the story about the paralyzed man and his friends in Matthew 9. This story was our story, too. Men carried their paralyzed friend on a mat to Jesus because they knew He could heal the man. In the same way, we needed our friends to carry us to the feet of Jesus. When we invite others into our hurts, we learn we're not alone after all. We become stronger when we have others to help carry our heavy burdens to the only One Who offers true healing.

For Queena, God offered a degree of healing through music. She had always loved listening to music, and whenever she heard it after the attack, music lifted her spirits, as if taking her away to a world where she could be herself again. Sometimes, she even squealed with excitement while listening to her favorite artists. When it came to Queena, every sound, every reaction, every smile signaled hope and accomplishment.

She absolutely loved country singer Luke Bryan's music. When she heard others talk about him, when his songs played on the radio, or when her caregiver played his album at home, Queena lit up, and her smile beamed. When she heard his voice, the sound likely took her back to September 2014, when she'd gone with Anna to see him in concert in town. Anna had written the country star and asked him to sign a shirt for Queena. She also made a practice of hanging signed t-shirts in Queena's bedroom for inspiration.

We are sitting in the wheelchair area, Anna wrote in her note to the country singer. *It would be an incredible and stimulating experience for Queena if you could come say hello in person. Hope we get to see you before you head out. We are so excited to be here and watch you perform all of our favorite songs. Good luck tonight, and thank you for helping Queena get better every day with your music!*

Luke Bryan wasn't able to meet Queena in person that night, but he did sign the t-shirt for her. A family friend who knows his manager took Queena's shirt backstage and got him to autograph it.

Queena's weekly music therapy sessions aimed to elevate her mood, help her communication skills, relax her muscles, and increase her eye contact, among other benefits. Music therapy also gave Queena the power to make decisions—a huge benefit. She picked the songs that the therapist played. She blinked her eyes once for yes and twice for no. By this time, she communicated best through her facial expressions.

When Queena chose a song or genre of music from a list read aloud to her, she listened patiently until she heard the song title or genre she liked, then grinned from ear to ear. The therapist was a musician himself. He brought his keyboard, guitar, and, sometimes, a small drum that fit on Queena's lap. Then he played either a recorded or a live version of her song choice.

To include Queena in the fun, the therapist gave her a set of bells and tied them to her wrists. He also encouraged her to stretch her arms by playing chords on various instruments. Her therapist called the chords she played "the Q-chord." Over the course of time, Queena started to maintain eye contact with her therapist for ten seconds at a time—a huge achievement because eye tracking is a good sign of increased comprehension and brain activity.

Music therapy was one in a long list of treatments in which I enrolled Queena. It was also one of the many therapies that our latest insurance program did not cover. Yet, by God's grace, and a slew of fundraisers, we stayed afloat.

Praying over the hearing - February, 2017

CHAPTER 28

A RAPIST SENTENCED—AGAIN

COURT OFFICIALS SCHEDULED KENDRICK MORRIS' resentencing hearing for February 2017. As the date grew closer, I tried my best to avoid it, at least emotionally. I didn't want to go through that again. I *couldn't* go through it again. Anna, however, prepared to speak and plead for a lengthy sentence. She asked if I wanted to read a statement as well.

"No," I told her. I would attend the hearing and speak with reporters if they reached out to me, but that would be the extent of my involvement. "It's so ridiculous and not fair that we have to repeat the same old thing again," I said. "I'm sorry you have to go through this again."

Still, the question lingered in the back of my mind. *Do I want to speak? No! Why would I want to speak?* Then another question emerged. *Should I speak?* The boy who hurt my daughter had asked for a reduced sentence. The thought stung like alcohol in an open wound. Could Queena receive a reduced sentence? No. Should he? Absolutely not!

Briefly, I considered taking Queena to the resentencing, forcing the now twenty-five-year-old Kendrick Morris to look her in the face and see all that he took from her. Yet I doubted the guilt, if he had any, would cause him to withdraw his request for less prison time. As my anger quieted, I thought about the implications for Queena if she were present in the courtroom. Attorneys would go over all the details of the attack as she sat there, listening, trying to comprehend. I recalled the counseling sessions and how she'd responded when we talked about the attack. I remembered the fear and pain on her face. No, I couldn't put her through the hearing. But I could go to the courtroom for her. I could be her voice. I could speak on her behalf.

Yes. I would speak.

A few days prior to the resentencing, I posted a request on the Join Queena Facebook page. I wanted to create a way for Queena's followers and supporters to show solidarity, whether they could be in court that day or not. I asked that everyone wear pink in Queena's honor and post pictures with the hashtags #queenawearsPINK and #JoinQueena.

The morning of the hearing, pictures of people in pink flooded our Facebook page. Also, a huge crowd of friends and family came to court to show their support. They filled the hallway outside Courtroom 15. We all donned different shades of pink but had a single message—hope and love for Queena.

Before entering the courtroom, we gathered to pray over the proceedings. A close family friend prayed words that felt like they came from my own heart. "Lord, today we ask for Your wisdom, Your peace, and Your justice to prevail. We ask for Your anointing on the proceedings, and we thank You for this outpouring of love for Queena."

Soon, Kendrick Morris was escorted into the room. I stared at him for a very long time and kept shaking my head. I really didn't understand why he and his attorneys had thrust our family into this painful situation all over again. I prayed for God's mercy on him. Whenever I watched Queena going through her therapy, just trying to get through her daily routine, I concluded that although I could forgive him for what he had done, I had no sympathy for him. He needed to stay in prison for a long time.

It's hard to recall the details of that day. I sat in the courtroom and heard much of what was said, but I succumbed to sensory overload. Anna's longtime friend, Katie Shook, summed up the happenings of the day in a blog post on JoinQueena.com.

As court was called into session, the defense began by bringing up two expert witnesses that testified that they believed
Kendrick was capable of being rehabilitated. As much as it
hurt to hear the suggestion that Kendrick's brain has the ability to recover, rewire, and rehabilitate from the life of abuse he
lived through, and the abuse he administered to his victims, I
couldn't help but hear what they were saying and see it as hope
for Queena's brain. There were many times they were speaking
of Kendrick and I wanted to jump up and scream, "That's great
that he is rehabilitating so quickly! Would you like to come evaluate my friend and tell me what her prognosis for rehabilitation
is? Perhaps, then, your opinion of whether or not he can truly
be rehabilitated may change."[40]

Morris had written in prison: "I am trying to learn to like myself. But
I have to think about what I did first."[41] His attorney, Pavlidis, said he had
shown tremendous remorse.

Clinical psychologist Berney Wilkinson, who had examined Morris
before his earlier sentence and again before this hearing, said that
Morris had lived in fear of White, whom he described as his stepfather.
Wilkinson related one memory Morris had shared whereon he'd said
White had broken all his Christmas presents in front of him as punishment for doing poorly in school. Morris' mother did nothing to stop the
abuse, Wilkinson testified.[42] The Department of Children and Families
had removed Morris from his home twice. Morris also told Wilkinson
about two incidents of sexual abuse he'd endured at the hands of a man
and a woman he knew.[43]

Another witness, James Garbarino, a psychology professor at Loyola
University Chicago, testified that all of Morris' past experiences made
him feel as if he lacked power and control in his life, which motivated
him to exert this over his victims. "I think Kendrick shows a recognition
of the crimes he committed to the point that it's hard for him to look at
it," he said.[44]

Each witness was asked by the prosecution during cross examination if they had even bothered to look into the details of the brain injury inflicted on Queena, the details of the crimes, or even photos from the crimes. Both times there was a "No" that resounded so deeply into my soul that it felt like I was being cut by a knife. If they had seen the pictures, read the reports, seen videos of her now, could they so unwaveringly sit on the witness stand and declare that he could re-enter society with the very victims whose lives he stole?

At numerous moments throughout the day, I glanced over to Kendrick, trying to extrapolate any kind of emotion that could dictate potential inward feelings. During the defense witnesses' testimonies I saw him wipe his eyes a few times during the descriptions of the abuse he lived through. As a mother of a little boy, my heart broke for Kendrick. Did he ever have anyone in his corner? All of the evidence given in the courtroom tells me that he was failed, time and time again, by those whom he held closest to his heart.

Regardless of the compassion I felt for him, his crimes can't be excused. There are people that have been in far worse situations, with much less to their name, and more repetitive and severe forms of abuse that haven't raped, strangled, threatened, and ripped away two women's lives. Many times, I thought about how his life now compares in contrast to Queena's life. Not many would ever wish to live in prison, but I have to wonder, if given the option to either live in prison or be crippled like his victim, would Kendrick trade places with Queena? I assume not. There were several times that the expert witnesses expressed Kendrick's love of reading. If he were to trade places with Queena, he would never be able to read again. And that's one of the more complex abilities he robbed from her. Swallowing, breathing, walking, eating, using the bathroom, showering, scratching an itch, being able to communicate when something hurts or you don't feel well—she can't do any of these things or even ask for them to be done for her.

The defense rested their case and we recessed for lunch around 1:45, as we processed through some of the most difficult topics from the morning and geared up for what we knew would be an emotional afternoon. We reconvened in the courtroom at 3pm. One by one, friends, therapists, and family members pleaded with the judge to impose the maximum sentence on Kendrick—life in prison. You see, in 2011, during the original sentencing, the judge could not impose a life sentence on Kendrick. There were laws that prohibited a juvenile from receiving a life sentence; however, the law has since changed and now allows juveniles to be sentenced to life with the provision that after a set period of time they would be permitted to have their sentence reviewed. I think for many, this may be the silver lining of having to re-open these wounds. In total, there were 14 different statements that were either read aloud into the court record or were submitted to the court. Each statement that was read was emotional and powerful.[45]

I wish that I could say I felt brave and fearless sitting through the hearing, but I didn't. Queena's friends read their statements, and I cried right along with them. My eyes were red, and my face was soaked with tears. Many times, I thought, *I'm not going to be able to do this. When it's my turn, I will just ask the attorney to read my prepared statement.* The attorney told me I needed to read slowly and clearly so the judge could understand me. I closed my eyes and repeatedly prayed, *Jesus, please help me!* When I opened my eyes, somehow, I felt amazing strength.

During the original trial and sentencing, I couldn't face my daughter's attacker. I feared my emotions and language deficiencies would prevent me from making it through my statement. So, Anna had read it for me. But this time, I found my voice. I walked to the witness stand, faced the judge, and calmly began to read. I had prepared a totally new statement. The one I had written during the first sentencing in 2011 felt dated now. I wanted to convey that although time had passed, my daughter still suffered. I proceeded to read the following words with confidence:

Nine years ago, my world was changed forever. You see me now speaking calmly, but if you could see inside me, you would see a broken heart and a fragile network of nerves.

Imagine for one moment that you received a call telling you that your vibrant, intelligent, beautiful, full-of-life young child, with the brightest of future in front of her, was viciously attacked and lucky to be alive. Then, when you think she will be okay, a series of unexpected seizures overwhelm her and render her helpless. As a result of the attack and seizures, you find out that the prognosis for her recovery is dim.

During this time, you wonder, "Who would do such a horrible thing? What kind of creature, not even a human being, could do such a despicable thing? What would drive someone to commit such a heinous crime?" The answer over and over again is an evil, evil person. No matter what race, no matter if male or female, and no matter how old or how young—this person is someone who has no regard for what will happen to the other person he is attacking. He only cares about himself.

When I found out who had done this to my daughter and that he had also raped a sixty-two-year-old woman, I knew this was an evil person. I am so glad they caught him because you know he would do it again. If you set him free, you will be gambling with some other potential future victim's life.

Each day of my life, I not only feel my own pain, but I feel the pain of my daughter, who will never recover. Our entire family, and so many close friends, feel the same pain. Queena fights and has made progress and keeps trying and trying to get better because she has no other choice. We must keep our faith strong, so she can be strong, too.

Nine years ago, this evil person administered a life sentence to my daughter. She can't speak; she can't walk; and she can't eat without help. Do you know that her muscles still remember the attack? Every day, she still struggles to swallow and breathe because he strangled her and cut off her oxygen during the attack. The fear he created will always be there in her memory. His life sentence is a piece of cake compared to hers. If you lessen his sentence, one day he will be free like you and me, while Queena will continue her life sentence until the end. Is that justice?

My faith says I should forgive him. I have come to accept our situation, but I will never accept letting this person go free—ever! If my daughter cannot get a resentencing, he shouldn't, either. He should stay in there for life, or until God says so. Judge Tharpe, on behalf of Queena and my family, I ask that you consider giving Kendrick Morris a life sentence. Thank you.

When I stepped down from the witness stand, I imagined how Queena would feel if she had seen and heard what I'd said. I sensed that she would have smiled with me. She would have been proud that her mother spoke on her behalf. As I turned, I saw Anna give me a look of reassurance, confirming that I'd done the right thing.

Then, it was her turn. She strode to the witness stand, and she began to read. Like me, she had written a whole new statement for the judge to consider.

Your Honor, it was almost six years ago that I first sat in this very seat. That was my first opportunity to tell Mr. Morris and the court how the attack on my little sister had impacted my family. Now, here I am again. I would give anything in the world, anything at all, to be able to report that things have changed, that things are better now. But that would be a lie. The truth is, these last few years have been filled with fear, worthlessness, depression, hopelessness, sickness, anxiety, and exhaustion.

Mr. Morris, since the first sentencing, how many books have you read or how many shows have you watched on television? How many times have you brushed your teeth or put on a pair of clean underwear? How many times have you stretched out your arms and legs or reached to scratch an itch? How many steps have you taken? How many meals have you eaten? How many words have you said?

If my sister were to answer those questions, which she can't, the answer would be zero. None. In fact, she cannot even be here for the sentencing today, yet here you are. Why can't she be here today? First of all, she would have to listen to the gruesome details of her rape and attack and relive the horrifying moment when she lost her life. Then, whom would she be able to confide in? How would she express her feelings to a therapist or even our mom or me? How would she ask for answers to questions that have been burning in her mind?

She wouldn't be able to. Her last words that were ever said were to me, almost nine years ago when she lay in the hospital bed in the ER. She was beaten so badly, she was unrecognizable. Do you know how hard it is to see your little sister in that condition? The bones in her face were fractured, and her teeth were knocked in. I used up almost a whole bottle of chamomile lotion on her body. She was covered in hundreds of ant bites all over her entire body, front and back, because you left her naked, on top of anthills, to die.

She was so swollen, she couldn't even open her eyes. But when she finally managed to peek one eye open, she realized all she could see was darkness, a void. Those were her last words to me, the last time any human being has ever heard her speak. She slurred her words. She used up what energy was left in her to say every syllable. She could barely make her lips move.

She said to me, "Why can't I see? I am so itchy everywhere. Can you scratch me? I cannot move. What happened to me?"

I told her that a very bad person had attacked her. She then asked me, "Did they catch him?"

I told her that the police had found him. I then told her what I now know will never come true. I told her that everything was going to be okay and that she would be back to normal in time for the prom.

She then asked me, "Am I safe? Are we safe?"

I said, "Yes."

And that was the last time I heard her little voice. What am I supposed to tell her tonight after the sentencing if Kendrick Morris's sentence is reduced? She is waiting on me to come over. How can I tell her that she is safe? That we are safe?

She cannot be here herself to hear the sentence being read out loud. She is bound to a wheelchair and a diaper. Spending more than three hours sitting in a wet and dirty diaper will cause infections and sores. Also, how would my mom feed her? Lift up her shirt in front of everyone so that she can pump liquids and crushed medicine down a tube stuck into her stomach?

If she were here, she wouldn't even be able to see her attacker, because her vision has been gone for eight years now. She would not even be able to look him in the eyes. She would just be sitting here listening and screaming, crying out and tensing up every muscle in her face and body until her jaw pops and her hips are crushed from trying to explode through the seatbelt of her wheelchair. Unlike you and me, she has lost her ability to control her emotions and her anxiety. We can sit quietly and fake a smile or refrain from yelling out by calming ourselves down. Queena does not have that luxury.

Like her body, her mind has also been severely damaged. She is trapped inside a body that she cannot control, and her mind replays the horrible scenes over and over again, and she will never be able to shut it off or vent to anyone about it. She has to live with the fact that she does not have much of a life, that her body is practically useless, and that our mom is dying a little every day inside and out. That, to me, is truly cruel and unusual punishment.

Almost nine years ago, you took my sister's life from me. You took my mom's life, too. I am left alone now. They have been replaced by two people I have never known before. It is like parts of the eighteen-year-old Queena that I knew have gone missing, have been downgraded to the physical abilities of a newborn with the cognitive functionality of a young child. Most likely, her life span has been greatly reduced. Her body will start to shut down from the lack of activity and real food.

My mother is just a shell, walking around mindlessly, having not showered in days or skipping two to three meals in a row. Her mind is completely consumed by thoughts of how she can bring the old Queena back. She has developed severe anxiety, obsessive compulsions, and has lost the ability to think about anybody but Queena, not even about herself. Her health has been noticeably declining. If she were to get very ill, I would be the one taking care of both of them, side by side in hospital beds.

We have all been harmed by the crime you committed. I am a victim. My mom is a victim. Our whole community has been victimized by your crime. We have spent our days desperately trying to rise above, holding on to each other, rejoicing at any tiny evidence of progress, clinging on to every ounce of hope that Queena will get better and that justice will be served. It is only by the grace of God and the blood, sweat, and tears of the people who have come to our aid that we have been able to consider some battles won.

Today is one of the biggest battles we will ever face—I will ever face. I am here to speak on behalf of my sister, who has lost her voice, and on behalf of the many other victims out there. We do not accept excuses, and we do not feel sorry for those that have made decisions to rape and assault innocent people. No matter if young or old, it takes an adult-like mind to be able to come up with and execute such a horrific attack.

Your Honor, I am asking that you please consider a life sentence for Kendrick Morris. We should never allow him the opportunity to ever hurt another person like my sister again.

During the resentencing, Morris' attorneys talked frequently about his exploration of spirituality. He was trying to determine which religion fit him best, they said. I didn't know if he had access to a computer and the internet in prison, but if so, I wished he would go to the Join Queena Facebook page. There, he could see how our God had used Queena and her injuries for His glory. I was sure he would like her God and accept Him as Savior. I whispered a prayer similar to the one I had prayed six years earlier when I first met him. *Kendrick, He is waiting for you to receive His forgiveness and to walk in a relationship with Him.*

After both sides had spoken, Judge Tharpe announced that he needed time to consider the changes to the law and to review the attorneys' arguments. He would render a decision on March 9, 2017—a full month later. We would have preferred to know right then, but we found peace with the judge's wisdom in taking his time, rather than making a rash decision.

Back in 2011, when the law restrained him from issuing a life sentence, Judge Tharpe had said, "If ever there was a case that cried out for a life sentence, this is the case." Then he'd sentenced Morris to sixty-five years in prison. I didn't see a reason why his view of Morris or our case would change drastically in the time since.

While we waited for March 9 to arrive, we filled our time with activities to distract our minds. Queena attended a prom for people with special needs, sponsored by Tim Tebow. We took a day trip to her favorite beach with some of her friends. We held a prayer vigil to ask for peace over the upcoming sentencing decision. Meanwhile, the outpouring of support from the community kept our spirits uplifted. Queena's Facebook page overflowed with supporters posting pictures of themselves wearing pink.

I didn't go to the courtroom to hear the sentence read. The nurse who took care of Queena mentioned on the day of Morris' resentencing hearing that Queena had seemed unsettled because she didn't see me when she woke up. So, I thought it best for Queena if I stayed home to help the nurse. Truthfully, I preferred staying home with Queena over sitting like a ball of nerves inside the courtroom. Besides, I'd already said what I wanted to say. I needed to be at peace, regardless of the outcome. So, I asked Anna to call me when she heard the decision.

While I waited, I found out that a local reporter was tweeting live from the courtroom. His updates posted to Twitter and to Facebook simultaneously. I nervously waited for his brief descriptions of the scene. Finally, at 9:46 a.m., he tweeted: "'Life sentences are the only appropriate sentences in this case.' Tharpe has sentenced Kendrick Morris to life in prison."[46]

I closed my eyes silently. *Thank God!*

I would not describe the moment as particularly joyful. The sentence did not change anything for Queena or our family. But at least it brought us some level of peace regarding our personal safety and the safety of the community. It demonstrated that the wrongful behavior of this young man warranted a life sentence.

I went up to Queena's old room, still decorated the same way it had been during her senior year of high school. Those were the days when she and her peers were excited about what was to come next in their lives—the days when they were making decisions and strategizing about the future. Queena had fully embraced all of her dreams and was ready to become the woman she hoped to be. Standing in her former bedroom, I remembered the goals she'd had for a career, a home, marriage, and even having her own children someday.

I saw my daughter as an amazing young woman, a fighter who proved to be braver than most. Still, her daily struggles were not ones that any human being would want to face.

Once again, tears flowed down my face.

Once again, I was reminded that grieving what was, what could have been, and what would never be is a slow and crooked process.

Yet tomorrow would come.

Life would go on.

Queena ready to dance the night away with Derrick - April 8, 2017

Derrick, Queena, and Anna, Bloomingdale High School Prom, Atlantis -
The Regent, Riverview, FL, 2017

A TREE OF VICTORY

A FEW WEEKS FOLLOWING THE resentencing, Queena's friend Derrick asked if he could come over to see her. Derrick, a senior at Bloomingdale High School and president of the school's film club, had produced several films already that local theaters and festivals around the Tampa Bay area had featured.

Derrick often came to the house to visit. Each time he did, he brightened Queena's day. Seven months prior, Derrick asked my permission to take Queena to his senior prom. I asked him if he was sure he didn't want to take another friend who could dance with him the whole night.

He responded, "Going with Queena would be way better, and I would have way more fun!"

I gave my permission. Still, I knew he had to get special permission from his school for Queena to come as his date, since she was older than twenty-one. I didn't mention anything to Queena because I didn't want to get her hopes up if the school rejected the idea.

One afternoon, Derrick came through the door holding a pink teddy bear and a sign. He handed it to Queena and said, "I got you a little teddy bear—pink, because I know you like pink." Then he held up a sign and read it aloud to Queena. It said, "Queena, prom would be unBEARable without you!" Queena laughed and smiled as her way of accepting Derrick's "prom-posal."

Derrick explained that not only had he gotten permission to bring Queena, but Bloomingdale High School had donated the cost of her prom ticket. An anonymous donor also gave Queena $250 to buy whatever she needed to attend the prom. News outlets found out about the prom, and soon, we received more donations, including services from a local hairstylist and makeup artist.

This moment was nine years in the making. The lavender dress that Queena had picked out for her own prom one week before her attack had hung in her closet, gathering dust. A seamstress named Dawn saw our Facebook post about Queena attending the prom. She reached out to us and came to our home. I showed her Queena's prom dress from 2008, and she indicated that she thought she could alter it to make it work. Then we took the dress downstairs to show Queena. We asked her if she wanted to wear it, and she beamed. *Yes!* I felt so emotional and happy.

The dress had to be altered to accommodate Queena's feeding tube. It would also need slits on both sides for the wheelchair's seatbelt to be inserted underneath the dress. Dawn offered to donate the cost of the alterations and even fashioned a shawl from leftover fabric. Finally, Queena would get to wear the prom dress she'd purchased weeks before her attack. This would be perfect, a beautiful ending to a terrible nightmare.

We topped off the dress with accessories and a pair of beautiful open-toed shoes from Nordstrom that we bought using the donated money. The outfit came together beautifully.

The day of the prom, we dressed Queena. Then the hairstylist and makeup artists performed their magic, sweeping her hair into an elegant updo. Derrick slid a corsage with a rose around her wrist. The crystal beadwork on the front of Queena's gown glimmered against the lavender fabric, and a sheer gossamer chiffon underskirt sparkled as it draped to her ankles.

When we finally left the house, sixty riders from the Old Town Chapter of Brandon Harley-Davidson greeted us on their bikes, lined up along our street, waiting to give Queena a special escort to her prom! They all stood and clapped as she got into her van. Then thirty motorcycles lined up in front of the van and thirty behind. It was truly incredible.

Derrick, the bikers, and everyone who donated may have seen their contributions as simple good deeds, but to me, they meant so much more. They created an extraordinary trip back to a normal life for my little girl. Her bright smile lit up the neighborhood. The laughter and the happiness flowed from her heart. This was the true joy of the Lord!

With the exception of Anna's wedding, Queena didn't get a lot of opportunities to be treated like a real princess, to appear on the outside just as amazing as she is on the inside. On average days, her life is marked by sweatpants, therapy sessions, and doctor appointments. But on this day, it was all about dressing up for a special evening. For just one night, Queena was the princess—no, she was the queen she was born to be—and sixty men on Harleys were her cavalry.

Now, every time the anniversary of Queena's attack creeps around, I struggle with the question of whether I will ever feel unabashed joy—the kind of joy that holds nothing back. A joy that becomes a consistent and permanent part of my life. I wonder if a lasting smile will creep across my face and stay there. I'm not talking about the smiles you force for picture-taking, but a *true* smile—the kind that emerges from the inside and can't be held back.

The last words Queena said to me before her attack were, "I love you." I never thought the events of the next twenty-four hours would change our lives forever. The anniversary date also carries a mountain of emotions for Queena's dear friends. The young women feel as if they lost a crucial piece of their tightly knit friendships.

Our family continues to need home health nurses twenty-four hours each day. I must be present as well to advocate for Queena's care. My salon business continues, but I manage it mostly from afar. Caregiving is an around-the-clock job that leaves little time for anything else. I would be lying if I didn't admit that my heart is scarred and, at times, still breaks open and bleeds. The anniversary of Queena's attack is always a bittersweet reminder of why our family was forced to adjust to a new normal, but I am grateful my daughter is still alive and progresses daily.

I'm still learning to rejoice in small victories. I'm finding ways to redefine the word *joy*. Perhaps it is defined as the joy I feel when Queena laughs at a joke, or when her eyes light up because we've placed a precious baby in her arms. Maybe it's the joy I feel when she smiles so big, she almost locks her jaw. Or it might just be the joy that comes when witnessing the love between two sisters. My heart swells when I watch Anna care for Queena, or when she talks with Queena and treats her as though she were not disabled but a whole and beautiful soul exactly like the rest of us.

"When Mom's away," Anna wrote on Facebook while I was attending a writers' conference, "we . . . walk the mall until they kick us out, listen to Eminem on high volume, binge-watch *Bachelor in Paradise*, drink Rum Runners in pineapples while listening to live music, pet all the dogs, take her credit card to Bed Bath & Beyond . . . xoxo, Anna & Queena."

Whenever I focus on the good times, I am able to see the glory in our storm. I can push past the negativity and embrace all that I have learned over the past decade. The biggest lesson I learned through this nightmare is that if we trust God with our brokenness, God's grace and healing will mend our lives, and He will delight in our restoration.

One day, I watched a video Queena and her friends had made in her senior year of high school. Her laugh was exactly the same in 2008 as it is now. The sound warmed my heart to know that nothing, absolutely nothing, can silence her joy. I love my daughter with all that I am.

Today, we have not lost faith nor sight of the big picture, no matter what obstacles have come our way. Queena is the definition of inspiration and, most of all, perseverance. Through a horrible tragedy came an amazing story of hope, miracles, determination, and faith. Queena's life is motivation for others to keep going, to not give up.

God constantly amazes me by using Queena's story to touch the hearts of people she has never met. We receive messages frequently through her website and the JoinQueena Facebook page with personal stories that would bring many to tears. The world is full of people who fight through evil and challenges—sexual abuse, substance abuse, physical restraints, mental challenges, and so on.

One story in particular stands out. Anna and I noticed that every few days for several months, we received donations from a young woman we had never met. Anna reached out to thank her and asked how she knew Queena. The woman said she attended the University of South Florida in 2008 and heard our story. From then on, she kept Queena in the back of her mind as life carried on and she graduated.

Then, in 2013, this young woman began drinking recreationally and soon found herself drinking a lot. She stumbled across an update on Queena in the *Tampa Bay Times* that compelled her to visit JoinQueena.com. Testimonials featured on the website inspired her to stop drinking altogether. She vowed that any time she felt the urge to buy alcohol, she would send the fifteen dollars she would have spent on a bottle of liquor to Queena instead.

She began emailing us, sharing her life, and we grew very close, although we never met in person. She sent audiobooks for Queena, birthday gifts, and Christmas cards. To this day, she still periodically sends money but has increased the amount to twenty dollars. Her life improved after she stopped drinking, she said. Lately, she began writing a children's book. She also joined the U.S. Army.

Yes, Queena's story planted a seed; the Lord cultivated it; and over time, it blossomed into a beautiful tree of victory that branched out to touch so many lives she never knew. The silver lining is that while a complete physical healing has not yet happened for Queena, we see shimmers of hope in the achievements God has allowed through her partial brokenness.

I am encouraged by how God uses people differently based on their talents and abilities. God's Spirit seems to use stories like Queena's—stories of deep grief and darkness—to shine a light into someone else's dark place. Many times, just when I feel like I cannot trudge any farther through the muck and mire of daily caregiving, God sends support through a neighbor, or some old friend of Queena's, or a stranger in the community who cares.

Our family will always miss the Queena we once knew. Yet we are so proud of her today. She is a blessing to anyone who has had the privilege of meeting her. She has changed people's view of the world, the fleeting nature of life, and the importance of seizing the day. Often, one can read a news story, feel a temporary emotion, and return to life as usual. But Queena's story—our family's story—has remained ever-present in the minds of many people.

Through the past decade, my family has learned many lessons. The first is to focus on making the best of each day rather than allowing fear to guide our thoughts about the present or the future. With God so close to us in our heartache, we learned that the impossible is truly possible. We discovered that barely surviving can turn into a new way of thriving. Despite the stark changes to our lives, I now know what it means when people say, "God will never forsake us!" God is with us and has not left our side. God's grace is beyond words.

I still believe that if we set goals, work hard enough, and stay positive, focused, and patient, we can achieve anything. At some point in our journey, however, all of us will face adversity. Some people understand the thoughts and feelings I've experienced because they are also warriors in their own battles. Others may have a long way to go to feel like a conqueror. Whatever stage of the battle we are in, we must hold on to the idea that adversity need not define us. The troubles we have endured do not define us. It is how we respond to the adversity we face that ultimately shapes who we are and who we will become as we reach for victory over defeat.

I've come to believe that the reality of God has been proven over and over again in my own life story. I believe I have benefitted from developing a personal relationship with my Creator. I was baptized on this belief. My personal conversations with God usually concern my needs, the needs of others, or simply thanking God's Divine Spirit for getting me through life's thick and thin spots—for being an amazing Source of love and power.

More times than I can count, I thought I couldn't make it through one more painful day. Still, I made it because God is always with me. The busyness and the adversity that comes with living in this world can creep in and cloud our vision, causing me to miss the love notes God leaves for me. When this happens, the solution is always to pray, "Lord, give me eyes to see You!"

To other people who may be travelling with me on a similar path, I humbly offer the following words of wisdom:

To those with disabilities: It takes a lot for many people to feel beautiful. But to feel beautiful, happy, and blessed while living with a disability is something else altogether. I encourage people to do as my Queena has done—keep smiling and hold your head high. Strive to capture each moment of each day. Show the world how beautiful and blessed you truly are. Reach for the fruit that hangs on your personal tree of victory.

To caregivers: It took me a long time to lean on God and other people. But leaning helped me muster the strength and courage to go on. I understand the hardships of caring for someone and would not have made it without looking up to the heavens as well as out to my neighbors. It is a great sacrifice to care for our loved ones in their time of need. There is no better way of showing our love, but we can grow weary in doing this work. Ask for help. Give yourself time to be you. Reach for the fruit that hangs on your tree of victory.

To parents: I can't help but think that if Queena's attacker had experienced understanding and love in his own life, this tragedy could have been avoided. Listen to your children, not just with your ears but with your hearts. Tell them they are loved and wanted and that there is a special place for them. If your child has a friend who is not receiving this at home, show them the same love. Show love to everyone, even the ones who are difficult to love. We must all reach for the fruit that hangs on our collective tree of victory.

To teens and young adults: Talk to trusted adults, counselors, teachers, or mentors about your feelings. Tell people about your dreams and fears. Talk about your day—good or bad. Express your feelings. Crying is not a weakness. Sadness and anger are normal emotions. It's okay to feel sad or angry. The darkness is only temporary. It will pass. As you find trusted people to talk to, you'll understand that you are not alone in your adversity. A community of supporters will listen. Reach out beyond yourself for the fruit that hangs on your community's tree of victory.

Despite my ever-growing faith and all the evidence I've seen of God's love, I sometimes wonder what our family did to deserve our situation. That is a question that cannot be answered. The truth is, bad things happen to good people. God does not prevent nor cause calamity, but God does promise to walk with us, abide with us, and love us through the hardships of life.

ACKNOWLEDGMENTS

*Whatever is good and perfect is a gift coming down to us from God our Father,
who created all the lights in the heavens.*

James 1:17

I am thankful that God is always by our side and am grateful to everyone who lifted us up throughout this tragedy and subsequent grief.

I thank You, Jesus, my Lord, for restoring our joy, hope, love, faith, and peace; for defying all odds to become Queena's strength; and for sending Your people to support Queena over these past twelve years. May You continue to send angels who reveal Your power in the world.

Thank You, Holy Spirit, Who lives within us, guiding us in God's new life each day. Thank You for intervening and making my dreams better than I ever could have imagined.

Thank you to Pastor Dave and Bahia Vista Church for baptizing our family. Your role during the hardest time in our lives has left a spiritual mark that causes us to be eternally grateful.

THE MEDICAL TEAMS

Thank you to all who provided care for Queena: Hillsborough County Fire Rescue Station 27 and the first responders who came fast enough and made the right decision to take Queena to Tampa General Hospital. Thank you to Queena's doctors and nurses, who calmed my daughter and our family on the night she was attacked. You continue to make a difference in the life of our Queena. Your kindness, sincere caring, and concern make everything better. You are a great encouragement!

Thank you to Queena's therapists, who taught us to find courage in vulnerability. You helped my daughter cope with the loss of her physical abilities, understand her emotions, and to let go of control every now and then.

Thank you to the advocates who stood unwaveringly beside us. I want to express my heartfelt gratitude for the home health aides throughout the years of caring for my daughter. You loved her as much as her family loves her. We appreciate the extra care shown to Queena. I'm so lucky to have each of you who took such wonderful care of my daughter. I will remember this always. Thank you for your patience with Queena and our family over the last twelve years.

THE LEGAL TEAMS

Thank you to the detectives who listened to our family. Thank you to the Hillsborough County Sheriff's Office. Your bravery, kindness, and generosity never cease to amaze us. Twelve years have gone by, and you have never stopped supporting our cause. You were there for Queena from the night of the attack and have never let go. You sat with us every night in the emergency room and in the ICU. You brought us coffee and Cuban sandwiches. You held Queena's hand through her seizures. You worked tirelessly on her case and helped bring about justice. Thank you, HCSO!

Thank you to the State Attorney's Office 13th Judicial Circuit—those who prosecute criminals throughout Hillsborough County. Thanks to Michael Sinacore and his team. Special thanks to Rita Peters, my idol, who fought tirelessly and never doubted our Queena.

Thank you to Hillsborough Circuit Court Judge Chet A. Tharpe, who proved himself to be an honorable and fair judge. To the jurors, and everyone else involved in the trial, thank you for your time and attention.

To the most wonderful business lawyer, Brent Britton. Thank you for being by my side with all of your advice, support, contributions, and friendship you have given me during these past five years. I'll be forever grateful to you.

OUR FAMILY TEAM

I thank my family for their continued support. A special thank you must be sent to my soulmate, Robert, for his unwavering help and support over the last twelve years. You are the most special person in my life—my best friend, philosopher, guide, and much more. Thank you for entering my life!

Thank you to my unconquerable oldest daughter, Anna—the other half of my heart. I know that it is not easy for you to be the hand-holding daughter and the sister of someone who suffered a traumatic brain injury. I am proud of your strength, Anna. Thank you for always pitching in to help Queena feel better and for everything you do for our family. I love you, Anna!

I also thank your husband, Jonathan Donato, for his continued kindness, acceptance, and support both intellectually and emotionally. I couldn't love you more if you were my own child!

To my sister, Tina, who broke down with us on that horrible night, I thank you for being there and sharing our pain. Thank you for taking care of my business and for bringing food to me every day. Thank you to my sister, brother, and cousins who live out of state but who follow us daily and encourage us with words of support. I am grateful for each of you. I am thankful also for my mother's bravery as she watched her daughter and granddaughter face this horrific event.

Thank you to my two adopted daughters, Rachel Brinton and Katie Shook. Thank you for your gifts—whether wrapped, spoken, or written—and for making our lives a true celebration of faith and love!

OUR FRIEND TEAM

Thank you to the friends who have sent uplifting words and support and continue to be by my side, including John and Cheryl Zemina, Caryn McDermott (Go, Gators!), Paula MacDonald, Cathy Cabeche, and many others who have walked through the dark halls with me—the entire way.

I am also thankful to friends who chose to remain anonymous. We can know you through your heart and through your gifts. We appreciate your giving spirit. Thank you for those who email support and prayers on a daily basis via Queena's website. God bless your heart!

Thank you to Queena's best friends who have always been there for her from day one. Most importantly, thank you to Rachel, Priscilla, and her family, who saved my daughter's life. She sleeps with your pictures that I framed in her bedroom to remind my daughter there are heroes in this story—proof that we are looking out for one another. Your love for Queena is something I will never forget. Thank you for being brave enough to be the voice she couldn't be. Thank you for being so strong when she was weak.

They say that friendship is the most valued treasure in the world. So, please accept my grateful appreciation for being a valuable treasure for my daughter. "Life is partly what we make it, and partly what it is made by the friends we choose" (Tennessee Williams). Thank you for allowing Queena to choose you!

OUR SPONSOR TEAM

Thank you to the sponsors that have supported our family during every fundraiser in the past twelve years. Special thanks to Guy Harvey, Inc., for your donation of Guy Harvey products for each of our events! And you never forget birthday gifts for Queena every year.

Thank you, Steve Stock, former President of Guy Harvey, Inc.! We don't even have the words to say. You have been supportive of Queena since day one.

Deep in the scar of our hearts is our love for you and your family. You will never know what you mean to us! Thank you so much for your generosity!

MEDIA TEAM

Thank you to FullMedia for donating an amazing website to Queena. We absolutely love JoinQueena.com! Thank you to Facebook, which enables JoinQueena to be an inspiration to others and provides the platform for Queena's world to be more open and connected to her nearly seven thousand followers. We are grateful for every one of her fans.

Thank you to the news media, local newspapers, and community for your words of hope, donations, acts of service, and love shown to Queena and our family. Thank you for your support and prayers over the past twelve years and your continued effort to share JoinQueena.com with the public. We are so grateful for the media who are there for us every time we need them. You help us find courage to keep going day after day.

Thank you for the TBI social media groups on the internet. A special thanks to Anoxic Brain Injury CareGivers and Polytraumatic Injury Family Support Group. Although I've never met most of you from around the world, your messages lifted me up and inspired me every day—grinding sorrows, losses, and funny moments. We've laughed, cried, encouraged, complained, expressed opinions, fussed, shared information, and loved just like the family we truly are!

NATIONAL AND WORLDWIDE SUPPORTERS

Thank you to everyone across the nation who wrote cards to my daughter and our family. Thank you to those who showed us *the kindness of strangers*. We thank you for caring about us.

Special thanks to all my editors, who encouraged me to write and then transformed my "broken English" into a beautiful memoir. I don't know what I would do without their advice. Thank you for helping us share our powerful message with the world. Thank you for your hard work of bearing our message so that the memoir of Queena's brave journey could come to life in the world.

Of the many, many people that made this book possible, I would like to express my great appreciation to the entire staff at Ambassador International Publishing: to Bethany—Office Manager, to Anna—Chief Operating Officer, to Katie—the editor who chose to select my work, to Liz—Publicity Director, to Sara—marketing specialist, to Hannah—the greatest cover and interior designer I could ever imagine. A very special thanks to Mr. Sam, the Publisher. I want to say thank you for your kindness, thank you for all your help, and thank you for the job you have done on my book. Thank you!

In closing, to my family and friends who continue to walk this journey through grief with us: This book and our current lives would be impossible were it not for the kindness and dedication of thousands of people, including each one of you. Thank you!

Lastly, I am deeply thankful to my daughter, Queena—for her forgiving spirit and her willingness to give me permission to tell her story. She is truly an amazing fighter! That's why thousands of people have followed her story over the past twelve years—the Bloomingdale Library Attack Survivor. I love you!

strength means
NEVER
GIVE UP

ENDNOTES

1 *Wikipedia, s.v.* "Nguyễn Văn Tường," https://en.wikipedia.org/wiki/Nguyễn_Văn_Tường (accessed August 12, 2018).

2 No relation. *Nguyen* is a fairly common surname in Vietnam.

3 Dong-Phuong Nguyen, "My Soul Is Broken," *The Tampa Bay Times*, July 11, 2008.

4 Dong-Phuong Nguyen, "Squeals of joy rise, tears of sorrow fall when friends visit rape victim," *The Tampa Bay Times*, July 26, 2008.

5 Donna Koehn, "East Bay Students Survive Year of Lessons in Loss," *The Tampa Tribune*, June 6, 2008.

6 Editorial, "Victim Deserves Help to Recover," *The Tampa Bay Times*, October 22, 2008.

7 Dong-Phuong Nguyen, "Bloomingdale rape victim has reunion at Abercrombie store she once worked," *The Tampa Bay Times*, March 25, 2009.

8 Dong-Phuong Nguyen, "Small steps to victory over evil," *The Tampa Bay Times,* April 26, 2009.

9 D'Ann Lawrence White, "'Improvements every day': Teen, family stay positive a year after brutal rape," *The Tampa Tribune*, April 24, 2009.

10 Dong-Phuong Nguyen, "Teen victim in brutal 2008 Brandon library sex assault can suddenly see color and pictures, her mother says," *The Tampa Bay Times*, July 29, 2009.

11 Yvette C. Hammett, "Gators Gear Brings Smile to Huge Fan," *The Tampa Tribune*, September 4, 2009.

12 Yvette C. Hammett, "Trip to UF Swamp a 'Super' Success for Brandon Teen," *The Tampa Tribune*, October 17, 2009.

13 Sarah Young, "July 14," in *Jesus Calling*, Nashville: Thomas Nelson, 2016.

14 Mike Wells and D'Ann Lawrence White, "Kin contest rape charges; Suspect was abused, accused of animal cruelty, reports say," *The Tampa Tribune*, April 30, 2008.

15 Ibid.

16 Dan Sullivan, "Ex-Buc Steve White disputes assertions that he abused Bloomingdale rapist," *The Tampa Bay Times*, February 14, 2017.

17 Thomas W. Krause, "Mother, Son Appear Before Same Judge," *The Tampa Tribune*, May 21, 2008.

18 Alexandra Zayas, "Kendrick Morris guilty of raping day care worker," *The Tampa Bay Times*, September 2, 2010.

19 Carol Wimmer, "When I Say I Am a Christian," http://whenisayiamachristian.com (accessed September, 2010).

20 "Kendrick Morris Guilty of Brutal Attack at Valrico Library," *The Lakeland Ledger*, October 6, 2010.

21 "Surveillance Time Stamp Crucial Evidence," *Vintech High-Tech Security Systems*, November 19, 2010.

22 Ibid.

23 Mike Wells and Thomas W. Krause, "Details emerge on library attack victim," *The Tampa Tribune,* June 7, 2008.

24 "Kendrick Morris Guilty of Brutal Attack at Valrico Library," *The Lakeland Ledger,* October 6, 2010.

25 Ibid.

26 Alexandra Zayas and Jessica Vandet Velde, "Kendrick Morris found guilty of brutal 2008 rape at Bloomingdale Library," The Tampa Bay Times, October 6, 2010.

27 Steve Otto, "Help running out for Bloomingdale victim," *The Tampa Tribune,* February 27, 2011.

28 "Tail-less Dolphin Helps Crime Victim," Dolphin-Way.com, https://www.dolphin-way.com/2011/05/tail-less-dolphin-helps-crime-victim/ (accessed May 31, 2011).

29 Alexandra Zayas, "Kendrick Morris guilty of raping day care worker," *The Tampa Bay Times,* September 2, 2010.

30 Alexandra Zayas, "Kendrick Morris sentenced for rapes, 65 years total in prison," *The Tampa Bay Times,* May 21, 2011.

31 Ibid.

32 Ibid.

33 Ibid.

34 Ibid.

35 Ibid.

36 Steve Otto, "Finally, a big win after tragedy," *The Tampa Tribune*, June 3, 2011.

37 *Wikipedia, s.v. "butterfly effect,"* https://en.wikipedia.org/wiki/Butterfly_effect (accessed August 12, 2018).

38 Marlene Sokol and Richard Danielson, "Former Plant High football coach and principal Vince Sussman dies at 63," *The Tampa Bay Times*, October 8, 2013.

39 Laura C. Morel, "Appeals court overturns 65-year sentences for Bloomingdale Library rapist," *The Tampa Bay Times*, August 22, 2015.

40 Katie Shook, "The Re-Sentencing of Queena's Attacker," http://www.join-queena.com/the-re-sentencing-of-queenas-attacker.

41 "Doctors Say Bloomingdale Rapist Kendrick Morris Could Be Rehabilitated as State Seeks Life Sentence," *The Tampa Bay Times*, February 9, 2017.

42 Ibid.

43 Ibid.

44 Ibid.

45 Shook.

46 Dan Sullivan, Twitter post, March 9, 2017, 9:46 a.m., https://twitter.com/TimesDan.

ABOUT THE AUTHOR

Vanna Nguyen is a refugee from South Vietnam and the mother of the Bloomingdale Library Attack Survivor, Queena. She devotes her life to Queena's full-time care and advocates for special needs and justice for victims of domestic, sexual, and physical abuse. She lives in Florida with her partner, Robert; Queena; and her two Shih Tzu dogs, Charlie and Princess. Her other daughter, Anna, lives nearby with her husband, Jonathan.

Follow Vanna and her family through the "Join Queena" page on Facebook, Twitter (@joinqueena), or the Join Queena blog.

Vanna's wish is that this book's proceeds can support ongoing expenses through Hope Heals the Brain, Inc. and Queena's Medical Trust Fund. If you would like to make a donation to help Queena, please visit www.joinqueena.com/donate.

For more information about
Vanna Nguyen
&

The Life She Once Knew
please visit:

www.thelifesheonceknew.com
www.joinqueena.com
www.facebook.com/QUEENATrueStory
@QUEENATrueStory
@VannaNguyAuthor

For more information about
AMBASSADOR INTERNATIONAL
please visit:

www.ambassador-international.com
@AmbassadorIntl
www.facebook.com/AmbassadorIntl

*If you enjoyed this book, please consider mentioning it on your social
media and leaving us a review on Amazon, Goodreads, or our website.*